The Economic Survival of America's Isolated Small Towns

PUBLIC ADMINISTRATION AND PUBLIC POLICY

A Comprehensive Publication Program

RECENTLY PUBLISHED BOOKS

The Economic Survival of America's Isolated Small Towns, Gerald L. Gordon

Public Administration and Policy in the Caribbean, Indianna D. Minto-Coy and Evan Berman

Sustainable Development and Human Security in Africa: Governance as the Missing Link, Louis A. Picard, Terry F. Buss, Taylor B. Seybolt, and Macrina C. Lelei

Information and Communication Technologies in Public Administration: Innovations from Developed Countries, Christopher G. Reddick and Leonidas Anthopoulos

Creating Public Value in Practice: Advancing the Common Good in a Multi-Sector, Shared-Power, No-One-Wholly-in-Charge World, edited by John M. Bryson, Barbara C. Crosby, and Laura Bloomberg

Digital Divides: The New Challenges and Opportunities of e-Inclusion, Kim Andreasson

Living Legends and Full Agency: Implications of Repealing the Combat Exclusion Policy, G.L.A. Harris

Politics of Preference: India, United States, and South Africa, Krishna K. Tummala

Crisis and Emergency Management: Theory and Practice, Second Edition, Ali Farazmand

Labor Relations in the Public Sector, Fifth Edition, Richard C. Kearney and Patrice M. Mareschal

Democracy and Public Administration in Pakistan, Amna Imam and Eazaz A. Dar

The Economic Viability of Micropolitan America, Gerald L. Gordon

Personnel Management in Government: Politics and Process, Seventh Edition, Katherine C. Naff, Norma M. Riccucci, and Siegrun Fox Freyss

Public Administration in South Asia: India, Bangladesh, and Pakistan, edited by Meghna Sabharwal and Evan M. Berman

Available Electronically

PublicADMINISTRATION*netBASE*

http://www.crcnetbase.com/page/public_administration_ebooks

The Economic Survival of America's Isolated Small Towns

Gerald L. Gordon

CRC Press
Taylor & Francis Group
Boca Raton London New York

CRC Press is an imprint of the
Taylor & Francis Group, an **informa** business

CRC Press
Taylor & Francis Group
6000 Broken Sound Parkway NW, Suite 300
Boca Raton, FL 33487-2742

International Standard Book Number-13: 978-1-4822-4882-1 (Hardback)

Library of Congress Cataloging-in-Publication Data

Gordon, Gerald L., author.
The economic survival of America's isolated small towns / Gerald L. Gordon.
pages cm. -- (Public administration and public policy)
Includes bibliographical references and index.
ISBN 978-1-4822-4882-1 (hardcover : alk. paper) 1. Small cities--Economic aspects--United States. 2. Urban economics. 3. Regional economics--United States. 4. Community development--United States. 5. Municipal government--United States. 6. United States--Economic conditions--2009- I. Title.

HC106.84.G667 2015
330.973009173'4--dc23 2015026069

Visit the Taylor & Francis Web site at
http://www.taylorandfrancis.com

and the CRC Press Web site at
http://www.crcpress.com

The dictionary defines *community* as a group of people who live in the same area, such as a city, town, or neighborhood, and who have the same interests (www.merriam-webster.com).

In seventeen of the fifty-one case studies in this research, the interviewees were asked what lessons they had learned from which others might benefit. One-third (seventeen) immediately said that economic growth in a small town is a team sport and that everyone must be in on the planning and execution of the plans.

This text is dedicated to the elected and appointed officials of America's small, isolated cities and towns—and all of their neighbors who get involved. Indeed, they all have the same interests and they all take part—because they are part of the community.

Contents

Preface

The economic history of the recent decade has been volatile at best and devastating at its worst. It has rather depended upon where one sits. If your community has either fared well and weathered the storms, or managed to recover, it's been tolerable. However, if you live in a city that was devastated once, twice, or three times, or that lost relatively high numbers of jobs and has not been able to recover, then this period of time has been damaging for your communities, employers, workers, and families.

If you live in a large city or metropolitan area, although there may have been significant job fluctuations, you may have weathered those same storms a little better simply because there is a greater mass of jobs near you. In small towns, the impacts have tended to be greater. In the small, isolated cities of this great nation, the impacts have tended to be significantly more severe.

Still, some cities survived while others did not. This research has examined which is which and why some cities are in good shape while others have not returned to their earlier highs in population, tax base, or employment opportunities. Did some do things right? Were some simply better positioned? And finally, are there some basic lessons that the leaders of these cities and towns learned that can benefit other leaders in other cities as they confront similar issues and situations?

Acknowledgments

Many people have contributed to my professional success. They have made it possible for me to succeed in my life and in my career. Others have made it possible to successfully complete my books. At the risk of repetition, I gratefully acknowledge the support of Alan Fogg and Vicki Reeve in my office as well as my right arm, Cheryl Martelli, without whom I simply would not have finished this.

I have the privilege of working for a board comprised of seven men and women from the business community who support me in all my endeavors, professional and otherwise. One could not have a better board than Steven Davis, Mike Lewis, Ronald Johnson, Cathy Lange, Mark Lowham, Bud Morrissette, and Sudhakar Shenoy, and their predecessors of thirty-one very productive years. A very special thanks goes to Dr. Johnson, who grew up in a rural area of Virginia and who tutored me (a city kid) in the ways of rural communities and their economic foundations. The lessons were invaluable as I conducted my research.

The photo preceding the main text of this book is courtesy of Abby Gentry.

About the Author

Virginia Business Magazine named **Dr. Gerald L. Gordon** the 2010 Virginia Business Person of the Year, and Leadership Fairfax, Inc., named Dr. Gordon the recipient of its 2011 Northern Virginia Regional Leadership Award.

Dr. Gordon is the president and chief executive officer of the Economic Development Authority in Fairfax County, Virginia, one of the largest office space markets in the United States. He has been with the FCEDA since late 1983. In that time, office space in the county has grown from 32 million square feet to nearly 120 million square feet and jobs in the county grew from 243,000 to approximately 600,000. As a result, the real estate tax rate has decreased from $1.47 to $1.07.

In 2005, the FCEDA was named by *Site Selection Magazine* as one of the Top Ten Economic Development Organizations in North America and, in 2007, *Time* magazine called Fairfax County "one of the great economic success stories of our time." In 2011, *The Washington Post* wrote, "Fairfax County remains the economic wunderkind of Virginia and in many ways of the Washington area."

Dr. Gordon previously taught at the Catholic University of America, the University of Maryland, George Mason University, and Virginia Commonwealth University. He has consulted with numerous city and state governments throughout the United States as well as the governments of the Republic of Poland, the island of Vieques in Puerto Rico, and the Federated States of Micronesia. He has also served as a consultant to various government agencies, the US Navy, businesses, nonprofit organizations, associations, colleges and universities, and the United Nations.

Dr. Gordon holds a bachelor's degree from The Citadel, a master's degree from George Washington University, and a doctorate in international economics from the Catholic University of America. He is also the author of thirteen books and numerous articles on strategic planning and economic development. His most recent books are *Reinventing Local and Regional Economies* (2011) and *The Formula for Economic Growth on Main Street America* (2009).

Dr. Gordon is the 2003 recipient of the prestigious Israel Freedom Award of the Israel Bonds organization. In 2006, he became the first American to address the All-Parliamentary Exports Group in the British House of Commons.

In 2007, he was accepted for inclusion on the roster of Fulbright Senior Scholars and was named a Fellow of the International Economic Development Council. In 2010, he received the James Rees Award from the Fairfax County Chamber of Commerce, and in 2012 he was named the TrendLines Trendsetter of the Year for the Washington, DC, metropolitan area.

Chapter 1

Introduction

Previous Research

I have authored three books in the past four years relating to the growth of local economies, ranging from those of major cities to regional economies to micropolitan-sized cities, the latter having between ten thousand and fifty thousand residents. These were *The Formula for Economic Growth on Main Street America* (New York: CRC Press, 2009), *Reinventing Local and Regional Economies* (New York: CRC Press, 2011), and *The Economic Viability of Micropolitan America* (New York: CRC Press, 2013).

In each book, differing perspectives on economic development and comebacks from economic decline were derived. This was accomplished by assigning to each set of research cities of different sizes. The first of the books looked at general principles of growth and recovery. The subsequent books considered large cities and major metropolitan regions and micropolitan communities.

In this way, the research was designed to help us understand better what makes local economies of varying sizes either grow or contract, and why some cities can recover and thrive while others cannot. Finally, the ultimate exercise was designed to identify the best lessons from each of those municipal settings in order to extract the most valuable lessons that could be replicated in other communities of similar sizes and economic conditions, as well as to clarify which of the lessons learned are more or less applicable to cities of certain sizes and circumstances and which are more generally applicable to municipalities generally.

As one might expect, the conclusions in each successive component of the research indicate that there are some commonalities between cities of different sizes when it comes to economic growth and economic development, as well as to the decline that many cities confront over time. Much of these distinctions are the result of ever-changing conditions—macro and micro—while other factors can play a key role as well.

But here's the tricky part: not all of the impacting factors are within the control of the cities' leadership. Global commodity prices, cheaper overseas labor, and the legislative actions of the states within which they are located can be among the most important of the many considerations. For that reason, the cities in the research long ago concluded that, first and foremost, they must address those issues over which they are able to exercise some degree of control. Otherwise, time, energy, and precious resources can be squandered on activities that are the least likely to yield positive returns. This becomes increasingly clear in this study and increasingly clear to the leaders of these smaller cities and towns because their options—and their resources—are far fewer than those at the disposal of larger communities, and especially those of major cities and metropolitan regions.

There are, of course, many differences *between* cities of the same or similar sizes as well. That is where the lessons learned have proven most instructive for other municipal leaders. Another reason for the presumed value for municipalities and their leaders is that this is not an anthology of lessons gleaned from research or theories. It is not even a larger reflection of the purposes of a single author. The research for each of these books has been done primarily through extensive discussions with the leaders of the communities identified for inclusion in this book. The stories told and the lessons learned—and thus reported—are theirs. They are taken from direct interviews with those men and women who actually lived and worked through the city histories involved. It was their collective stories I told, in the case of one book, seventy mayors and other community leaders, including college presidents, chambers of commerce, executives, and more; and in another case, seventy mayors of micropolitan cities across America.

The next logical consideration—following large urban regions, primary cities, and micropolitan cities and towns—is the small towns that dot the US map. As these small towns attempt to build or rebuild their economic bases, what lessons have they learned? What are the common elements of those lessons as relates to what worked and what did not work? And finally, what guidelines may be extracted that could be instructive to the leadership of other small cities and towns that could enable them to grow faster or better, or to recover more quickly? To be true to that objective and the presumption that it would be *their* conclusions that would be of greatest benefit to their peers in other communities, each of the fifty-plus interviews concluded with the same question: "If you were speaking to a room full of other city managers/mayors from other, similarly sized municipalities that have similar sets of circumstances, what lessons would you offer them?"

As such, this research is, once again, the result of detailed studies of the histories of these experiences through the eyes and words of those who lived them. Interviews with city administrators or fifty mayors of small cities and towns with common challenges and common interests have generated a base of intelligence from which to conclude what are generally more effective approaches to economic development, economic growth, and economic revitalization in other small towns across the United States.

Of course, this does not imply that there can be established a formula that, once applied, can guarantee small cities and towns of future economic success. It simply implies that when similar approaches have been relatively effective in certain settings, they are worthy of consideration by others in similar sets of circumstances. As well, that which has been ineffective with some consistency provides a message to other similar cities that while such a strategy might work for them, there are certain pitfalls to avoid when trying. There is no "one size fits all" in economic development.

According to a publication of the International City Management Association (ICMA), there are 3142 nonmetropolitan counties in the United States, of which roughly two-thirds are rural. These areas, however, contain seventeen percent of the nation's total population and represent about seventy-five percent of the total land area (ICMA, 2012). Further to this point, Huston wrote that eighty-seven percent of all American cities in the census report of 2000 had fewer than ten thousand residents (Huston, 2009).

Clearly, rural America is an important part of our national makeup, and its needs and economic challenges need to be given due consideration by legislatures at all levels. Once the backbone of the nation, many of these cities and regions had gained their initial prominence because they were located at or near major intersections or waterways. The advent of the railroads, and eventually the airports, diminished the value of some of those locations.

Even infrastructure improvements that would seem to benefit small towns often had a detrimental side to them. As a positive, the interstate highway system, for example, meant that the small and isolated areas could be reached more easily. But it also meant that their residents could reach other areas more easily. Several of the small town leaders interviewed in this study mentioned that because interstate highways represent significant pass-through traffic, major national retailers located nearby. This includes, most notably, Walmart. While new jobs became available as a result and residents had enhanced shopping available, there were also harmful effects that resulted.

A national chain like Walmart meant problems for the main street merchants in small town America, which simply could not compete. The result was lost revenues, closed shops in small city downtowns, and even decreased revenues for those cities in which sales taxes are a primary source of general fund resources, and hence the public services the cities can provide to their residents and visitors. Of course, these "big-box" stores locate where the tax benefits are best. This means that they often locate near the interstate highways but just over the lines between the cities and their neighboring counties.

This leads to the question of where the revenues go. In such cases, small town residents spend their earnings and, rather than resulting in enhanced public services for their communities, simply enhance the profits of far-flung corporations.

These kinds of considerations have caused many to ask what such communities can reasonably do to generate local retail opportunities. Again, this is of particular importance if the city in question derives much of its local general fund from income tax revenues. One study wrote that "not every small town commercial center can come back; some may be just too far gone" (Benfield, 2012). And more than one analyst focused specifically on Walmart as one chain that, when it went nationwide, seriously hurt many main street merchants in small towns, even referring to the corporate giant as "main street killers" and other very negative terms.

These small towns, while highly diverse, demonstrate some patterns to their main street development as well. Traynham (2009) wrote: "The usual small town of twenty-five hundred people has two grocery stores, two food stores, a couple of veterinarians, a 'good' restaurant, a beauty shop, a lawyer or three, an insurance agent, a hardware store, and a pharmacy." But, decades ago, many of them had strong agriculture-based economies. So important to many small town economies was agriculture that one writer quoted an interviewee who said, "Two bad wheat markets will touch my business quicker than the tightening of the national credit market." When local farmers near small towns sell their produce, they do so to the local grocers, and when they had poor crop years, the local grocers suffered because they had to import the produce to sell to local residents (McCray, 2013).

As will be detailed in the summaries of the interviews, when small family farms declined and the industry went the way of large corporate dominance, communities needed to find other means of employment and tax generation. Given the education levels and skills sets of the local workforce, and the availability of land, the saving grace for many cities seemed to be manufacturing. As has been well documented, much of that subsequently went overseas where land and labor costs made the US home markets much less competitive, and new opportunities needed to be uncovered for America's small cities and towns. Over that time frame, the service and technology economies had become the great strength of the United States, but they generally required higher education levels and potential new employees in greater numbers than typically available in small towns.

Indeed, for many small towns, a single employer was sufficient to sustain the economy indefinitely—as long as that industry itself could be sustained. The danger is, of course, that when a primary employer leaves a small town, its dependency is exposed. Not only are jobs and tax revenues at stake, but typically these are the businesses that support all manner of local functions, ranging from churches to Little Leagues and scout troops to chambers of commerce. When they depart or close operations, all such organizations—and the community at large by extension—also suffer. The impact then becomes felt by the citizens of the community and begins to affect their general sense of worth.

"Concrete, Washington was named for the local cement industry. When the last cement plant closed down, the town lost not only the big employer but much of its sense of identity" (Moltz and McCray, 2012). Many of the leaders interviewed for this research noted a malaise that settled over their towns. For many of the cities, this became a loss of hope that led to little or nothing being done to try to rebuild the local economies. People simply gave up. In essence, they knew the better times were over and that they would not return, so why even bother trying?

So emphatic was this latter reaction in small towns that several city managers who were asked to participate in this research replied negatively to the request for an interview, saying simply that neither they nor their cities had anything to offer. The request had been couched in terms of discussing the "positive lessons you have learned from which others can benefit." If there is a sense that nothing positive had happened, or was happening, in their local economy, they felt that they had nothing to offer. The most extreme of those reactions implied that nothing positive looking was planned for the near future as well.

These unfortunate situations have a cause and also represent the effect. As will be noted later, the brain drain caused by the loss of good employers can damage a small town much more quickly than their big city counterparts because one employer leaving can be such a significant percentage of the overall local economy (and tax base). There also seems to be something of a general recognition that the best and brightest of young people will leave smaller towns to seek better opportunities in larger cities and regions. This is registered as a loss of the cream of the labor pool, but there should also be recognition of what is left behind: the lowest skilled in the workforce and the workers who cannot leave. This creates a terrible "double whammy" for small towns because, at the very time tax revenues are declining, the demand for public support for individuals and families is increasing. The consequence: "Scattered throughout the nation thousands of towns find themselves twenty, ten, or even five years away from extinction because there are too few tax payers, consumers, and workers to keep things going" (Carr and Kefalas, 2009).

The resolution for this kind of concern may lie in the advent and application of technology, especially the broadband infrastructure that could enable many of these isolated locations to serve as hosts to technology workers whose employers are at considerable distances. Alas, many of the cities in this study cited this as still being a current barrier to growth and possibly even their ultimate survival. Yet, they are still cities and towns in which people live their lives and raise their families and somehow manage to make a living.

Is this a contradiction? Will these cities ultimately simply give way? One of my board members at the Fairfax County Economic Development Authority, Ronald Johnson, has a rather unique perspective on this question. He is a businessman whose company works on broadband infrastructure, and he is an advisor at many levels on these issues. Perhaps most importantly, he grew up in Virginia's rural Amelia County, so he knows whereof he speaks: "In the country—even in the little cities and towns—you learn to rely on each other, and simply put, you somehow just learn to cope."

But, why do small town residents even *want* to remain when their community can no longer provide them with gainful employment? Repeatedly, I was told by those interviewed for this research that small towns are safer, have better schools, and that the sense of a closer-knit community implies a healthier lifestyle for residents. In the interviews, I heard this so often that I began to accept the veracity of those statements without question.

However, one must consider one of two possible explanations. First, one must question whether the smaller schools, with fewer opportunities, are better than their urban and suburban counterparts. In a small school system, the technology may be outdated or the numbers and types of course offerings so relatively few that it is limiting for the students. One could also make the argument that the criminal activity exists in small towns, albeit possibly different than what one might encounter in a more populous area. Similarly, the small town leaders in this research often maintained that "in a small town, you know all of your neighbors." Again, that may be a good thing or not. Furthermore, as a city kid, I know that on your block in major American cities, people also know all of their neighbors. And, I will argue with any small town denizen that rural residents are quicker to lend a helping hand.

The conclusion is that the reader must be careful not to accept such sweeping statements as "the quality of life is better in a small town." The fact is that the quality of life is so personal that one must conclude that it is only different and not better. Quality of life, like beauty, is in the eye of the beholder. That being the case, it becomes important to understand what the definition of a small city or town is.

What Is a Small City or Town, and Who Lives in Them?

All of the cities that have been included in the current series of books on urban and rural economic development have a common feature: they are comprised of people and neighborhoods. Men and women, being inherently social beings, need to interact with other people. They do so largely on a given scale. Residents of New York City, for example, might think of themselves as New Yorkers, generally, but they also have a sense of the neighborhoods in which they live. Someone from the Village has a far different neighborhood than does someone from Soho or Washington Heights.

New York City is entirely too big to feel like one large neighborhood. The cities in my recent book on micropolitan economic growth are different. Micropolitan cities have between ten thousand and fifty thousand residents. At the high end, they too are too large to comprise a single neighborhood. Even at the lower level of ten thousand residents, micropolitan communities are still too large to form a single cohesive neighborhood. People live in the Terrace Park area or on the North Side.

This is where small towns are different: they can be regarded a big neighborhood. Everyone knows everyone else and the mayor has to adopt policies with the knowledge that he or she will see the issue's opponents tomorrow at the grocery store or at church on Sunday. Or, that he or she will leave office and go back to running his or her own business. Today's opponents may also be customers. Small towns may have issues similar to those of larger cities, though on a different scale, but the dynamics are all very different. This underlying sense of small towns was cited repeatedly in the interviews for this research. But, small towns can be regarded in one of two ways: numerically and psychologically.

The term *small town* has a different meaning for different people. For those who have ever lived in or near one, it would almost have to be a more realistic reflection of true small town life in America. This would be especially so if the small towns with which those people are familiar are also isolated from other urban areas to an extent similar to the cities and towns of this study.

For the rest of us, our impressions of small town life and small town economies are probably misinformed, at a minimum. In fact, they are as likely as anything to be advised by television shows that depict the people and the communities of fictional places like Mayberry, Green Acres, and Petticoat Junction. For me and the rest of this group of misdirected individuals, the towns are sleepy, the people are either kind or kooky, and the employment base is sufficient that there are never recessions. Neither are there poor schools, issues around poor or insufficient water supplies, or substantial crime. If someone needs something, the good folks of the town come together and support the cause.

Further, many of these invented towns exist for no apparent reason. The train connection in Petticoat Junction would seem to be the exception to that rule. Indeed, many of the small towns that now dot the nation's map have their origins in proximity. That could mean proximity to a resource, but more likely initially meant proximity to a river or a railroad because those were the primary means by which goods were shipped and dollars could be imported into the community. Those original strengths have gone away with the advent of more efficient rail lines, air cargo transport, and the interstate highway system. Other cities may own that strength today, leaving these small cities to find new means of developing and sustaining the local economy.

Neither do natural resources always hold the same economic development asset strength that they once had. Many of the cities in this study tell of having to replace the timber industry or the mills or textile operations or other manufacturing because those industries went overseas in search of cheaper labor. Even natural resources such as minerals and oil are not a guarantee of small town economic stability. Frequently, those resources are spent and can no longer sustain the economic base of these small, isolated cities and towns.

Who lives in these small towns? As a result of the fifty interviews conducted as part of this research, it appears that many of the residents of these small and isolated cities and towns are men, women, and families who have lived there for many years, or even generations. The second largest group appears to be people who lived in similar settings, although not in the specific small town in which they now reside. Third would be the folks who arrived for a job and decided to stay, some of whom have done so because of the great differences between the small town and the larger urban areas from which they hailed. Then, there are the occasional individuals who are there because they married someone from that community or because they happened to be there one time and fell in love with it.

The groups that do not seem to exist in large numbers are those who moved to these small towns and cities because they wanted to enjoy the lifestyle specifically offered. In fact, judging from previous research, it appears that those who seek a small town lifestyle are really in search of communities that are not quite this small. Many move to micropolitan cities (ten thousand to fifty thousand residents) because they can capture all that is good about small towns and some of what is good about larger urban areas, including educational opportunities, cultural offerings, and a stronger overall quality of life, however they individually define that.

In several of the interviews conducted for this research, the city manager or mayor noted that when their economies declined and the workforce departed for new opportunities, the city was left with an older population, with less earning power, and with greater demands for public services. In such cases, the quality of life can shift quite rapidly from a thriving community to an aging community with a future that is far less bright and optimistic than before.

The double whammy here is that the city has a lower base of income tax revenues, a smaller base of retail-generated sales taxes, and the potential for much greater—and different—demands for public services. This might include increased needs for public health, day care, and various forms of recreational opportunities. Indeed, many of these small cities and towns exist in states, such as Pennsylvania, that have eliminated income taxes for pensioners in an effort to repopulate small towns.

The loss of the job base has other damaging effects on small towns. It has already been noted that these companies were often the greatest supporters of Little Leagues, scout troops, churches, and other institutions in town. But, an additional loss is that many of the corporate executives were leaders in their respective communities as well. This means that economic decline can very rapidly lead to community decline, and even community dissolution. For evidence of that cause-and-effect relationship, one need only count the number of ghost towns that can be found across the United States.

All of the small cities in this book have met a certain definitional standard for being relatively isolated from another larger urban area. Of course, some are isolated and some are *very* isolated. The greater the degree of isolation from larger urban areas, the greater the sense of need to serve as a hub for other small cities in the region and for those who live in the more rural areas, on farms, and so forth. In those situations, the hub city must be all things to all people. It becomes an employment center, a retail center, and the source of medical services, cultural opportunities, recreational pursuits, and more.

Given the size of the communities in this study and the relative isolation from larger urban areas, regionalism and collaboration become much more likely than in more populated conurbations. Helping one's neighbor becomes a way of life. It is one means of survival, but it is not a guarantee of survival.

Regionalism can have numerous applications in theory. In some settings, it can mean the joint, cooperative funding of municipal services that enable the elimination of redundant functions and services in those areas where common support for common offices can represent both greater effectiveness and greater efficiency. Again, on the surface, this would appear to be an obvious strategy for municipalities that are proximate to one another but that are, collectively, somewhat isolated. Why, for example, would a county and two small towns need separate water treatment facilities when one such plant could serve all?

Many have suggested that this type of redundant service provision is simply the consequence of egos, politics, or even a historic separation of services. Others will point out that cooperative funding of common municipal services and facilities will have to happen, if only because communities cannot afford to do otherwise. Indeed, on the surface, regionalism of this type may appear to be what today's slang classifies as a no-brainer. And, many of the leaders of small, isolated cities and towns who were interviewed for this study indicated that they either had or would be moving in the direction of shared services in their respective reasons either because it makes good sense or because they could no longer afford not to do so.

But, things are not always as they appear to the outside observer. There are, in fact, situations in which regional collaboration of this type is discouraged by the tax policies of the states in which the region is located. In several of the interviews conducted for this text, city and town leadership described the key situational variable that stands in the way of regional funding of common services. This is the case in states where the tax policies unwittingly pit city and town against the counties that surround them in a "competition" for tax revenues. For example, in some states, counties may be authorized to collect the sales taxes or other tax streams, while cities and towns may have to rely on property taxes or an array of fees or other collections to provide public services.

In several of the communities reviewed herein, the respective state's tax policies unintentionally make business locations in the county less difficult due to the tax burden relative to a similar location within the city limits. If a company can simply locate one block over the boundary between city and county, and thereby reduce its tax obligations, it will likely do so. It can still gain access to the area's workforce and amenities, so there is no need for company leaders to assume the greater costs of locating one block closer to the city center.

The consequence is that the county generates the greater or more consistent tax revenues, while the city is obligated to provide the core services the residents of the region expect from localities. These services may include parks, libraries, public education, and more. Most prominently however, this will include much of the infrastructural requirements for water and wastewater treatment, road construction and maintenance, and other critical, but very expensive, public service needs.

Albeit an unintentional consequence of state taxation policies—some of which stretch back decades, or even centuries—the result of these situations has frequently been a form of competition between counties and cities. This creates a scenario in which the joint funding of common services can be difficult to negotiate and budget. The outside observer might react by encouraging those states to reconsider their taxing structures for municipalities. While this may seem entirely reasonable to an outsider, it undoubtedly seems unlikely to those living within the situation. After all, the problem represents long-term policies and structures, and if they were to be changed to enable the cities and towns to benefit more, someone else (the counties) would have to agree to benefit less. Unless new taxes can be created or old tax rates increased, the revenues represent a zero-sum game. Any changes will have winners who will be happy and losers who will be unhappy.

The only remaining option is to generate new revenues for the cities and towns that need greater resources. Some of those interviewed referred to this as "increasing the size of the pie." That is, the same relative share of all taxes generated will provide greater resources to everyone if the total is enlarged. This is why economic development is so vital to these small towns. It is the only way for many of them to generate the increased revenue streams that will help to pay for public services for their residents, businesses, and visitors.

For many communities, this creates quite a conundrum. They know they need to grow. They know that residents often cost more in services than they pay in taxes. They know they need businesses to grow because they generally require less in services than they contribute in taxes.

They know they need to attract and retain and grow companies. They don't always want to. Growth after a given point represents less of a gain and potentially more of a loss of another kind: the loss of the small town environment, their own sense of community.

Thus, the issues of growth do not always relate to questions of what or how, but if. In these cities, the proper balance must be struck between essential growth, desirable growth, and too much growth.

The reader is also advised to keep in mind while reading this study that any of these small, isolated cities can become ghost towns. The challenges for policy makers are whether to work to ensure that more cities do not become ghost towns in the future, and how best to be sure that doesn't happen for a lack of effort and support.

Numerous mayors and city managers in this study noted that the people who live in these cities and towns really *need* to like some specific element of the lifestyle or they simply will not last. In International Falls, Minnesota, the mayor said that it was fifteen degrees below zero on the day of the interview. The city manager of Breckenridge said that one really has to love the big sky or have some other reason to be there, or they just are not going to be happy with the other climactic conditions prevalent in west Texas. They both said the same thing: "It's definitely not for everyone."

The term *rural* is equally difficult to pin down. Despite all of the research that surrounds the definitions of urban, suburban, exurban, and even micropolitan areas, there remains no universally regarded definition of what a rural community is. Indeed, the term *rural* is more often described in terms of what it is not rather than what it is, and even that is indistinct. Actual population levels don't generally enter into the discussion. Rather, one is advised merely to assemble all of the other areas, and whatever is not included in those must be rural.

Given this paucity of description, one can surmise that a rural community is something less than a micropolitan community that, according to the US Bureau of the Census, and along with several other defining factors, has a population of no less than ten thousand souls. When considering the rural community therefore, one can presume the outer limit to be 9999 residents. Presumably, inasmuch as one person does not constitute a community, the other extreme is a community of two. For the purpose of this research then, a small town will be understood to have no more than ten thousand residents.

For the purposes of this research, greater definition was necessary in order to establish the list of case study towns. My presumption was that the challenges of a town of fewer than one thousand are far different than those of a town of nine thousand. For that reason, the "sweet spot" for the case studies was set closer to the midpoint, with a focus on five thousand to nine thousand people.

And surely, there is more to the requisite definition than simply the size of the population. A city of five thousand people that is located adjacent to other cities of varying sizes within a larger metropolitan area would not have the same issues—or solutions—as a city of the same size but that is more isolated from other cities or towns. Thus, the second criterion for case study selection will be that the towns must be located at least twenty-five miles from the next largest category of cities: micropolitan (ten thousand to fifty thousand inhabitants). Indeed, many of the cities included in this research are not only the largest cities in their respective counties, but comprise half or two-thirds of the total population of the counties in which they are located. For that reason, many of the cities herein have been designated as the seats of their counties. This can sometimes be a good thing because it means that all county tax dollars pass through the city and that there are numerous additional jobs associated with the administration of the county, as well as city employment.

Even when the discussions turn to considerations of what cities and towns need to survive and thrive, a general list of needs can easily be compiled for cities, suburbs, and exurban communities of various sizes. But, for rural communities, the summary is more typically one of *what is not present* rather than what can be found in town. It is actually rather easy to identify what assets and amenities are missing in America's rural communities. One merely has to Google *rural associations* and up will pop statewide a variety of associations addressing rural issues related to health care, public education, broadband capacity and Internet service, electricity, water, transportation, and growth.

If one goes back to the Internet and this time searches for books about ghost towns, there will be numerous sources cited, including stories of western states with century-old ghost towns as well as books and articles that discuss the towns in various states across America that are in such decline today that they could one day become ghost towns as well. Most have been threatened by either fires, floods, or other natural disasters, or the loss of an industry or railroad line. Some have lost the agricultural land that was once so important to their local economies, or have seen their natural resource assets run dry, or have witnessed the departure of a primary company or the death of a primary industry. Perhaps this is why two authors have noted that "economic development is often concerned with diversifying the rural economy" (Woods and Sloggett, p. 1).

The more modern equivalent of those types of disasters for isolated small cities and towns has been the advent of big-box retailers. These stores have many advantages and do good business but, as has been noted, do not leave the revenues generated by sales in the local communities in which they reside. Those go back to the headquarters location. Of course, the sales generate sales taxes, but not every small city gets to keep what they earn; those often accrue to the benefit of the state budget or are redistributed statewide on a formula basis that may or may not benefit the point of generation.

Another, rather disappointing, trend in small towns, especially those that are also isolated, is a tendency to quit. That is, there can be a sense that follows economic decline that nothing will succeed in turning around the fortunes of the city or its inhabitants, so why keep trying? This is a refrain heard in a relative few of the interviews conducted herein, but then I was in search of the most positive of examples and lessons that could be emulated by others, so the discussions were not directed toward the decline. Perhaps even more importantly, some took themselves in that direction quite naturally.

Small cities that have experienced the loss of the major employers, or several large employers, have responded in different ways. Some have overcome the loss and focused on recovery strategies, while others have given in to a sense that there will not be a recovery.

Cities are comprised of individuals, and individuals react to challenges and loss in different ways. But, understanding why some people react in one way while others react differently is not as easy as simply assigning the conclusions to human nature. Some situations are more clearly recognizable as being able to be turned around. As will be seen, it is possible that the economic environment enables some small cities and towns to have options. These may include the loss of a large employer working with the natural resources of the area. In such a case, a new employer or a different use of the area's resources may be feasible. Several examples of this will be seen in the interviews.

Unfortunately, there seem to be more examples of barriers than opportunities. For example, the greater the isolation of the city, the more difficult it may be to identify legitimate reasons for business to locate. The greater the distance from transportation networks, the more difficult it will be to resurrect the local economy. Often, the taxation policies of the respective states can make economic growth and recovery more or less difficult. States are also cited by those interviewed in this research as placing undue focus on the promotion and economic development of their primary markets. The explanation that accompanies that recognition is that larger markets generate greater returns on the states' investments. While true, the arguments offered are that a proper balance of expenditures to support the growth of large cities and small towns needs to be reached.

Because much of the environment in which recovery must be understood and conducted is often out of the control of the leadership of these municipalities, it becomes easier to understand how, in some of these communities, it is a natural reaction to become resigned to one's fate. In such situations, recovery is hampered or even defeated altogether. In those communities, when the jobs leave, the workforce also leaves. The result can be the loss of the very asset needed to attract new employers. The corollary outcome is that cities are left with greater demands for public services and public support at times when the tax revenues and budgetary resources are rapidly declining.

Despite all this, there are many examples across this great nation of rural communities that remain in existence and even seem to be flourishing today. Why have some communities thrived—or reversed declines—while others have continued to spiral downward? Are there lessons that can be learned from the successful that are replicable in other rural communities as they try to move forward?

What are the responsibilities of the governments of these small, rural cities and towns? How do they generate the tax base that enables them to provide the public services they are required to provide? How do they relate to the counties and states within which they reside? What can they do to further the advance of the local economy in order to generate additional revenues for the locality and to enhance the quality of life for their citizens and visitors? And, what are the roles and responsibilities of the state and federal governments to ensure their ultimate survival and growth?

Clearly, every small town in America is different and has different possibilities. To select the relevant sample of small towns to include in this research, data from the Bureau of the Census was used to identify all of the cities and towns across America—by state—that have between five thousand and nine thousand inhabitants and that are located no closer to a micropolitan or larger city or town than twenty-five miles. Having thus narrowed that list, further focus was needed. I wanted to ensure that all regions of the United States were represented. By ensuring a comprehensive geographic spread, it may be possible to identify any regional issues that impact economic development and economic growth or revitalization.

At this point, with approximately fifty cities to be included as case studies and forty-eight contiguous states to consider, the average per state would be presumed to be about one; however, that was not assumed as a criterion. Further, while small towns in border states would be fine, small towns in locations immediately proximate to the border with either Canada or Mexico were considered carefully because it was assumed that too many of the issues with which their leadership would be involved would relate to the borders themselves. Thus, the cities and towns that were, with one exception, ultimately selected for the study are generally inland by a distance of at least twenty-five miles.

At this point in the selection process, the universe of potential cities and towns for inclusion numbered more than twelve hundred. Further culling the list from this point became, of necessity, increasingly less scientific. There needed to be enough commonality between the sample towns to ensure enough mass in the data to reach common conclusions; yet, there needed not to be so much in common between the case study towns that other situations are not considered. And, in complete candor, the final decision to be included or not was often made by the leadership of the towns themselves. Some mayors and council chairs were excited to be included while some—although only a few—expressed skepticism and asked to be excused from further consideration.

One important reason for assessing the economic vitality of these small cities and towns is that there is a great sense expressed in the literature that these towns are actually essential to the very national character of the United States. People regard the presumed slower pace of life, the healthier and more wholesome environment, the lower costs and safer neighborhoods, and the longing for a sense of community that is not readily found in more urbanized areas, and express a tug to try that type of lifestyle and raise their families there. Moreover, a strong sentiment was repeatedly expressed that we are collectively a nation of people who expect choices. To those who choose to live in small towns, their preservation is an absolute.

Another clear reason for nonparticipation is that cities and towns of this size, while incorporated, do not always have elected (and possibly even appointed) officials who are full-time or who have the time to devote to inquiries of this nature as they are trying to manage their businesses and family lives as well.

This should, in no way, be regarded as a lack of interest or pride in their cities. To the contrary: these are some of the most dedicated public servants in all of America. It is their stories that follow; it is their lessons we will hope to learn.

What Does It Mean for a Small Town to Be Isolated, and Why Is That Important?

Prior research in this series targeted seventy micropolitan cities across America. The designation of micropolitan was developed by the US Census Bureau in 2007 and includes municipalities with between ten thousand and fifty thousand residents. The research concluded that there are three types of micropolitan cities. Metropolitan micropolitans exist within the orbit of, and are dependent upon the economic fortunes of, major metropolitan areas. A good example of this would be

Paramus, New Jersey, an inner suburb of New York City. The second type is the hub micropolitan, which is perhaps up to fifty miles from a major metropolitan area and can draw upon it for some of the services its residents require, such as educational opportunities, culture, and medical attention. Galesburg, Illinois, is one such city. Third, there are isolated micropolitans, such as Twin Falls, Idaho, which, as a result of their greater distances from larger urban areas, must ensure that they can provide all the services their constituents require, in or near their cities. In effect, they need to be almost entirely self-sufficient.

The lessons learned about being that isolated are indeed transferable to the much smaller cities in this study, but the order of magnitude of their effects can be significantly greater. Being isolated *and* small means that the requirement for being self-sufficient is much greater. This is because a smaller group is less likely to have all the requisite services than a larger area to be able to generate the demand necessary to attract them. This means that the residents of small and isolated cities or towns are often required to drive great distances to obtain some of the medical, educational, cultural, shopping, or other services that they either need or want. The same can be said of advanced education or recreational and cultural opportunities.

While much of the discussion above addresses the negative elements of isolation for small towns and their residents, it is not all bad. Many of the interviewees expressed the benefits of living in areas that are distant from larger urban regions. These benefits tend to include the outdoor opportunities that are readily available, the closeness of neighbors and townspeople who *must* rely on each other, and the perception of diminished access to drugs, crime, and other urban problems.

It was with considerable interest that I listened to mayors and city managers talk about the drug and crime issues in their cities. Many of these small town leaders indicated that their isolation from larger cities and metropolitan areas has meant that there is less likelihood for their residents to have drug issues (per capita) and that the relative crime metrics are also lower in the smaller cities and towns. None addressed issues related to alcoholism in their cities. The implication seemed to be that these evils that are more typically associated with large inner cities were far away from their havens of safety. Another perspective expressed seemed to imply that in cities and towns of less than ten thousand residents, the troublemakers and drug usage tend to be more obvious and known rather than able to remain hidden. Many respondents made the point that small town school systems are smaller and generally have smaller class sizes that make it difficult for students to hide. The argument they make is that poor performance in small city schools is spotted and addressed early and often.

However, there was also a distinct group of small town leaders who participated in the interviews for this study who noted, to the contrary, that such difficulties are not that unknown in their cities as well, and that those are not problems only of larger urban areas, other than in terms of the orders of magnitude. Those individuals also noted the direct relationship (as is well established by research) between crime rates and substance abuse on the one hand and unemployment and underemployment on the other. Thus, as the economies of these cities rise and fall, they are as susceptible as anyplace else in terms of these issues.

That really brings this discussion full circle: Why do people choose to live in these smaller cities and towns? The overall conclusion must certainly be that cities of all sizes have great appeal for some but not for everyone: in short, to each his own.

One of the consequences of a city where the economy is on the decline is that it ultimately begins to lose the very institutions and pillars of the community that would be needed to re-create a vital and growing economic base. That may include the workforce, doctors, or other personal services. In one interview, it was noted that the city had lost its optometrist and residents now had to travel long distances for eyeglasses. In another interview, it was noted that the hospitals had downsized and patients who needed MRIs had to travel substantial distances to obtain such service. More serious medical treatment options were certainly located in larger urban areas.

But, these losses are just part of the story for a small, isolated city or town on the decline. Retail opportunities move away and people either have to travel or become significantly more self-sufficient. In the long run, residents begin to consider relocating to communities where these basic needs are available. One loss that is less common but equally devastating is that of a local press. In July 2013, an article appeared in the Raton, New Mexico, newspaper, *Raton Range*. Its publisher wrote the heartrending piece that is included in part in Chapter 4. After decades of publication and numerous last-minute attempts to rescue the paper, it was closing—at least, temporarily. An interview with the publisher of *Raton Range*, Ms. Paula Murphy, also appears in Chapter 4.

What is happening in many of our small cities and towns is indeed heartrending. And, it is happening with a greater frequency than one may imagine. "A record number of US counties—more than one in three—are now dying off, hit by an aging population and weakened local economies that are spurring young adults to seek jobs and build families elsewhere" (Yen, 2013). The 2012 census data that is the basis for the article indicates that 1135 counties are undergoing what the author refers to as "natural decrease"; that is, deaths in those communities are more numerous than births. In the 2009 census data, reports the article, not even nine hundred counties fell into the same category, and the ratio that represented was only one in four, not one in three.

Yen also reported that "the population of non-metropolitan areas ... declined by about 0.1 percent, compared with growth of one percent for large metropolitan areas and 0.7 percent for small metropolitan areas" (Yen, 2013). Clearly, the question of small, isolated cities and towns, and their potential for survival, must be a serious—and growing—policy concern for local, state, and federal officials.

Some of the communities included in this research are experiencing natural decrease, while others are faring reasonably well or even very well. What sets some communities in one economic direction and others in the opposite direction? And, what can we learn from both histories?

Selecting the Case Study Cities

Data from the US Bureau of the Census (Department of Commerce) was used to identify the cities in each state that had between five thousand and nine thousand residents. This initial screening yielded a list of 1121 cities in the forty-eight continental states, including three that had none (Rhode Island, Massachusetts, and Connecticut).

The map was then divided into seven regions and the states within each of those regions tallied to indicate the total qualifying cities and towns that met the specified criteria. The Northwest region includes five states and a total of sixty-eight qualifying cities and towns. The North Central region includes five states with a total of ninety-six municipalities meeting the criteria of the population filter. The Great Lakes region, which is also comprised of five states, has a total of 239 such locations. The Northeast region includes eleven states with a total of 246 cities and towns with the cited population base. The Southeast region is home to ten states with a total of 252 such locations. The South Central region, with six states, includes 206 cities and towns of this size. And finally, the Southwest region includes six states and 114 such communities.

Following this analysis, the second criterion was applied: the case study cities should be no closer than thirty miles from another city with a population larger than ten thousand residents. This was done to ensure a significant degree of isolation. This process (which entailed the plotting of more than twelve hundred cities on forty-eight state maps) yielded a possible list of 144, which are listed in Table 1.1.

It was then decided to use as case studies the same number of cities from each region as the region bore to the list of "possibles." As a result, the case studies drawn from the following list of possible cities will approximate the following distribution: Northwest, 7; North Central, 8; Great Lakes, 3; Northeast, 2; Southeast, 12; South Central, 8; and West/Southwest, 10.

It should be noted that the population filter yielded numerous potential cities that were removed from the list when the second—the isolation—filter was applied. In the most densely populated regions of the United States, the population bases are spread broadly across the states, making it difficult to identify areas in which cities of the requisite size are located no closer than thirty miles from a larger urban area. This was the case most notably in the Northeast and Great Lakes regions. In other areas, such as the Southwest, it was much easier to identify cities that are both "small and alone."

Indeed, the second filter resulted in fourteen states being identified as having no city that met both qualifications. These include Connecticut, Delaware, Florida, Kentucky, Maryland, Massachusetts, New Hampshire, New Jersey, Ohio, Oklahoma, Rhode Island, and Vermont. Thus, roughly fifty case studies were to be drawn proportionately from the remaining thirty-six continental states, as shown in Table 1.1.

Table 1.1 City Data for Case Study Selections (Possibles)

State	City	*July 1 Population Estimates*	
		2010	*2013*
Northwest			
Idaho	Emmett	6557	6519
	Rupert	5554	5617
Montana	Havre	9310	9771
	Lewiston	5901	5902
	Livingstown	7044	7136
	Miles City	8410	8646
Oregon	Lincoln	7930	8040
	Milton-Freewater	7050	7099
	Umatilla	6906	7002
Washington	Ephrata	7664	7959
	Othello	7364	7631
	Quincy	6750	7242
Wyoming	Cody	9520	9833
	Douglas	6120	6469
	Lander	7487	7732
	Powell	6314	6476
	Worland	5487	5456
North Central			
Iowa	Algona	5560	5513
	Cherokee	5253	5186
	Clear Lake	7777	7692
	Estherville	6360	6126
Minnesota	Crookston	7891	7904
	Detroit Lakes	8569	8899

Table 1.1 (*Continued*) City Data for Case Study Selections (Possibles)

State	City	*July 1 Population Estimates*	
		2010	*2013*
Minnesota (*Continued*)	East Grand Forks	8601	8602
	International Falls	6424	6352
	Kasson	5931	6047
	Montevideo	5383	5219
	Redwood Falls	5254	5135
	Rogers	8597	11,983
Nebraska	Chadron	5851	5787
	Holdrege	5495	5527
	Sidney	6757	6829
North Dakota	Devil's Lake	7141	7246
South Dakota	Brandon	8785	9532
Great Lakes			
Illinois	Benton	7087	7054
	Carmi	5240	5208
	Mount Carmel	7284	7112
Indiana	North Vernon	6728	6703
Michigan	Ecorse	9512	9343
	Iron Mountain	7624	7601
	Kingsford	5133	5131
	Ludington	8076	8040
	Manistee	6226	6117
	River Rouge	7903	7676
	Walled Lake	6999	7127
Ohio	None		

Continued

Table 1.1 (*Continued*) City Data for Case Study Selections (Possibles)

State	*City*	*July 1 Population Estimates*	
		2010	*2013*
Wisconsin	Ashland	8216	8130
	Rice Lake	8438	8339
Northeast			
Connecticut	None		
Delaware	None		
Maine	Caribou	8189	7952
	Presque Isle	9692	9402
Maryland	None		
Massachusetts	None		
New Hampshire	None		
New Jersey	None		
New York	Canton	6314	6714
	Cedarhurst	6592	6646
	Lawrence	6483	6546
Pennsylvania	Bradford	8770	8630
	Corry	6605	6513
	Titusville	5601	5431
Rhode Island	None		
Vermont	None		
Southeast			
Alabama	Arab	8316	8050
	Brewton	5408	5436
	Hamilton	6885	6804
	Jackson	5228	5102
	Monroeville	6519	6289

Table 1.1 (*Continued*) City Data for Case Study Selections (Possibles)

State	City	*July 1 Population Estimates*	
		2010	*2013*
Alabama (*Continued*)	Roanoke	6074	6039
	Robertsdale	5276	5671
Florida	None		
Georgia	Camilla	5360	5084
	Sandersville	5912	5837
	Swainsboro	7227	7560
	Thomaston	9170	9081
	Waynesboro	5766	5809
Kentucky	None		
Mississippi	Booneville	8749	8759
	Kosciusko	7402	7315
	Louisville	6631	6463
North Carolina	Brevard	7609	7645
	Roxboro	8362	8344
South Carolina	Lake City	6675	6724
	Lancaster	8526	9045
Tennessee	Covington	9038	9052
	Humboldt	8452	8402
	Lexington	7657	7587
	McKenzie	5310	5578
	Milan	7851	7779
	Ripley	8445	8399
	Savannah	6982	7105
Virginia	Bluefield	5444	5392

Continued

Table 1.1 (*Continued*) City Data for Case Study Selections (Possibles)

State	*City*	*July 1 Population Estimates*	
		2010	*2013*
Virginia (*Continued*)	Emporia	5927	558
	Farmville	8216	8079
	Galax	7042	7035
	South Boston	8142	7989
West Virginia	Elkins	7094	7214
	Keyser	5439	5310
	Moundsville	9318	8887
South Central			
Arkansas	Berryville	5356	5465
	De Queen	6594	6723
	Greenwood	8952	9302
	Mena	5737	5723
	Newport	7879	7771
	Pocahontas	6608	6532
	Trumann	7243	7155
	Warren	6003	5882
Kansas	Chanute	9119	9255
	Colby	5387	5416
	Concordia	5395	5261
	Fort Scott	8087	7934
Louisiana	Leesville	6612	6637
	Marksville	5702	5593
Missouri	Boone Terre	6864	7232
	Charleston	5947	5921
	Chillicothe	9515	9318

Table 1.1 (*Continued*) City Data for Case Study Selections (Possibles)

State	City	July 1 Population Estimates	
		2010	2013
Missouri (*Continued*)	Dexter	7864	7938
	Macon	5471	5506
	Perryville	8225	8334
Oklahoma	None		
Texas	Atlanta	5675	5632
	Breckenridge	5780	5525
	Childress	6105	6091
	Crockett	6950	6621
	Dalhart	7930	8256
	Elsa	5660	5575
	Fort Stockton	8283	8384
	Jasper	7590	7656
	Pecos	8780	8903
	Seminole	6430	7027
Southwest			
Arizona	Bisbee	5575	5360
	Winslow	9655	9479
California	Calipatria	7705	7095
	Cloverdale	8618	8738
	Corning	7663	7592
	Crescent City	7643	7188
	Fairfax	7441	7607
	Fort Bragg	7273	7250
	Mammoth Lakes	8234	8073
	Yreka	7765	7605

Continued

Table 1.1 (*Continued*) City Data for Case Study Selections (Possibles)

State	*City*	*July 1 Population Estimates*	
		2010	*2013*
Colorado	Alamosa	8780	9562
	Craig	9464	8981
	Delta	8915	8860
	Gunnison	5854	5873
	Lamar	7804	7776
	Salida	5236	5409
Nevada	Winnemucca	7396	8002
New Mexico	Raton	6885	6537
	Socorro	9051	8911
	Taos	5716	5731
	Truth or Consequences	6474	6246
	Tucumcari	5363	5152
Utah	Roosevelt	6046	6750
	Vernal	9089	10,344

Source: US Department of Commerce, Bureau of the Census, http://www.quickfacts.census.gov.

All of the cities listed in Table 1.1 met the initial screening criteria of size and geographic isolation. In order to pare the list further—to the fifty or so case study communities—several additional screens were overlaid on the remaining universe of possible cities. The intention in doing so was more than simply to cull the total to a desired number; it was also intended to select a wide geographic distribution, including as many of the continental states as feasible, and—most importantly—to include cities that have confronted either declining or dramatically increasing populations or business communities over recent years. In this way, it will be possible to see both sides of the many issues involved as well as to identify both the challenges and some of the approaches that have been tested and yielded positive conclusions.

It is important to note that cities and towns, as well as counties, exist and operate within the contexts of the realities and the laws of their home states. State policies do not always seem to benefit localities, so it is important, when assessing municipalities' abilities to grow and sustain their local economic bases, to consider that which they cannot control, including the business-friendliness of their respective states. Table 1.2 lists the relative rankings of each of the states represented in the city case studies as determined by CNBC and Forbes.com.

Table 1.2 Relative Rankings of Case Study States as Business-Friendly

State	*Forbes.com*	*CNBC*
Northwest		
Idaho	25th	10th
Montana	26th	19th
Oregon	19th	17th
Washington	9th	21st
Wyoming	23rd	9th
North Central		
Iowa	12th	11th
Minnesota	8th	15th
Nebraska	6th	4th
Michigan	47th	29th
Wisconsin	41st	22nd
Northeast		
Maine	50th	38th
Pennsylvania	27th	39th
Southeast		
Alabama	44th	33rd
Georgia	10th	8th
Mississippi	49th	41st
Tennessee	15th	13th
Virginia	1st	5th
West Virginia	46th	48th
South Central		
Arkansas	35th	24th
Kansas	17th	14th

Continued

Table 1.2 (*Continued*) Relative Rankings of Case Study States as Business-Friendly

State	*Forbes.com*	*CNBC*
Missouri	30th	26th
Texas	7th	2nd
Arizona	24th	20th
West/Southwest		
California	39th	47th
Colorado	5th	7th
New Mexico	45th	33rd
Utah	3rd	5th

Source: http://www.cnbc.com and http://www.forbes.com.

To help identify the growth or decline of the respective population bases and numbers of business establishments in each of the cities, US Bureau of the Census data was used. To look for some of the strongest and most challenging situations, additional materials were employed, including the CNBC and Forbes.com ratings of the best states for business and a variety of online assessments of the best small cities in various states. From all of this, the fifty cities were selected and contacted regarding interviews with the mayors or city managers who were in place at the time of contact, as shown in Table 1.3.

For each of the fifty case study cities listed in Table 1.3, the population trends are provided, including columns showing the differences in the population bases between 2000 and 2010 in both whole numbers and percentages. For every city in which the change over that period was less than five percent a horizontal arrow is used to indicate the direction of the change: pointing to the left for decreases of less than five percent or to the right to indicate increases of less than five percent. Increases and decreases of more than five percent are illustrated by arrows pointing up or down, respectively.

To summarize, the data shows that, among the fifty-one case study cities, eighteen showed population growth in excess of five percent during the two-year period shown. Nine cities lost more than five percent of their population bases over the same period. Eight gained between zero and five percent, and sixteen lost between zero and five percent.

Data in Table 1.4 shows the number of business establishments counted in the 2007 economic census released by the US Bureau of the Census. Data for 2012 will be useful for comparative purposes and for identifying trends, but it will not be

Table 1.3 Case Study Communities, Population Trends

State	City	Population Estimate		Population Change		Direction
		2000	2012	No.	Percent	
Northwest						
Idaho	Emmett	5789	6529	740	12.8	↑
	Rupert	5645	5473	–182	–3.0	→
Montana	Lewistown	5813	5857	44	0.1	→
Oregon	Lincoln	7437	7965	528	5.0	↑
Washington	Ephrata	6808	7916	1108	16.3	↑
Wyoming	Cody	8835	9689	854	9.7	↑
	Douglas	5274	6280	1006	19.1	↑
North Central						
Illinois	Carmi	5408	5218	190	–3.5	←
Iowa	Algona	5741	5511	–230	–4.0	←
Minnesota	Detroit Lakes	7745	8823	1078	13.9	↑
	International Falls	6703	6357	–346	–5.2	↓
	Montevideo	5346	5247	–99	–1.9	↓
Nebraska	Holdrege	5655	5537	–118	–2.1	↓
	Sidney	6282	6808	523	8.3	↑
North Dakota	Valley City	6831	6601	–230	–3.4	↓
Great Lakes						
Michigan	Kingsford	5549	5147	–402	–7.2	↓
Wisconsin	Ashland	8216	8128	–88	–1.0	←
	Rice Lake	8401	8368	–33	–0.4	←
Northeast						
Maine	Caribou	8312	8051	–261	–3.1	←
Pennsylvania	Titusville	6146	5501	–643	–10.5	↓

Continued

Table 1.3 (*Continued*) Case Study Communities, Population Trends

State	City	Population Estimate 2000	Population Estimate 2012	Population Change No.	Population Change Percent	Direction
Southeast						
Alabama	Arab	7288	8264	976	13.4	↑
	Hamilton	6660	6841	181	2.7	→
Georgia	Thomaston	9558	9101	–457	–4.8	←
Mississippi	Kosciusko	7372	7242	–130	–1.8	←
North Carolina	Brevard	6874	7619	745	10.8	↑
	Roxboro	8627	8324	–303	–3.5	←
Tennessee	Covington	8463	9038	575	6.4	↑
	Lexington	7393	7791	398	5.4	↑
	McKenzie	5295	5383	88	1.7	→
Virginia	Galax	6837	6908	71	1.0	→
	South Boston	8491	8068	–423	–5.0	↓
West Virginia	Elkins	7032	7180	148	2.1	→
South Central						
Arkansas	Pocahontas	6518	6597	79	–1.2	←
Kansas	Colby	5450	5406	–44	–0.8	←
	Fort Scott	8295	7951	–344	–4.1	←
Missouri	Charleston	4732	5908	1176	24.9	↑
	Chillicothe	9026	9432	406	4.5	→
	Perryville	7667	8262	595	7.8	↑
Texas	Breckenridge	5868	5666	–202	–3.4	←
	Elsa	5549	6279	730	13.2	↑
	Pecos	9501	8785	–716	–7.5	↓
West/Southwest						
Arizona	Winslow	9520	9382	–138	–1.4	←

Table 1.3 (*Continued*) Case Study Communities, Population Trends

State	City	Population Estimate		Population Change		Direction
		2000	2012	No.	Percent	
California	Fort Bragg	7026	7252	226	3.2	→
	Yreka	7290	7697	389	5.3	↑
Colorado	Delta	8915	8813	–102	–1.1	←
	Gunnison	5409	5892	483	8.9	↑
	Lamar	8869	7836	–1103	–11.6	↓
	Salida	5504	5317	–187	–3.4	←
Nevada	Winnemucca	7197	7777	580	8.1	↑
New Mexico	Taos	5716	5689	–27	–0.05	←
Utah	Vernal	7714	9817	2103	1	↑

Source: Census Quick Facts, 2012.

Table 1.4 Number of Business Establishments (2007) in Case Study Communities

Region	State	City	Firms 07
Northwest	Idaho	Emmett	INA[1]
		Rupert	629
	Montana	Lewistown	1049
	Oregon	Lincoln	1092
	Washington	Ephrata	580
	Wyoming	Cody	2085
		Douglas	706
North Central	Illinois	Carmi	498
	Iowa	Algona	798
	Minnesota	Detroit Lakes	1141
		International Falls	602

[1] Information not available.

Continued

Table 1.4 (*Continued*) Number of Business Establishments (2007) in Case Study Communities

Region	*State*	*City*	*Firms 07*
North Central (*Continued*)	Minnesota	Montevideo	593
	Nebraska	Holdrege	642
		Sidney	437
	North Dakota	Valley City	941
Great Lakes	Michigan	Kingsford	434
	Wisconsin	Ashland	853
		Rice Lake	1035
Northeast	Maine	Caribou	831
	Pennsylvania	Titusville	581
Southeast	Alabama	Arab	804
		Hamilton	610
	Georgia	Thomaston	913
	Mississippi	Kosciusko	1153
	North Carolina	Brevard	1822
		Roxboro	1161
	Tennessee	Covington	732
		Lexington	929
		McKenzie	431
	Virginia	Galax	589
		South Boston	829
	West Virginia	Elkins	986
South Central	Arkansas	Pocahontas	438
	Kansas	Colby	<25
		Fort Scott	830
	Missouri	Charleston	264
		Chillicothe	1177

Table 1.4 (*Continued*) Number of Business Establishments (2007) in Case Study Communities

Region	*State*	*City*	*Firms 07*
South Central (*Continued*)	Missouri	Perryville	919
	Texas	Breckenridge	INA[1]
		Elsa	786
		Pecos	425
West/Southwest	Arizona	Winslow	899
	California	Fort Bragg	1163
		Yreka	1019
	Colorado	Delta	1224
		Gunnison	1076
		Lamar	749
		Salida	12,317
	Nevada	Winnemucca	738
	New Mexico	Taos	1886
	Utah	Vernal	1182

[1] Information not available.

Source: US Bureau of the Census, Economic Census, 2007.

available until 2016. Such information is worthy of consideration when regarding the economic health of a community, particularly small, isolated cities. However, care must be taken not to read too much into the data. The number of firms, for instance, is not nearly as important as the number of employees. Fifty firms of one hundred employees each will probably generate more jobs, income, and expenditures than will one thousand companies of two employees.

Another misdirection that results from a simplistic view of the relative numbers of firms in each city relates to the cause for company births. For example, an immediate and significant increase in the number of business establishments in a community may be the result of a larger company moving away. In that instance, many of its former employees may be forced to attempt to start their own businesses. In that example, the community was likely better off with the smaller number before the departure of that larger employer.

For each of the case study cities, the leaders who were interviewed are listed in Table 1.5. A map is also provided to illustrate the geographic distribution of the case study cities across the continental United States.

Table 1.5 Case Study Communities and Interviewees

City, State	*Interviewee*	*Title*
Northwest		
Emmett, Idaho	The Honorable Bill Butticci	Mayor
Rupert, Idaho	Kelly Anthon	City administrator
Lewistown, Montana	Kevin Myhre	City manager
Lincoln, Oregon	David Hawker	City manager
Ephrata, Washington	Wes Crago	City administrator
Cody, Wyoming	The Honorable Nancy Tia Brown	Mayor
	Jenni Rosencrance	City administrator
Douglas, Wyoming	Tony Tolstedt	City administrator
North Central		
Carmi, Illinois	Sandra Irvine	City administrator
Algona, Iowa	Keri Navratil	City administrator
Detroit Lakes, Minnesota	Bob Louiseau	City manager
	Larry Remmen	Director of community development

Table 1.5 (*Continued*) Case Study Communities and Interviewees

City, State	*Interviewee*	*Title*
International Falls, Minnesota	The Honorable Bob Anderson	Mayor
Montevideo, Minnesota	Steve Jones	City manager
Holdrege, Nebraska	Robert Rager	City administrator
Sidney, Nebraska	Gary Person	City manager
Valley City, North Dakota	David Schelkopf	City manager
Great Lakes		
Kingsford, Michigan	Tony Edelbeck	City manager
Ashland, Wisconsin	The Honorable Bill Whalen	Mayor
Rice Lake, Wisconsin	Curt Snyder	City administrator
Northeast		
Caribou, Maine	Austin Bleess	City manager
Titusville, Pennsylvania	Larry Manross	City manager
Southeast		
Arab, Alabama	The Honorable Bob Joslin	Mayor
Hamilton, Alabama	The Honorable Wade Williams	Mayor
Thomaston, Georgia	The Honorable Hays Arnold	Mayor
	Patrick Comiskey	City manager
Kosciusko, Mississippi	The Honorable Jimmy Cockroft	Mayor
Brevard, North Carolina	Joe Moore	City manager
Roxboro, North Carolina	Stephen Steese	City manager
Covington, Tennessee	The Honorable David Gordon	Mayor
Lexington, Tennessee	The Honorable David Jones	Mayor
McKenzie, Tennessee	The Honorable Jill Holland	Mayor
Galax, Virginia	Keith Barker	City manager

Continued

Table 1.5 (*Continued*) Case Study Communities and Interviewees

City, State	*Interviewee*	*Title*
South Boston, Virginia	The Honorable Ed Owens	Mayor
Elkins, West Virginia	The Honorable Van Broughton	Mayor
South Central		
Pocahontas, Arkansas	The Honorable Frank Bigger	Mayor
Colby, Kansas	Tyson McGreer	City manager
	Christy Preston	Director of economic development
Fort Scott, Kansas	Dave Martin	City manager
Charleston, Missouri	Richard Goode	City manager
Chillicothe, Missouri	Ike Holland	City administrator
Perryville, Missouri	The Honorable Deborah Gahan	Mayor
	Brent Buerke	City manager
Breckenridge, Texas	Andy McCuistion	City manager
Elsa, Texas	Joe Contu	City manager
Pecos, Texas	The Honorable Venetta Seals	Mayor
West/Southwest		
Winslow, Arizona	Stephen Pauken	City manager
Fort Bragg, California	Linda Ruffing	City manager
Yreka, California	Steve Baker	City manager
Delta Colorado	Justin Clifton	City manager
Gunnison, Colorado	Ken Coleman	City manager
Lamar, Colorado	The Honorable Roger Stagner	Mayor
Salida, Colorado	The Honorable Jim Dickson	Mayor
Winnemucca, Nevada	Steve West	City manager
Taos, New Mexico	Rick Bellis	City manager
Vernal, Utah	Ken Bassett	City manager

Similarities and Dissimilarities between the Economic Forces and Solutions Facing Large Cities and Small Towns

In previous research, the lessons learned in larger cities were generally repeated in micropolitan cities as well. However, there was also a general overlay of additional conclusions for the micropolitan cities and towns depending upon some of their essential characteristics. Some of the most influential characteristics that affected these conclusions included geographic location relative to larger cities and regions, and proximity to various man-made or natural attractions.

The primary lessons learned in the larger settings, as relates to the growth or redevelopment of the local economies, were as follows:

1. Ensure that a welcoming attitude exists that encourages businesses to locate and remain in the community. The support for business growth and economic development must be more than purely rhetorical; it must be translated into tax measures, local ordinances, and other municipal business-related decisions. In fact, it can be argued that if there is not an inherent consistency between public statements of support for business growth and reality that businesses will quickly see the ruse and will stay away in numbers. The long-term damage created by such baseless promotion tends to be a well-deserved negative reputation that is spread by the employers who have looked and felt deceived.
2. Undertake the strongest economic development strategies when the economy is strong; don't wait until it is necessary to act. Too many examples exist of communities that coasted through the fat times and only began to promote themselves during the lean. At that point, they are trying to explain away a negative situation rather than promoting the presence of economic strength and growth. Again, employers see through such inaccuracies very quickly and share the information with others. By promoting a strong economy, employers can be shown that this is a city in which they, too, can be successful.
3. Recognize that economic growth does not occur in a vacuum. Communities cannot remain in the same economic place, neither growing nor contracting. Too many locations want to stand pat: "We like things as they are." That is a very fine perspective, but standing pat requires attention and action, not just idle hoping. In the competitive environment that is local economic development, other communities of like size, geography, and assets are growing and contracting all around them. A city or a region cannot sustain its *relative* position or its comparable competitiveness because not everyone else will do so. No local economy is an island.
4. Regard the development or growth of the local economy as a long-term process. There are no quick fixes, and the decline of the local economy can occur at a far quicker pace than its positive recovery. When local officials sell their

constituents on the budget allocations for such efforts, they need to be careful not to oversell the results or the rapidity with which they may be achieved. This can be a difficult concept for officials—elected or appointed—who do not expect to be in place in the long term and who may want to deliver results in the short term. While that can be possible, the best-laid plans are those that lay a proper foundation, make the sale, and reap the benefits. This may take a while.

5. Much of what can make a community more successful in its economic development in the future relates to providing the assets and amenities that the businesses of the future will require. Communities must therefore fall into one of three categories when it comes to the conditions necessary for future economic development:
   a. The assets needed to attract the businesses that strategic planning has targeted already generally exist in the community.
   b. The assets considered to be important can and will be acquired or developed over time in order for the locality to become more attractive to those businesses.
   c. The businesses targeted for economic development attraction and retention are those for whom the *existing* assets are actually the ones they need in order to be successful.

   Too many communities promote themselves for an industry segment for which they are not right. In the latter instance, the community cannot expect to attract or retain other businesses, and run the risk of establishing a reputation for bluster or hopes rather than realistic expectations. Conducting an asset gap analysis to identify industries and the relevant assets for a city must be a critical feature of strategic thinking and strategic planning.
6. The leadership styles that are most successful for economic development are often different than those required for other municipal leadership purposes. Economic development typically requires courage on the part of those who use relatively scarce resources for marketing, travel, and staff at the same time that other competing demands for human and budgetary resources represent critical needs in the community. This could require the courage to absorb criticism by representing these programs as more than just expenditures; they can be characterized as investments for which the expected returns are greater than the costs and that, in the long term, will provide additional resources to support the other needs of the municipality. This means, however, that explanations must be made for promotion instead of smaller classroom sizes in the public schools or new road construction or additional police officers on the city's beats. In most of the cities investigated, strategic planning takes place around a number of key municipal issues, including land use planning, budgetary planning, public schools planning, utility planning, and much more. In a very few communities one finds that the plans are completely coordinated with one another. Economic development professionals have a great

deal of information that can help instruct land use planning in a community but are not always included in the process. Similarly, the planning for business targeting, attraction, retention, and development may be well instructed by those who determine where the relevant sites will be located and how they will be zoned.

7. As noted above, economic development, as a budgetary line item, should be viewed not as an expense but as an investment. Of course, that is only a valid assertion if the returns on that investment are greater than the original investments. It also implies that communities must have very clear and measurable objectives in mind for such investments as well as a system of measuring the outcomes over time. It may seem self-evident to assert that this also means that the arguments that there will be positive returns on these investments are not just "sellable," but realistic and quantifiable, but all too often those details were not considered in many of the cities included as case studies.
8. In many of the nation's cities, there has been an inexorable growth outward in contiguous circles. This pattern began after the Second World War when returning vets wanted homes and yards and were willing to move out of the cities to have them. The suburbs flourished as those who could afford to do so moved. Ultimately, the jobs moved with them. This has created a double whammy for the cities that are left with the lowest skilled or educated and the lowest wage earners. Those lower incomes translate into lower tax generation and higher transfer payments to indigent, unemployed, and underemployed individuals and families, yielding a greater demand for services from an ever-shrinking revenue stream. And, of course, there is a direct relationship between lower incomes and higher rates of unemployment on the one hand and criminal activity on the other. This can further exacerbate the budget pressure (for enhanced law enforcement budgets) and, at the same time, devalue the attractiveness of the area for business locations. The extension of these trends has often been the heightening of tensions between the inner cities and the suburbs.

When considering the results of the seventy interviews with micropolitan city mayors, the above, more general lessons, did seem to apply. However, there was also an overlay of additional factors that were consistent across the board as related to the growth or regrowth of these smaller (ten thousand to fifty thousand residents) urban areas. The lessons that are specific to the micropolitan cities were as follows:

1. The means by which the local governments of the micropolitan cities build the tax base from which they provide city services is a more critical question than it is for larger cities. This is because they have fewer options for generating a range of revenue options. For example, there is typically limited land available in these smaller towns. Thus, a state that allows local governments to tax real estate in order to constitute their budgets for public

services may find that they have only finite resources from which to serve their constituents. In states where sales taxes accrue to the micropolitan city's coffers, a logical strategy is to seek to grow the base of merchants that can provide additional shopping opportunities as well as sales tax revenues. However, if the state either caps the percentage that goes to the point-of-sale community or centralizes the collections statewide and then redistributes the revenues based on established formulae, these may be seen as disincentives to be more aggressive in retail attraction/economic development efforts. In these circumstances, cities could potentially find themselves generating additional resources that will ultimately accrue to the benefit of the state of other, even competitor, cities within the state.

2. Micropolitan cities must, by virtue of their very size, be far more collaborative than a larger urban area. People know each other and interact more frequently; this means that they must rely on each other to ensure growth and a strong sense of community. Involvement in such a setting was often described as more intimate. Residents in a small town cannot be as invisible as they might be in a larger community or region. When everyone knows everyone else, they all tend to have opinions about each other. Many mayors who were interviewed expressed the same sort of relationships for elected officials. Several noted that when they go to the grocery store or out to dinner with their families, everyone they see knows who they are and what they have or have not done relative to the issue or issues of particular concern to them. One told me: "There is no hiding in a small town. We all must rely on one another." Interestingly for the current research, the dependence upon one another in a small town seems to increase as the town itself becomes increasingly isolated from other urban areas.
3. Small towns with obvious resources for economic development often work very closely with them to further economic development. This may include hospitals, military installations, colleges and universities, natural resources and parks, special events, and more. Micropolitan cities cannot become too comfortable with these assets when they are dominant in the economy: military bases may have land use requirements that are outside of the community's perceived best interests, military bases can be closed or reduced in size and scope, and macro-economic conditions can affect visitation to parks, natural resources, and events, for example. While it is fair to say that such community assets can be used to enhance the local economy, they are like any other economic development asset. They need to be viewed as one component of a larger economic base. These communities need to ensure that their economies are diverse enough to sustain base closures, declines in expendable income, unseasonable weather, and other forces beyond their control.
4. The economic diversification referenced above can be even more vital to a small town than to a larger community. In a large urban area, the departure of a dominant employer can be damaging to individuals and to the local

economy. In a small town, such a loss can be devastating and could potentially destroy the entire economic base of the city and even that of the region. On the other hand, a new large-scale employer that comes to the community can also have a more dramatic impact on a smaller city than it would have on a larger one.

5. Related to the above-referenced loss of a large employer was the oft-stated concern of the loss of the best and brightest young people from these cities, sometimes, though not always, in the wake of the loss of a major employer. Several of the mayors who were interviewed, however, indicated that the people who left the city and the region when very young in order to enjoy a different style of living will return when they reach the family stage of their lives. This is because they appreciate the values of their hometown and want their children to enjoy the same type of childhood they had enjoyed. Still, the numbers of those who leave tend to outweigh the numbers who return by a significant level, and the importation of a sufficient workforce to these smaller cities often becomes a constraint to further or faster or more desirable economic development over time.
6. Not surprisingly, the mayors of the micropolitan cities unanimously stressed the growing attractiveness to people of the small town values their communities offer. This may include lower crime or good neighbors or other manifestations of small towns where people know each other and get more involved because they have to do so. More than one mentioned the reduction of stress and the available outdoor activities as contributing factors to greater health and longer lives for their residents. Quality of life is one component of the "pitch" for every economic development professional in the United States. Of course, that quality has as many definitions as there are people who were asked. It is, as many interviewees pointed out, a matter of choices. One may not find all of the opportunities in a small town that are immediately available in a larger one, but the sacrifice of opportunities works in both directions. Small town leaders are very proud of what their cities have to offer and what they do not offer as well. Many of those who were included in the evaluation indicated a belief that Americans were beginning to rediscover small towns and the benefits they can offer.
7. Mayors of micropolitan cities are themselves as distinctly different from their larger city counterparts as are the cities they each represent. Only three of the seventy micropolitan city mayors who were interviewed acknowledged an interest in further or higher office. This seems, on the surface, to be atypical in larger urban settings, where local leadership may be seen as a stepping-stone to elective office at either the state or federal levels. The other sixty-seven men and women who were interviewed relate how they became mayor just because they felt needed or saw an opportunity to help the community in which they have lived, often for several generations, and where they hoped that their children and grandchildren would remain and raise their families. For the most

> part, they simply wanted to accomplish their objectives so they could get back to their families and their jobs. This also consistently seemed to mean a greater dependence than one might find in larger cities on the strong leadership of their professional city managers and staffs. The outcome typically was felt to be a less political, more professional process of municipal management.

The key question now involves the extent to which these (general and micropolitan city) lessons apply to the next level of cities, as measured by their population bases. That is, do these lessons still apply when the communities under consideration have only five thousand to nine thousand inhabitants and are isolated from other, larger urban areas? If they do not, which are not applicable and why? And, what are the new lessons relating to economic growth and economic development—or redevelopment—that apply specifically to the many small, isolated cities that span this great nation?

Chapter 2

Fifty-One of America's Small and Isolated Cities Examined

This chapter includes a research-based summary of the current economic situation of the fifty-one small, isolated cities that serve as case studies in this research. To a very great extent, an Internet search produces little on many of the cities. The best sources are their (often overly promotional) websites and Wikipedia. Because they are small and isolated, their often rich histories garner little attention, and economic successes or challenges are not given great coverage.

Following those somewhat scant stage-setting descriptions are summaries of the discussions held with the city's mayor or city manager. In this way, the stories of their economic growth, decline, and revitalization are told through their own words and experiences. It will be clear to the reader which of those descriptions are told from first-person experience and which are tales related by those who are relative newcomers to the city. This is not the case with the mayors included herein, but it is reflected in the interviews of the professional city managers included herein who have moved to their respective homes by way of several moves throughout their professional careers in public administration.

In the conclusions that follow these case study descriptions, summaries of the responses from city leaders help identify larger trends for small, isolated cities in general.

Northwest Region

Emmett, Idaho

Emmett, Idaho, is a quickly growing community. Between the decade of the 1990s and 2000, the city's residential population grew by more than 12 percent. The following five-year period saw another 19 percent growth. Yet, the city's unemployment rate remains below the national average at 5.6 percent, compared favorably with the US mean of 6.3 percent, at the time of this writing. This provided fodder for the discussion with the city's mayor.

A key area to explore with the mayor of Emmett is what has enabled the city's economy to grow fast enough to accommodate these additional residents. Are new jobs coming into Emmett? And, how has housing been increased to support the new families? Has the infrastructure and school system—and much more—been able to serve such a quickly growing residential base?

This small, isolated city sits at nearly six thousand feet above sea level and was initially settled as the result of the 1860s discovery of gold. Little else can be found through an Internet search about the local economy other than the loss of a Boise Cascade manufacturing facility that closed its doors in 2001. What has replaced it?

The largest sawmill in the city had closed but was purchased by a new owner who restarted operations, assisted by $4 million in federal stimulus money. The second life of the sawmill, however, was even shorter than the first. Employees were dismissed after seven months, and they and the city were devastated again. How has the employment rate remained relatively low when there have been so many new entrants to the labor force at the same time that major employers have closed their doors?

The city now hosts a variety of festivals to attract visitors. This includes, for example, the Cherry Festival, which is reported to attract fifty thousand people for a week in June. The interview with the city's leaders covered whether this has been an effective strategy.

In March 2010 (Gem County, 2010), the community gathered to create a strategy to plan for the growth of the local economy. The key background elements cited included the following:

- The rivers and dams in the area produced a quality of agriculture and a quality of life worth preserving.
- Low taxes and a skilled labor pool were attractive assets for business.
- Rail and air service are sufficient to support commerce as well as tourism.
- There is increasing migration to Gem County because of the rural lifestyle.
- Growth of the employment base in Boise, a little over thirty miles away, could establish Emmett as a bedroom community.

- Traditional resource industries are not strong growth industries for the future of the city. Entrepreneurialism holds greater promise for Emmett.
- Big-box retailers are affecting the ability of the local retailers to succeed.

Is there a tension growing between those who wish to retain the local, rural flavor of the city and the region with those who seek growth? This was a primary topic for the interview with the city's leadership.

Photo courtesy of Erika Harmon.

Interview with the Honorable Bill Buttucci, Mayor of Emmett, Idaho

Emmett, Idaho, is a city of nearly seven thousand residents within a larger region that is home to an additional seventeen thousand people. The city is close to the lower end of the continuum in terms of the definition of the case studies in this research. It is also near the lower end of the spectrum in terms of its relative isolation from other larger urban areas. Emmett lies only forty miles from a number of other cities. This has resulted in Emmett becoming essentially a bedroom community in which people live and return at the end of the workday.

Such was not always the case. Emmett was at one time the home of a large Boise Cascade plant that employed up to five hundred workers. After one cutback, the employment base declined to three hundred. Ultimately, the business closed its doors in Emmett completely. That was followed by a canning facility—the jobs in which were only seasonal—closing its doors as well.

At one time, the stronger employment base in Emmett enabled the city to support three grocery stores and three car dealerships. Today, there is one grocery store and one car dealership, which sells used vehicles. Retailers who provided such basic needs as clothing, household appliances, prescription refill services, and more to the people of Emmett are all gone now as well. This prompted Mayor Butticci to note, "People go to work and shop elsewhere, and then come here to come home."

Today, Emmett's largest employers are the public school system, which has 115 employees, and the county government, which employs about 100 others. The remainder of the city's economy is comprised of small businesses. Thus, the city is focusing its economic development efforts on ensuring that the downtown shops are leased and that their customer base is growing or stable. As they are "somewhat off the beaten path, the shops will need to be more than what can be found elsewhere." They need to provide the kinds of items and services that people cannot find elsewhere. This includes antique shops and other specialty item retailers. The city's leadership also feel that agricultural tourism also has potential for Emmett; a local produce represents healthy food alternatives that can be marketed in a way to attract visitors.

Following on that concept, a grant was obtained from the US Department of Agriculture that will support the feasibility planning for, and architectural designs of, a facility from which local organic foods can be packaged and sold. Further, the city's industrial park is the site for which marketing is taking place as the city seeks to attract or create companies of between fifty and seventy-five jobs each. Hopes are high for the park's progress because rail connections already exist to the site.

Fueling the hopes for the growth of businesses in Emmett is the ability to offer the residential base as potential workforce. Mayor Butticci notes that the residents who commute to other areas for daily employment greatly dislike the requisite commuting times, the high costs of gasoline, and having to deal with substantial snowfalls along their commutes during those seasons. The mayor believes that such individuals would jump at the opportunity to stay closer to home for employment opportunities. For the mayor, this represents a workforce that can be "offered" to prospective employers.

The city leaders feel that Emmett offers a community for families. Like so many of the communities involved in this research, Emmett wants to offer potential employers an attractive place for their workforce to live. It is quite likely that being an attractive small town is not an unusual offering to many businesses. It is quite correct, however, that the *absence* of appeal in a small city can deter a site location executive from pursuing a given location any further. There are simply too many alternatives from which to choose.

Mayor Butticci easily cites the advantages of his city, and they are not unlike those itemized by many of his peers in this research: good schools, a hospital, and entertainment. But, there is more to Emmett: a river in the city's limits, parks, mountains within forty miles, major cities within forty miles, an abundance of clean water, strong power supplies, branches of colleges and community colleges in close proximity, and more.

The greatest asset gap for business attraction, according to the mayor, is easy access to the major highways in the region. "If there is anything that seems to hamper us, the lack of a better connection to the highways would be it."

The mayor expressed a further concern regarding the tax base, which is heavily dependent upon property taxes. The seasonal and generally fluctuating nature of commercial revenues has meant that the city cannot rely on a constant level of resources from which to provide public services. Much time is spent in planning for off-seasons and poor years.

The need for greater constancy in the economy and in the city's revenue streams remains a prime motivator for Emmett's economic development program and applies equally to its attraction, retention, and expansion efforts. "The residential base brings in too little revenue to fund the public services we need. We must have the commercial and industrial taxes to help pay for the services our residents require."

Mayor Butticci believes that small cities and towns always need to be prepared for economic development in advance. This means that "the infrastructure needs to be in place, and the city must be clean and presentable, and the schools must be in good shape. Businesses may come in to look, but they won't stay if things aren't right for them. We always have to think ahead!"

Issues for economic growth	• Loss of retail
	• Connections to major highways
	• Seasonality of commerce
	• Tax base dependence on real estate
Strategies for economic growth	• Agritourism (pick your own)
	• Enhance the quality of life
Lessons learned	• Prepare for economic development
	• Residents must buy into expenditures for new infrastructure
	• Attractiveness of the city is critical

Rupert, Idaho

Rupert, Idaho, enjoys a relatively low rate of unemployment—less than 7 percent at a time when the national average exceeds 8.5 percent. Yet, the population growth has not been consistent over the recent past. Between 1990 and 2000, the total population of the city increased by 3.5 percent, only to decline in the ensuing five year period by more than 7.5 percent.

It is possible that the unemployment rate has remained low either because people left town or simply because the incoming jobs outpaced the in-migration to the city. This is a common concern when strictly looking at the numbers without greater explanation of the details. It is a research challenge in smaller cities and towns more than in their larger counterparts. In a smaller city, a small number represents a greater percentage change.

In the interview, the city's leadership was asked to shed light on the causes of that inconsistent growth. Situated more than 150 miles from the state capital, and miles from other cities of greater size, the relative isolation may also be a factor. The mayor was asked how the distances from other, larger urban areas have affected the economic growth and stability of Rupert over time.

The economy appears—through online research—to be both diverse and stable, even expanding. In 2013, a company headquartered in Portugal—Frulact—selected Rupert, Idaho, as its location for a processing plant, delivering one hundred jobs in the first wave of employment. The comments by the company noted that Rupert was the "ideal location" for this plant, although no greater specificity was provided. This is a key consideration for small cities; the interview with the mayor can help focus the reader on the factors that made the city ideal.

It was also interesting to learn whether and how this announcement has been used by the city's leadership to encourage other businesses to consider a location in Rupert or the region. If one large corporation found the city to be ideal, other cities of similar size and geography might be encouraged to do so as well. The city's reaction to the announcement was recorded by the media: "Rupert, Idaho is on the map right now. It's caused quite a buzz in different places. We've had press all over Europe. The Secretary of the United States Department of Commerce mentioned us in a speech a month ago. We've had a lot of exposure" (Dayley-Smith, 2014).

One online article indicated that the recent (2012) significant upgrade of the city's wastewater treatment facility was an important factor in the company's decision, although it did not indicate why that is the case. This too was a topic for discussion with the city's leadership. It certainly gives credence to the many comments by city leaders throughout this study that it is vital already to have the necessary infrastructure for business in place when courting businesses.

Other economic development assets appear to be found in Rupert, including a short three-mile distance to Interstate 94 en route to Pocatello and Twin Falls, and the varied and plentiful outdoors activities that exist in and near Rupert. These include the Snake River, hunting and fishing areas, skiing, and natural and human history.

The economy of the region appears to be dominated by farming, a Kraft Cheese factory, a potato processing plant, and an Amalgamated Sugar plant only five miles east of Rupert with one thousand seasonal positions. While the diversity represented therein is impressive, it must be noted that the seasonality of much of that employment base represents potentially severe challenges for the workforce as well as for the revenue base from which the city provides public services to its residents and its visitors.

The city of Rupert has obtained authorization from the surrounding county to expand its urban renewal district into the county in an effort to attract additional businesses to the greater region. At present, the entire city lies within an established urban renewal zone. This was a topic for conversation with the city's leadership as well.

Photo courtesy of the Renaissance Arts Center in Rupert, Idaho.

Interview with Kelly A. Anthon, City Administrator of Rupert, Idaho

Rupert, Idaho, is an agriculturally based community that got its initial growth spurt as the result of federal homesteading legislation that helped to populate the area and provided the resources necessary to construct a dam that could help support the residential needs of the city as well as support the irrigation of its fields. As a result, sugar beets became an immediate success and still are a large part of the local economy. Consequently, the Amalgamated Sugar Company now operates in Rupert, representing what is believed by City Administrator Anthon to be the largest sugar factory in the world.

Other local crops include an exceptionally diverse array, including wheat, corn, and hay. These crops are complemented by a number of local fish farms. This range of products within the agriculture sector represents what the city administrator believes is sufficient diversity to offset uneven markets and prices for individual crops. Indeed, Rupert proclaims itself to be the world's "most diverse food basket." The growth of dairy farms has been so positive that Chobani yogurt recently opened a plant in the city.

This diversity is worthy of notice. Most of the literature addressing business diversity relates to diversity in terms of several different industries. The above description relates to diversity *within* a given economic sector, in this case, agriculture. This is much more likely to be the case in a small town, especially one that is relatively isolated from other, larger urban areas. In a small city or town, there is unlikely to be sufficient workforce or infrastructure to support multiple-industry diversification.

Within a small city, however, it is feasible to grow several components of an agricultural or other base economy. If, in fact, the objective of economic diversification is to ensure that the periodic peaks and valleys of economic cycles that impact various sectors can potentially be offset by the alternate (peak or valley) in other, co-located sectors, then this form of economic diversity is equally valid as an objective and certainly more likely to be found in small, isolated communities.

However, despite the validity of this form of economic diversification, there is a flaw in the logic as applies to agriculture as the single, though diversified, economic segment. The question raised is whether a disastrous weather event or season could potentially damage *all* of the sectors at the same time, thereby making the entire city, its businesses, and its region susceptible to economic hardship. After all, Rupert also asserts that it has more food-related jobs per capita than anywhere else in the United States.

City Administrator Anthon notes that although the city does not feel overly susceptible, it would like to diversify away from just agriculturally related businesses. He acknowledges that such a disaster has occurred before: a Kraft Cheese plant closed several years ago, costing the city a lot of jobs, but soon thereafter, the plant was purchased by a Portuguese company, Frulact, which not only replaced the lost jobs and helps support the local farmers, but also represented the first foreign direct investment into the state of Idaho.

The selection of Rupert as the site for their first US-based plant relates to a number of factors, including the proximity to water and input products, but was also made possible by the city's, and the voters', decisions to approve bond financing to increase the capacity of the wastewater treatment facility in town. "We had the infrastructure in place and were ready to go. They could come, get set up, and get started right away."

For attraction purposes, businesses related to agriculture obviously lie within the city's sweet spot. Thus, city planners devote much of their economic development efforts to the retention of the existing non-agriculture-related businesses that have the ability to go elsewhere. "The loss of Kraft left us all feeling pretty vulnerable. We know that they can leave. We must be attentive to the needs of our businesses always!"

One manner in which the city works to retain its existing businesses relates to the municipally owned power company. The city often negotiates "extremely low rates" for the utility as an incentive for businesses to remain in Rupert. This does not overly diminish the city's general fund—from which public services are provided—because that is comprised largely of the personal property tax base and funds received from the state of Idaho through established revenue-sharing formulae.

When asked if the state was a helpful partner or a hindrance in local economic development, Anthon noted, "It is a mixed bag. The Department of Commerce has programs that are very useful and foresightful. But, there needs to be a better understanding of the value of tools like tax increment financing for urban renewal."

The College of Southern Idaho has a very positive impact on economic development in and around Rupert because it is "very agile and can retool quickly to create workforce training programs needed by local employers." Anthon also believes that the expansion of these programs could be an additional contribution to the growth of the city and the region if they could include training and support for agriculture and food research. This would be a particularly important contribution for two reasons: local companies are spending more time on this (notably Frulact), and because it would help to reverse the brain drain as students finish school and are forced to relocate to find positions outside of the production side of the agricultural businesses in the region.

In addition to the brain drain from which many of these small, isolated communities suffer, Rupert's other challenges for further economic growth include the ever-rising costs of developing and maintaining the infrastructure of the city and the longer-term concern over potentially limited water resources throughout the western United States. Although not a direct problem now for Rupert, it is indeed a large regional issue that may ultimately impact all of the cities and towns in the area.

City Administrator Anthon cites one lesson he has learned from his experience as a leader in a small, isolated town: "To compete with larger cities that have more

Issues for economic growth	• Brain drain
	• Costs of infrastructure
Strategies for economic growth	• Economic diversification
	• Develop activities to offset nonpeak seasons
	• Offer low (city) utility rates
	• Expand workforce training programs
Lessons learned	• Infrastructure must be in place before businesses can be attracted
	• Be attentive to existing businesses
	• Economic diversification can be within a sector as well as between sectors

of everything, it is necessary to show off the city to economic development prospects through our own eyes. That is to say that we must show them Rupert as we see it, as we enjoy it, as we appreciate it."

Lewistown, Montana

Lewistown sits in the center of the state of Montana and, to some extent, draws its economic strength from its geography. Originally settled by the Blackfoot Indian tribe, the area eventually became the site of a fort that served to protect passing travelers, Fort Lewis, from which the present city derives its name.

The surrounding Judith Basin helps create the very fertile soil that supports several large cattle ranching operations and wheat farms. As a consequence, the unemployment rate at the time of this writing is recorded at less than 5 percent, while the national average is 8.6 percent. Is this the result of jobs in agricultural pursuits or does Lewistown support a more diversified economy? This was part of the discussion with the city's leadership. A further topic for review related to whether the region lost jobs as small family farms went out of business and were replaced by the technology available to the large agricultural conglomerates that have been cited by leaders in other case study cities.

Photo courtesy of Kevin Myhre.

Interview with Kevin Myhre, City Manager of Lewistown, Montana

City Manager Myhre started the discussion by noting that Lewistown, Montana, is located in the geographic center of the state. It is situated 105 miles from

Great Falls and 120 miles from Billings. The city owes its existence to the 1880s establishment of mining operations and the subsequent establishment of a trading post nearby. The city benefitted from the nearby Big Stream, which still provides freshwater to the citizens of Lewistown. Indeed, Myhre points out that its waters are so pure that it is brought to city residents for consumption without additional treatment.

Today, the county that surrounds Lewistown has the greatest number of head of cattle in the state of Montana. This means that a great deal of ranching still takes place in the area and provides some jobs for local residents. This is important for the city because the mining operations that had for so long sustained the economy have all closed down, and with them went many of the jobs in the support industries that were located nearby. As an example, Myhre cites the fact that the mining operations had been conducted 24 hours a day, every day. Because of that, a cluster of diners and other support services operated in proximity to the mines. They too operated all day long, every day. And, they too have long since closed.

The nonranching base of the local economy consists primarily of small manufacturers, including those that produce such diverse products as air doors, a variety of welding operations for military contracts, small heating units, and other small and mid-sized products. Most of these businesses, however, are located in the county, just a short distance outside of the city limits, due to the reduced tax burdens in the county.

This creates a considerable problem for the city and is one that has been cited in several of the interviews. The city is required to provide the support services, public services, and infrastructure within the city limits while not benefitting from any of the tax generation resulting from these operations. In Montana, city governments constitute their general funds (from which public services are provided) primarily from the real estate tax base.

At the same time, the technology used in farming has enabled larger farm operations to be much more efficient with many fewer jobs. Consequently, the family farms of days past are fewer each year, and those jobs are gone and will not return. One result of this has been the loss of some of the longest-term residents of the region.

Lewistown exists in an area of exceptional natural beauty. This fact, coupled with the fact that the state of Montana does not impose income taxes, means that people who have accrued equity in property in higher-cost areas can buy homes in Montana relatively inexpensively. As a result, many retirees have begun to locate in and around Lewistown. The resultant demand for public services creates a further problem for the city because there is no contribution to the city's coffers other than real estate taxes. This creates extreme budgetary pressures for the city, which has to provide an array of public services, some of which are particular to its older residents. "The state of Montana has not changed in this regard in years," says Myhre, "and it's a problem for us."

City Manager Myhre chairs the local economic development corporation, so he was asked about the target areas for the economic development strategic plan. He notes that the focus continues to be less on attempts to attract new businesses to the city and more on working with the existing business base to retain them in the city and to help them grow. In fact, in the discussions of the economic development corporation, no attraction targets—either industry segments or specific companies—have even been identified. The emphasis on business retention has meant that the city's leaders have needed to address some of the most prominent economic development and lifestyle gaps that exist. There is, for example, but one grocery store for the six thousand residents of Lewistown and the three thousand others who live in the region but outside of the city limits.

As a consequence of an economic development focus on retention and not attraction, the local institution of higher education, the Montana State University, Northern Campus, trains primarily nursing students for the local hospital. This means that there is no program that can be used to attract new businesses, although there are "some general business classes" that could benefit those interested in starting up new businesses.

After twenty-three years in Lewistown, City Manager Myhre was quick with logical and well-reasoned responses. He is clearly aware of the issues being probed and has given them great consideration. One question, however, caused him to pause: Can Lewistown survive? His reply: "Yes and no."

"In the 1970s, the city built a convention center and the hotels thrived and it literally saved the community." Today, the center is run down and is need of major renovations and modernization of the technology being used. "This might help to revive the city again if we can find a way to get it done."

"But," Myhre continued, "in the long run, Lewistown will decline like all of the small towns in Montana. We have lost more than twenty stores in our downtown in the last five years. Lewistown will survive because of the area's natural beauty, but that will hurt too because retirees will move to the city and that hurts us financially. We won't become a ghost town but other small towns in Montana will because the agricultural base of jobs is shrinking." His conclusion was that "unless you have a lake, oil or gas reserves, or are near railroad lines, or a major interstate highway, it will be tough to survive. Other cities like ours just might become ghost towns."

In terms of lessons learned, City Manager Myhre concludes that Montana needs to institute a sales tax. All of the surrounding states, save Wyoming, have a sales tax. Visitors to the area from other states use the infrastructure but contribute nothing to its support. In effect, 10 million visitors annually use the infrastructure that is built and maintained by the 1 million residents of the state. The imposition of even a small sales tax could provide support for the infrastructure, in part from people who are not residents of the state, while not being so burdensome as to deter visitors from coming.

The city hosts a variety of festivals each year to attract visitors to the area because they do make purchases and that helps the local merchants. These include an annual festival, a dinner train complete with a murder mystery, and a Christmastime polar train. These are designed to attract visitors to the city and to support the local merchants, and City Manager Myhre maintains that even a small sales tax would help the city provide infrastructure for its residents as well as the visitors.

Issues for economic growth	• Dependence on property taxes
	• Businesses locate in county for tax purposes while city has to pay for infrastructure
	• Loss of retail, grocers
	• Retirees pay little in taxes but take much in services
	• Decline of the downtown
Strategies for economic growth	• Business retention
	• Attract retailers
	• Refurbish city's convention center
	• Create festivals to attract visitors
Lessons learned	• Montana needs to allow a local sales tax

Lincoln, Oregon

The population of Lincoln, Oregon, has grown steadily over the past two decades. The city is surrounded by water, most notably to the west, where the city enjoys seven-plus miles of Pacific Ocean coastline. This would appear to be a strong asset for some forms of economic development, and that served as a topic for discussion in the interview with Lincoln's city manager.

A brief Internet search revealed two economic issues that bore consideration as further topics for the interview with the city's leadership. The first relates to the potential for tourism activities and supporting industries as the basis for current and future economic growth. This is possibly already in place, but there is little available information online in this regard. The second issue relates to the significant amount of detail on the city's website dealing with programs of urban renewal. Does this imply the need for city beautification projects or downtown revitalization programs, and if so, are these issues in the way of further growth?

Photo courtesy of Phillip Burnett.

Interview with David Hawker, City Manager of Lincoln, Oregon

David Hawker, Lincoln, Oregon's, city manager, characterizes the city's economic base as being "almost exclusively visitor based." The consequence of having year-round visitor attraction opportunities is that the full-time population of the city can, from time to time, expand regularly from the reported mid-eight thousand range to more than ten thousand. This can have both positive and negative impacts on the city, its resources, and its economy.

Because of the visitor numbers, Lincoln tends to trail by several months the other areas in the region both into and out of recessionary periods. Further, because of the city's dependence on visitors to the local attractions, the primary asset for economic development is absolutely and completely out of their control: the weather! However, although it cannot be controlled, the weather can be better reported and the region has made efforts to improve the technology for and the reporting of atmospheric conditions and weather patterns. This helps both the city and the businesses involved to plan better for variations in their operations and revenues. City Manager Hawker points out that this is particularly helpful as visitor levels tend to increase in Lincoln when the weather is hot elsewhere.

The city has also put into place a variety of activities to diversify its economic base. In this case, that means providing indoor activities for people during rainy times. These include a glass-blowing operation at which visitors can blow their own glass, a school that offers cooking classes, a cultural center with multiple activity options, and a casino that is operated by a confederation of local Indian tribes.

Given the number of visitor attractions and the hospitality businesses that support them, the leaders in other cities might attempt to attract sales tax-generating businesses to the city. However, this is not the case in Lincoln for two reasons. First, the city's budget does not benefit substantially from the sales taxes spent by visitors. The city's budget is more heavily dependent upon the revenues produced through the 9.5 percent hotel tax, much of which is used to fund the local Convention and Visitors Bureau, which works to attract more visitors to the city and its activities.

The second reason that the city does not attempt to bring in more tax-generating businesses is that it has a distinct and stated preference for growing its own new businesses locally rather than attracting established companies to come to Lincoln from elsewhere.

In Lincoln, Oregon, economic development attraction is defined in terms of visitors rather than companies. And, the city wants visitors to do more than come to Lincoln; it wants them to extend their stays. To encourage that, the city has provided greater broadband support to make it possible for businesspeople and others to extend their visits to the city and to the region a few days longer.

Additional support for the local hospitality industry is provided by a technical college in the city, which the city supports and which offers micro-enterprise development programs. In this way, local residents can learn to create and sustain new businesses, and can get access to the types of counsel and other support they need to be successful.

The one gap that exists for the city is in its hotel offerings. City Manager Hawker notes that while numerous budget and mid-range hotels do exist, there is a need for a few higher-level hotels to accommodate other visitors who have the wherewithal to afford more expensive lodging and who might be encouraged either to come to town or to stay longer if there were more accommodations that aligned with those to which they are accustomed. Similarly, a few white-tablecloth restaurants would also help round out the city's hospitality offerings, according to Lincoln's city manager.

Indeed, it is Hawker's sense that the city erred in allowing unlimited growth in the lodging base that did not help to round out the community's assets or improve the local economy. A lesson lies in not permitting an oversupply to occur, he feels, because the resultant overcompetition results in lower room rates for all. Further advice is that, for cities like Lincoln, where hospitality is critical to the local economic base, it is important to concentrate on attractions for what Hawker refers to as the "shoulder seasons." These are the less popular times of the year for tourism when the businesses need more travelers to come.

Finally, saving for a rainy day is important in a small, isolated city where a single industry is dominant. This is not only due to the seasonality for the primary industry in the economic base of the city and the region. Recessions hurt both the city and its merchants, and both suffer from diminished revenues over what are often significantly long periods of time. There was a great deal of deferred maintenance that does not help show the city in its best light. Those matters need to be kept up to date on a consistent basis in order to attract business and retain companies. "We need to put our best foot forward."

Issues for economic growth	• Dependence on property taxes
	• No high-end dining for visitors
Strategies for economic growth	• Create indoor activities to complement outdoor tourism
	• Seek to attract more upscale hotels and restaurants
Lessons learned	• Save surpluses for a rainy day
	• City attractiveness is critical

Ephrata, Washington

Ephrata, Washington, is one of the small, isolated cities in this research in which the population has been growing substantially and with consistency over the recent past (1990 to 2005). At the time of this writing, the city's unemployment rate of nearly 10 percent exceeds the national average by a full percentile point (http://www.usbeacon.com). This may be either the result of or despite the growing population of the last two decades.

The city of Ephrata was originally a stop along the rail line from Walla Walla heading northward during the 1880s. It was not, however, until the Grand Coulee Dam was completed on the Columbia River that the region's soils were made substantially more fertile and agricultural pursuits throughout the region began to improve noticeably. The area was converted into a government town through a series of actions, starting with the development of an Army airfield for training purposes at the height of the Second World War, in 1942.

After World War II, the county of which Ephrata is the county seat determined to construct two hydroelectric dams on the river to generate cheap electrical power. Those dams have created many jobs and have also resulted in the provision of cheap electrical power as an attraction for employers to the city and the region. A thread of conversation for the city manager was whether this has actually been used successfully as an asset for economic growth.

The Port of Ephrata, with more than two thousand acres of developable land, represents a potential economic development asset, but there are no buildings at present and the infrastructure to the building sites is not in place either. This was discussed with the city's leadership. Are there plans in place to develop the park to prepare for growth?

Photo courtesy of Wes Crago.

Interview with Wes Crago, City Administrator of Ephrata, Washington

Initially a small water refilling stop along the area's early railroad lines, Ephrata, Washington, has existed in one form or another for more than a century. Its city administrator, Wes Crago defines the geography: "We are at the top of the Columbia River Basin and the region is very arid. We need the river to irrigate the entire area."

Perhaps surprisingly, then, the economy has not been overly dependent upon the river. The city has built its economy and its growth on the basis of a series of government projects. These include federally funded projects as well as state and local programs. City Administrator Crago expressed it this way: "Our prosperity has always been tied to government projects."

Ephrata was a base camp for those working on the Grand Coulee Dam project. During World War II, an air base in the area provided both jobs and spending throughout the local economy. Irrigation projects along the Columbia River that were designed to irrigate local fields were funded by public monies. In the early 1950s, the county funded two projects to use the river as a source of power generation for Ephrata and the surrounding areas. Throughout all of this history, these public works projects provided the local economy with jobs and, ultimately, with the tax revenues from which city services could be supported.

Not all of the region's growth has taken place in Ephrata, but that which occurred nearby also benefits the city. This includes the regional airport in Moses Lake and the high-tech business community that is throughout the region. The major employers include Microsoft and Yahoo, which have created data centers in the region. These kinds of employers also provide stability to the city's and the region's economy because they are across such diverse industries and industry segments.

Even much of the private development that takes place in the city and throughout the region is ultimately the result of government projects. The former air base is now in use by private industry. The steel fabrication plant has contracts with the Department of Defense to provide high-precision elements for a variety of systems.

The city focuses its current economic development efforts not on large wins and hundreds of jobs; rather, the targets are smaller businesses in technology areas, including, prominently, light manufacturing as well as various services companies. The city leaders feel that, in this way, the economic base can become a positive mixture of federal and state projects and small, locally generated entrepreneurial businesses across a wide range of business areas.

Unlike some of the cities included in this research, Ephrata does have an area within the town limits that remains available for further development. However, City Administrator Crago noted that it is "disadvantageously located." For him this means that the city needs to "build in advance of growth." The feeling is that, in most instances, businesses do not want to find a location and then begin building their facilities and backfill the necessary infrastructure. Rather, they need to have the site up and ready to go to the maximum extent possible.

In the past, the city's infrastructure has been oriented to the needs of the residential areas and not the commercial districts in the town. As a result, people tend to live in Ephrata to take advantage of the excellent quality of life but commute to employment in other locations. Crago believes that today's businesses have an expectation that the community will be a partner in the development of the needed infrastructure.

The city is now preparing a strategic plan to assess what it wants to be like in the future and how best to prepare itself for the optimal vision. Says Crago, "We are at the tipping point." The city will decide through this planning process what types of businesses it wants and how best to make itself an attractive location for them.

One point of interest concerns the seemingly ever-present Walmart. In 2000, a Walmart Superstore located in Ephrata. Unlike other cities in this research, however, Crago did not feel that the presence of the store damaged the smaller, local shops. "Our small businesses just adjusted to the new situation and picked niches for themselves. For the most part, they remain in business and are doing well." This is interesting because it is in direct contrast to the comments of city managers and mayors in many of the other cities in this research, who noted the negative impacts of Walmarts in terms of damage done to local retailers who could not compete, as well as with the concern over revenues from the store going to corporate headquarters rather than staying in and being re-spent throughout the community.

In terms of lessons offered for other small, isolated cities across the country, Crago emphasized the critical importance of community involvement. "Communications with our citizens has been very important. We involve them in the discussions and in the decisions. We have a very public process here. It's important because it gets the citizens involved." Crago adds that it is also important because in a small town, leaders are also neighbors. "There's no hiding. We go to church together. We all sit together at the baseball games. When the team goes to the state championships, we all go, and a fire truck leads the way."

A second bit of wisdom related to a topic that had not been raised in the interviews with the leadership from the other small, isolated cities in this study: Crago and his team and the community have considered what the core mission of the city government should be. As a result, some prior city services have been privatized because they could be provided more efficiently and without costing taxpayers resources. Two of these services included trash collection and the ambulance service.

According to Crago, in the case of trash collection, there is no question that the decision was a good one and that the newer rates are even with the old, or even perhaps a little better. Ambulance service is a little more difficult to assess the impact of the changes, but there have been no complaints with the current situation. Not only does this involve some savings, but it has also generated some business for local small businesses.

Issues for economic growth	• Remaining areas for development not located near infrastructure
Strategies for economic growth	• Privatize some city services
Lessons learned	• Involve the community through ongoing communications
	• Privatize some city services

Cody, Wyoming

In spite of steady population growth in Cody, Wyoming, the city's unemployment rate is a very healthy 4 percent. This is at a time when the US national average stands in excess of 8.5 percent. The interview covered this topic and sought to determine the causes for both the economic stability and the population decline.

The city possesses numerous economic development assets. It lies fifty-two miles from one of the primary entrances to Yellowstone National Park. As a consequence, it has a thriving hospitality industry, an airport, and a booming retail sector. In recent years, federal budget cuts have created problems for local commerce (Prevost, 2013). Reductions in the federal allocation to Yellowstone National Park in 2013 equaled \$1.75 million of the \$35 million total. This resulted in a two-week delay in the opening of the park, which in turn meant millions lost in revenues for local businesses and in tax revenues for many small cities in the greater region. The city of Cody estimated its losses at one hundred thousand visitors and \$1.3 million in spending.

Complementing the tourism assets are several other strong economic sectors that include agricultural production, oil and gas extraction, some light manufacturing, and numerous rodeo competitions that attract visitors. In light of the federal budget cuts, it appears that economic diversification should be in the planning stages in Cody. The interview with the city's leadership addressed this issue.

Photo courtesy of the city of Cody, Wyoming.

Interview with the Honorable Nancy Tia Brown, Mayor, and Jenni Rosencrance, City Administrator of Cody, Wyoming

No less a personage than Buffalo Bill Cody founded the city that now bears his name. Mayor Brown noted in the discussion: "You need to understand what it takes to live in a place like this. It's a small town. Most people work several jobs to make ends meet. But, if you are willing to do that and you are an outdoors person, there is an extraordinary quality of life here. Buffalo Bill's spirit is still alive here."

Cody had a vision of a community that would be able to survive the conditions. To that end, he established what is now known as the Buffalo Bill Dam and Reservoir that provides water to the city and the surrounding area. As the region is located in the high plains, water provision is a critical issue. It is necessary for use by both ranchers and residents.

The dam is found at the convergence of the north and south forks of the Shoshone River. While this originally enabled a permanent location for a city, and today sustains it, the real reason Cody thrives is that it is located fifty-two miles from one of the main entrances to Yellowstone National Park. There is also a national forest in the region that helps attract visitors to the city. These attractions have helped the local hospitality and retail sectors thrive.

Despite the proximity to very popular tourist attractions, the city's leadership has long seen a need to diversify the local economic base. As such, these assets have been complemented over the years with other industry segments, including agriculture and energy. These have helped to offset a key economic development challenge: the cyclical nature of the tourist seasons. Local businesses need to make enough in a few short months to sustain themselves throughout the rest of the year. The city also has to prepare itself to avoid the negative effects of cyclical revenue streams to the general fund. One means by which it feels it has done so is by paying off its entire municipal debt. "Being debt-free means that we will not be in trouble when revenues go down because people aren't coming to the area to see the sights."

Revenue diversification for the city is a possibility, but as yet an unrealized one. The state of Wyoming passed legislation that enabled areas in the state to increase the sales tax by as much as 2 percent. The current level of 4 percent goes to the state's coffers. If the majority of local jurisdictions in a county can agree to place the issue on a referendum, the people can elect to add up to the remaining 2 percent for the enhancement of local public services. To date, most of the areas in Wyoming have elected to do so. The area in which Cody is located, however, succeeded in placing the measure on the ballot, but the people did not support it when it went to referendum. As a consequence, the city has had to reduce the preexisting levels of municipal services rather than enhancing them.

The city's leadership knows that it must work diligently to find high-paying jobs for the residents to offset the effects of the cyclical parts of its economy. An energy company, Husky Oil, opened a facility in the city and became what the mayor describes as a "huge underpinning to the city's economy," but it has since departed, leaving the cyclical nature of the remainder of the economy to resurface as an issue. This led the mayor to note that, for the city of Cody, not just any jobs will do; it wants jobs that pay well and will be in place year-round.

Mayor Brown cited a new strategy that she believes will "put Cody on the cutting edge in Wyoming." Lannette Pharmaceuticals, which is based in Philadelphia, acquired a local firm and created Cody Labs, which could create as many as several hundred jobs over the years. In part, the attraction of Cody was that the state of Wyoming does not have an income tax, for either employers or their workforce. Cody is hoping to trumpet that fact in an effort to attract other employers to join Lannette. This is an important consideration for a small town in which these kinds of successes can be few and far between. When one does occur, public relations efforts can make it known to other companies that may wonder what it is about this particular town that made it attractive to a colleague or a competitor? Perhaps, this is a city they should consider as well.

To support the attraction of new businesses and to help existing local companies succeed, the city is home to two assets in higher education: Northwestern College and a branch of the University of Wyoming. While "they have not been players, historically, there is new leadership at the university who sees this as part of the institution's role." It remains to be seen precisely how that interaction and support will actually play out.

Creating businesses that are not oriented essentially to supporting the tourist trade is also important for the city because about one-third of the revenues to the city's general fund come from the sales tax base, which is, as noted, seasonally and even annually variable.

The natural beauty of the area helps to bring people to Cody, but Mayor Brown and City Administrator Rosencrance note that the city has lost its brightest kids, who have to leave town to find employment opportunities in other disciplines. The efforts of the local economic development program—Forward Cody—are focused on job creation that will not only help retain the next generation workforce, but also bring back some of those the city has lost over time. To do so, they must complement the area's natural beauty, a great public school system, and the cultural and outdoor opportunities of the region with employment opportunities that are in a wider range of sectors and skill sets, and that have the absence of seasonality that will provide stability to young families.

Mayor Brown reminds her peers that economic development should be entirely focused on "what the community needs and wants." In short, the employers that will come to Cody need to bring "jobs that fit." They should not be just any jobs. "They need to be right for this city." Further, there needs to be a professional economic development agency or individual. This work is vital and cannot be assumed by other groups or volunteers.

Finally, it is important in small towns to partner with other groups. "In a small community, you can't do it all by yourself. Besides, in a small city everyone knows everyone else. In Wyoming, with fewer than six hundred thousand people, everyone knows the key players. I can call the governor and he'll take my call. We just have to be able to work together."

Issues for economic growth	• Budget impacts of the cyclical nature of tourism
	• Revenue diversification needed by the city
	• Brain drain
Strategies for economic growth	• Economic diversification
	• Use recent successes to generate more
Lessons learned	• Do not pursue "just any jobs"
	• Community involvement through ongoing communications
	• Save surpluses for a rainy day

Douglas, Wyoming

Douglas is a city of fifty-six hundred in the east central portion of the state of Wyoming. The population base has remained fairly constant over time with small but steady increases. The rate of unemployment at the time of this writing was roughly half of the national average. Like many of the cities in this study,

Douglas—due to its isolation—is the largest city in its region and serves as the county seat. The city is located on the North Platte River and has two major highways that pass by the city's limits, serving as drivers of positive economic development. Another transportation asset for economic growth includes a regional airport that boasts of significant capacity at present as well as potential for further growth of runways and service facilities.

Water is always a consideration for communities in this part of the country, but the city of Douglas has a source of drinking water that is estimated to be sufficient for a city three times its size. The North Platter River is not only a source of water supply for the city and the region, but also an attraction for water sports enthusiasts who bring spending money to the city's merchants and hospitality industry. One question for the interview with the city's leadership was whether there are plans to increase the tourism and the city's hospitality business base, or whether the size of the city and tourism has reached the growth limits desired by city planners.

Substantial wealth has been realized by the residents of Douglas due to discoveries of oil and natural gas reserves in the region. The extent to which this is expected to continue well into the future, or even grow further in its economic strength, were also topics of conversation for the city's leadership.

Photo courtesy of Gary Plumb.

Interview with Tony Tolstedt, City Administrator of Douglas, Wyoming

City Administrator Tolstedt explained that the city of Douglas, Wyoming, is probably best known as the "home of the jackalope." Although fictitious, the cross between an antelope and a jackrabbit has brought some notoriety to Douglas.

One might, as first observation, imagine that the city's strategic location would have much to do with the economy and the types of business that are conducted in the city of Douglas. Along the highway from Casper and Cheyenne, Douglas would seem to be in a position ideally suited to warehousing, distribution, and storage, but City Administrator Tolstedt focuses instead on agriculture and energy as the economic mainstays of the region.

Oil and gas extraction in the region has created a significant financial boom for many residents but has created some difficulties as well. Housing to accommodate the rapid influx of new workers and families for these companies has lagged behind the growth in the workforce. This has created rising values for existing and new homes, making the proposition less attractive for the newer residents. Tolstedt acknowledges that it has been hard to keep pace with that aspect of the boom. "This is important to a town with such a positive quality of life."

Another difficulty created for the city and the region by the boom periods in the oil and gas fields relates to the workforce and the needs of other local employers. The energy companies pay much higher salaries and are thus able to attract workers from the ranks of police officers, schoolteachers, and others with lower pay scales to work for them. "When a young person can earn as much as $150,000 in the oil fields and a police officer makes about $42,000, you really have to want to be a police officer to stay on the force!"

Tolstedt also notes that there will be more growth coming. Estimates run as high as one thousand more wells that will receive operating permits over the next ten years. "We need to keep our infrastructure going and be able to stay ahead of the pace of growth." Toward that end, the city of Douglas paid off all of its preexisting long-term debt. This will enable the city to grow without some of the normal financial constraints that cities of this size often face in boom cycles. "We have to be sure that we can sustain public services at all times."

Public services in Douglas are paid largely through the city's sales tax revenues. This revenue stream is growing at present due to the fact that the sales of oil and gas are taxed and some of those tax revenues go into the city's budget. However, estimates often range as high as one thousand new residents in-migrating to Douglas in a single year. In such times, "housing, public safety, and infrastructure are all-important to the community." When asked whether those increased needs include the city's public school system, he noted that those costs are borne by the state of Wyoming, which has managed the growth. However, the city experiences serious financial strains in such times.

A significant need for the city of Douglas is additional retail. Although the distances to neighboring cities may seem to some to be rather substantial, the driving times are small enough that residents can and do much of their shopping in larger urban areas that have greater retail opportunities. These include Cheyenne, which is a ninety-minute drive; Casper, which is a forty-minute drive; and Gillette, which is a two-hour drive from Douglas. Tolstedt notes that, in their part of the country, driving such distances is more commonplace than might be the case on the highly densely populated East Coast.

As a lesson learned, Tolstedt offers that "the good times won't last, but neither will the bust periods." By not overextending themselves when the times were good and the budgets flush, the city was able to balance the costs of city services to its residents in a consistent manner through both cycles. It requires experience-based planning and constant awareness of cycles and trends, but it can be done well.

A second lesson offered by Tolstedt relates to the city's generally high quality of life. "We have a great school system and a strong hospital and medical community. We have additional land on which to develop. It's a good place to live. But, we have to work hard to keep it that way. We need a new recreation center and a new joint judicial center. Douglas is a great place to live and we work hard to keep it that way."

Issues for economic growth	• Housing availability and affordability
	• Shortage of retail
Strategies for economic growth	• Build housing
	• Add and maintain infrastructure in the best of times
	• Attract retailers
Lessons learned	• Don't overextend in the good times

North Central

Algona, Iowa

The unemployment rate in Algona, Iowa, at the time of this writing was 3 percent. This may be a reflection of a strong economy or simply a diminution of the numerator in the unemployment rate calculation: the number of residents in the labor force. As the population has experienced marginal but steady decline, this is a possible explanation and was a topic for discussion with the city's leadership.

The city is located on the northern border of the Iowa River, where it separates the states of Iowa and Minnesota. In this region, agriculture is king and Algona is no exception. Not only does agriculture account for 10 percent of employment, but a recent survey in the area indicates that residents feel that the best bet for future economic development will also be in the agricultural area. Today, 23 percent of employment is in retail and 10 percent in services. Manufacturing accounts for another 11 percent, and real estate and insurance account for another 16 percent of all local jobs. Do the city's leaders agree that the future lies in agricultural output, or is economic diversification part of the strategic plan for economic development in Algona?

Photo courtesy of Bradley Jensen.

Interview with Keri Navratil, City Administrator of Algona, Iowa

City Administrator Navratil characterizes the economic history of Algona, Iowa, as "fortunate." A Snap-On Tools plant supports four hundred jobs in the city and the Pharmacist's International Insurance Company another three hundred. Hormel adds two hundred more positions to that base, which is rounded out by a metal fabricator, agricultural feed research facilities, and a variety of agricultural pursuits.

Navratil is quick to point out that while there is already significant diversity in the economic base, agriculture dominates the financial outlook. However, the agricultural entities in the region are largely technology driven and do not generate nearly the same job numbers as had been the case in the past.

The stable job base and the diversification in the economic base enable the city to be less focused in its strategic plan for economic development on what to attract and more focused on how to retain its existing employers—large and small. The efforts of the community to do so are complemented by the involvement of the Iowa Lakes Community College, which supports industry growth through job training programs that are highly targeted to the existing job base in the current operations, with an emphasis on the job classifications that are the most difficult for employers to fill.

A state grant was recently secured that enabled the retention of a local business by providing the training for skills sets that were otherwise unavailable in the area. This enabled the company not only to remain in Algona, but also to expand its operations and increase its hires. In exchange, as is the case with most incentive programs, there are requirements that the company remains in place for a specific length of time and that it keeps the job numbers at the agreed-upon levels or higher.

In terms of educational opportunities, the state of Iowa perennially tops the lists of states in terms of a variety of quality factors for kindergarten through twelfth grade education statewide. City Administrator Navratil acknowledges that as being one of the factors that brought her family to the state. "We make a big investment in our kids." This is an attractive asset that must also bring employers to the state. Employers want to be able to attract the best workforce from any location to their jobs, and they know that those individuals will want excellent educational opportunities for their children.

Navratil notes that other marketable assets for economic development attraction—and retention—for the city of Algona include a stable economy and a safe environment. Further, although Algona is indeed rural, it serves as a hub for a wider region and thus provides a full range of business and personal services as well as recreational and cultural opportunities. If there is a gap in those offerings for residents, it would be that there has not been sufficient planning for "succession" in the downtown. To keep the downtown area vibrant and attractive, Navratil believes there will need to be new stores ready to come in as the older retailers close their stores or move on.

Another concern of City Administrator Navratil is that the city needs to remain visually attractive for families. The young people from Algona often finish school and want to try living in other types of environments. Frequently, they will return when they have families because they want to raise their children in the same type of environment in which they were nurtured. However, Navratil warns, this can only happen if the city remains economically vibrant and attractive for families and others. In response to those needs, the city has built parks, bike trails, walking paths, and other family-oriented recreational opportunities.

In order to finance these kinds of improvements, Algona focuses its attraction efforts on businesses that will generate property taxes—the prime contributor to the general fund of Algona—as well as jobs and income. This may be particularly important for Algona because the state of Iowa passed a law that rolled real estate taxes for the commercial and industrial sectors back to 90 percent of the levels at the time of its passage. While the intent was to make the state more attractive for business attraction, it has also had the effect of diminishing the tax base revenues for its communities, which now have to worry about how best to provide quality public services to residents, businesses, and visitors.

City Administrator Navratil offers, as a lesson learned, that the city needs to ever be watchful for the changing needs of the business community generally and of the employers individually. This can only happen when the city's leadership maintains a strong relationship with business leaders in the community. By knowing ahead of time when a company has concerns, they can be dealt with before becoming more serious. It may even help to identify employers that are considering relocation away from the community.

Finally, Navratil says, "We make our own destiny. We have a hospital. It supports a couple hundred jobs, but it also means that people don't have to go too far for treatments. We want residents to find what they need right in town. It's like that here." As evidence, she cites a chamber of commerce study that indicated that there is absolutely no retail leakage from Algona. Of course, part of that is due to the distances that one would need to travel to purchase items elsewhere, but importantly, the absolute need to leave Algona to find what one needs is minimal. Fort Dodge and Mason City are within a one-hour drive, so it would not be overly burdensome for one to go to those communities for his or her purchases. The benefit lies in not having to do so. "You can get what you need here in Algona."

Issues for economic growth	• Succession planning for stores downtown
	• Tax implications of state-imposed cap on property taxes
Strategies for economic growth	• Business retention
	• Attract retailers
Lessons learned	• Keep the city attractive
	• City–business community relations should be nurtured constantly

Detroit Lakes, Minnesota

The city of Detroit Lakes, Minnesota, was established in the early 1870s and began its initial growth spurt shortly thereafter when the Northern Pacific Railroad built a line through the area. The city gives credence to the state's moniker, "Land of Ten Thousand Lakes." The numerous lakes in the region provide Detroit Lakes with an economic asset that generates tourism for water sports and activities in both the winters and the summers. It is estimated that the year-round population of the city of around eighty-five hundred can surge to as high as thirteen thousand during the high tourism seasons.

Not surprisingly, the economy is driven in part by the attraction of several resort areas and retail establishments. Complementing this are large job numbers in sectors unrelated to the tourist attractions, including health care and public administration, the latter aided by the city's status as the county seat of Becker County.

The tourism destinations in Detroit Lakes are supported by several major highways, including US Routes 10 and 59 and Minnesota Highway 34. The economic base of the area is further diversified by agriculture businesses, a variety of services businesses, and two industrial parks that house a large number of manufacturing entities.

Finally, the city has, for many years, hosted an annual camping and country music festival in August that attracts large audiences. This has also helped to support the retail outlets throughout the region.

Detroit Lakes seems to be home to a viable and sustainable economy relative to most of the other cities included in this research. As such, the focus of the interview with the city's leadership was on how the city reached that situation and what lessons were learned in the process that may be transferable to other, similar communities facing similar economic challenges.

Photo courtesy of the Detroit Lakes Regional Chamber of Commerce.

Interview with Bob Louiseau, City Manager, and Larry Remmen, Community Development Director of Detroit Lakes, Minnesota

Like many of the cities included in this study, especially midwestern cities, Detroit Lakes was established (1871) in response to the advance of the railroads moving America westward. Today, the core of the economy in this part of west central Minnesota is based in tourist attraction to the region's many lakes and other natural amenities.

Tourism is not the only component of the Detroit Lakes economic picture. Although it is the anchor, it is supplemented by several manufacturing operations and the types of business and personal services that serve a wide region with great distances to other urban areas. As such, people come into Detroit Lakes to access the services that are not available elsewhere within easy reach. Finally, there are additional contributions to the city's economy that derive from its designation as the county seat, which is also due, of course, to its prominence in the region as the largest urban setting.

The city's leadership indicated that they are interested in further expanding the services sectors of their economy because the demand exists for more, although that does not imply that there are major asset gaps for the constituents of the city and the region. For instance, the medical sector has grown substantially in response to the needs of the populace of the wider region. Today, Detroit Lakes is home to two major clinics, a hospital, and an elder care facility. Retail establishments in the community include a Walmart and a K-Mart.

Thus, the community is also focused on developing other parts of its economic base, notably the manufacturing sector. Existing businesses provide metal fabrication, tool and die operations, parts stamping, and welding. To facilitate the attraction and success of these types of businesses, the local technical college works closely with both city officials and the business community. By taking an active part in the attraction of new businesses, the technical college demonstrates how it can quickly tailor course offerings to accommodate the workforce training needs of the employers. This now extends to working with the high school in Detroit Lakes to ensure that the future workforce and students at the technical school receive education in the proper prerequisites to prepare them to meet the specific needs of the employers.

When asked if the community has always had such a diverse economic base, the leadership responded that such had not always been the case. Rather, their predecessors in the city had concluded that it was important to smooth out the peaks and valleys of the local employment picture, and began to pursue a range of employers for Detroit Lakes, a policy that the current leadership still endorses.

The most instructive part of that part of the economic history is that the planning and initial diverse economic development in Detroit Lakes was initiated during "a down economic time." During the 1970s and 1980s, the city began to develop an industrial park to attract employers. In western North Dakota, the oil industry created several "spin-off" opportunities for the larger region, including parts of Minnesota, and Detroit Lakes sought to be one of the beneficiaries of that growth. As a result, a small tool and die business was attracted to the city and represented an early success.

When asked how the city could afford to invest in an industrial park during a recessionary period, City Manager Louiseau replied, "People sacrificed for it. We saw that it was important and we did it." The city had another opportunity to demonstrate that type of resilience. In 1992, a major employer shut down and the city lost 525 jobs. The response was to develop additional lands for industrial parks to "attract jobs that were more relevant." In some other cities that experienced such dramatic upheavals, people moved away, but not so in Detroit Lakes. Louiseau and Remmen said that the city responded by attempting to upgrade and modernize itself. "This is one of the most beautiful places in the country. No one ever gave any thought to leaving."

The lesson that was learned from these experiences was that "you can't wait till things are in bad shape to get things done." The city's budget is dependent upon property taxes as the principal source of revenues. The city has agreed to allocate $50,000 per year for the next five years to match a fund of $6 million raised privately to upgrade and rebuild bike trails and streets in the city. The lesson learned in this respect was that city leaders must "look at the economic development side and the community development side as well as workforce development concurrently." From an economic development planning perspective, this has meant looking at the numbers and types of jobs as well as the salary levels for those jobs at the same time as considering the generation of property taxes for the city's budget.

To attract and retain businesses, two key issues for Detroit Lakes are workforce development and the availability of sufficient housing for the workforce of today and tomorrow. An additional significant area for the leadership of Detroit Lakes and their economic development efforts is the need for greater highway frontage for the city. At present, there is a two- to three-mile frontage to the largest highway in the areas. Louiseau points out that this is only about half of what a community the size of Detroit Lakes typically has. People must cross rail line to access the frontage. All of this, if improved, could increase the development potential of the city, and thus its ability to generate additional resources for city services.

Another concern for the planning of economic development in and around the city of Detroit Lakes relates to the environmental policies of the state of Minnesota. It was pointed out that employers can simply locate in other states where the permitting process is less onerous.

The primary economic development lesson learned in Detroit Lakes has been that one cannot wait to do that which is vital. "We have to do what we can with what we have now. That means that we have to engage the entire community." In Detroit Lakes, that has meant creating community-wide events that are in seasons other than the heavy tourism seasons. This helps the city's retailers as well as the revenue forecasts for the city. "We have to work together."

Issues for economic growth	• Greater highway frontage
	• State environmental policies
Strategies for economic growth	• Economic diversification
	• Increase workforce training through the local technical college
Lessons learned	• Don't wait for the good times to invest; do what you can now
	• A close working relationship with the business community is important

International Falls, Minnesota

The city of International Falls is, not surprisingly, so named for its location across the bridge from Ontario, Canada. The presence of the bridge has economic significance, as it is a crossing point to and from the two nations. This means that the region is home to a contingent of Customs officials who generate economic activity as well as an economic cluster that exists to provide services to the passengers crossing from one nation into the other.

Initially, commerce in the area resulted from the harnessing of the Rainy and Lake Rivers, which are spanned by the International Falls Bridge. The resultant power became an abundant energy source for mill production, and the abundance of timber made paper production a natural business line for the area. The original mills were ultimately sold to Boise Cascade in the mid-1960s and paper production remains the largest industry in the region.

One of the obvious considerations for the growth of business is the extreme weather conditions that prevail in the area. These might appear to relegate being small and isolated to the status of lesser barriers to growth. Being known as the "Icebox of the Nation" probably doesn't help economic development matters. Perhaps the city's leadership can indicate whether that challenge can also be seen as an opportunity by some businesses and some industries.

Another avenue of inquiry for International Falls' leaders is the rather steady decline in recent years of the city's population. Between 1990 and 2005, census data shows that the total population of International Falls has declined from more than eighty-three hundred to just over sixty-three hundred residents. Additionally, nearly 95 percent of the residents are classified by the Census Bureau as white. Does the town have plans—or hopes—to regrow or diversify either its residential or its business communities?

A 2013–2014 "Statement of Goals by the International Falls Economic Development Authority" emphasizes the value of local highway and truck routes as business attraction assets. Much of the resulting industry targets are in the retail space, and much of the geographic focus is on the city's waterfront as an area of opportunity. The additional economic potential of these assets was a topic of discussion with the city's leaders.

Another topic for the interview with the city's leadership was the conclusions of an informal survey conducted the Minnesota Public Radio (Arts) in which people were asked how the city would be impacted by layoffs in Boise Cascade. Respondents feared population losses, the loss of support for local institutions and programs, the loss of image for the city, lower tax base revenues and the decline of city services, and the possibility that International Falls could become a ghost town. Finally, one respondent answered that this would carry a strong "psychological component as well."

Photo courtesy of Bob Anderson.

Interview with the Honorable Bob Anderson, Mayor of International Falls, Minnesota

Mayor Anderson offered a piece of advice for other cities that are small and isolated: make the best use of your resources. That is an interesting piece of advice from a man who was, on the January day of the interview, in a city with fifteen degree below zero temperatures. "Oh, I guess we're used to it here. No one really slows down until it reaches about forty below." Of course, Mayor Anderson is a native Minnesotan.

In that kind of an environment, how does one take advantage of what is naturally presented to him or her? The answer: in some very interesting and definitely instructive (for other small, isolated cities) ways. The kind of creativity in economic development that Mayor Anderson described was a necessity. The city of International Falls sits on the northern border of Minnesota across the International Bridge from Fort Frances, Canada. On either side of the border, one can find similar cities and similar economies and a shared sense of community and friendship despite being located in separate nations.

In both cities, there is a paper mill that has supported the respective economies for generations. However, the electronic information age has meant that paper for newsprint is in far less demand than in the past. As a result, the mills on both sides of the border have fallen on difficult times. The International Falls mill, which has four paper-producing machines, has idled two of those operations at the cost of 265 jobs. "This placed the local economy in a position of significant jeopardy," said the mayor. That is indeed a lot of jobs in an area of such size and isolation. International Falls and Fort Frances both have about sixty-five hundred residents with another twenty-five hundred nearby, for a regional total of about fifteen thousand people. So, how can the region recover those jobs?

Due to the location near the border crossing, retail is important to both communities, and while there is some overlap, much of the retail—especially restaurants—is sufficiently distinct to attract patrons from across the border. Given the natural attributes of the environs, and Mayor Anderson's admonition to use the resources available, tourism is a promising industry sector. People fly into the area to fish on Rainy Lake. This is a tremendous attraction, as the lake itself is approximately forty miles by forty miles. People fly into the area, rent cabins, eat in the restaurants, shop, and go home.

Other strategies include emphasizing the timber industry, as the region has an abundant supply of hardwoods. Further, because some types of timber cannot be used in the paper manufacturing process, there is now a study being conducted to assess the viability of a business based on using that timber to produce pellets for heating fuel that can then be exported to Europe where that type of fuel usage is popular.

Other existing industries are also located in International Falls. The mill, despite having eliminated 265 jobs, still employs six hundred people. United Health Care operates a forms processing function in International Falls at which several hundred workers are employed. Local summer camps for boys and girls—the latter of which is expanding—provide jobs and attract expenditures to the region in the summer months. Finally, a local community college is well connected with industry and the specific needs of the local employers. For example, it is now training students in preengineering (electrical, mechanical, and chemical) to support the needs of the timber industry and the paper mill.

Mayor Anderson himself worked at the paper mill for fifty-one years. His jobs varied and included being the head of public relations as well as doing college recruiting for the mills. He noted that people were often attracted to International Falls but left after a year of two, so it became clear that the city needed to grow its workforce to keep them in the area.

The need to train students for preengineering points to a strong need for these small and isolated cities: they must train and retain the workforce their employers do and will require. Otherwise, the resident companies will not grow and may not even be able to stay in place. International Falls is more than one hundred miles from any town as large as itself, and even farther to a significant urban area. The mayor spoke of the need to ensure that residents could find the services they need locally. There is no secondary or tertiary health care facility in the region. There are only two optometrists in the city. "People need to know they can obtain those things for themselves and their families."

And, the city needs to be able to provide the public services that residents require. One-third of the city's municipal budget is derived from a property tax, while the remainder comes from state contributions that go to all cities in the state as the result of a needs-based formula distribution. Some citizens voice concerns about growing too much and damaging the quality of life they all enjoy, but Mayor Anderson believes that economic development is an important function up to the point that it ensures that the city can remain a full-service community for its residents. He felt that it could grow from its current size of sixty-five hundred to perhaps twelve or thirteen thousand, ensuring the provision of public and private services and keeping the tax coffers full enough to remain self-sufficient.

Mayor Anderson has recently begun his second term as the mayor of International Falls, having served on the city council for fourteen years in the seventies and eighties as well as one four-year term as mayor at that time. In his second time around, he feels very positive about the future of the city and its economy. One million people cross the bridge into and out of Canada every year; they spend money locally. A local airport enables tourists to come to the area easily for the fishing and other outdoor activities. There are abundant natural resources on which to base a sustainable economy.

The mayor repeats this mantra consistently: "Use your natural assets." One of the obvious features of International Falls is the cold weather. Can that be seen as an asset? Numerous manufacturers come to International Falls during the winter months to test their products' abilities to function in such conditions. The list includes Hyundai, Jaguar, and Bell Helicopters. Clothing is another item that has been tested there, and its manufacturers have subsequently marketed the items as "cold weather tested in International Falls." This provides good business for the hotels, restaurants, garages, retailers, and others in town during what had previously been regarded as the off-season.

Even the festivals in International Falls take advantage of this "economic development asset." The Arrowhead Ultra Marathon includes biking, skiing, and running. It has grown to be so popular that the planners now cap the number of entrants at 180. The event lasts two days and three nights and provides significant revenues for the local hospitality and retail industries. Another such festival is the "Freeze Your Gizzard Blizzard Run," a ten-kilometer run that attracts participants from around the world and has the same kind of impact for local businesses. The mayor relates that one participant—a woman from Brazil—arrives in town each year three weeks prior to the event to become acclimated. Three weeks of stay in the city translates into revenues for room, board, and personal services.

The local assets, including those that one might, at first, consider barriers, have enabled International Falls to sustain its economy year-round and provide not only revenues for local businesses but also taxes for the public services of the city. "Use your natural assets."

Issues for economic growth	• Workforce issues
	• No health care facility
	• Image
Strategies for economic growth	• Regionalism
	• Attract retailers
	• Take advantage of natural assets
	• Workforce training
Lessons learned	• Make the best of the natural resources nearby
	• Regional cooperation is vital
	• Prepare workforce with training before attracting employers

Montevideo, Minnesota

Initially established as a fur trading outpost due to its proximity to the region's many navigable waterways, Montevideo later based its economic strength on the transport of the region's agricultural output. Over more recent years, the city's population has declined fairly consistently to its present level of about fifty-three hundred. This was a fruitful area of inquiry in the discussion with the city's leadership. What is causing the decline, and what is being done to create the economic growth that may reverse that trend?

The unemployment rate in Montevideo is rather low (about half the national average at the time of this writing), but it is unclear whether that is due to a significant level of available jobs or the departure of potential participants in the labor force. The Montevideo Industrial Development Corporation has purchased nearly three hundred acres and built sixteen buildings with about three hundred sixty thousand square feet to accommodate new business growth.

The city's industrial development website posts its annual goal as the creation of twenty-five new jobs that can be either in new or existing industries. Is the city being realistic about its potential for further economic growth, or is its leadership simply pleased with its current position and not interested in more substantial growth?

Photo courtesy of the city of Montevideo.

Interview with Steve Jones, City Manager of Montevideo, Minnesota

Montevideo sits in the middle of the prairie in the Minnesota River valley, near the border with the state of South Dakota. It sits at the confluence of the Minnesota and Chippewa Rivers, which have blessed the region with excellent soil for agricultural pursuits, notably the farming of sugar beets, soybeans, and wheat. Further, being in the valley provides some protection from the harshest of the winter weather patterns.

As such, agriculture provided the primary source of economic growth over the years of the city's existence and until the 1970s, when a substantial diversification of the local economy began in earnest. City Manager Jones explained that much of the economic and other history of Montevideo can be trifurcated by the seventies due to the changes in the community's business base, and the nineties when the region suffered through a major flood.

That experience drove the city's leadership of the day to pursue other industry sectors. Today, the economic sectors that enjoy prominence and growth in Montevideo include electronics manufacture and small motor production. A turkey production plant provides another 250 jobs, and other manufacturing plants in Montevideo produce such varied items as the modular home sections produced by Friendship Homes and various medical devices. This is not only a strong job base for a small town, but a diverse one as well.

The growth of these industries has created a housing shortage in and around Montevideo. This is not an unusual comment from the city leaders included in this research. The housing shortage is exacerbated in Montevideo, however, by the fact that there are not enough people to fill all available positions, which leads employers to recruit. Thus, while there is an interest in attracting more workers to the city and the region, Jones expressed concern about where they would all find places to live.

One of the potential solutions to the workforce supply comes from the migrant populations—largely Hispanic—who used to pass through the area to work on the farms. Those previously transient individuals are now being encouraged to stay and be trained for the new jobs. It remains to be seen at this time whether this will have the desired impact of reducing the workforce shortages.

But, diversification for the city of Montevideo has two considerations. The first, as described above, relates to the industry sectors represented in the area. The second relates to the physical location of the businesses. Some are in the downtown area, while others are outside of the city limits and near the highways that pass through the area. They are designed to capture some of the pass-through traffic.

Jones explained that the retailers that are located near the highways are general purpose in nature. A Walmart is located there and is a place at which people can buy, for example, a good bicycle. However, if they are cycling enthusiasts, they may want to visit the specialty bike shop in the downtown. Other businesses located in the downtown area include other specialty stores, banks, and restaurants. Both types of retail opportunities are important.

Although Montevideo does not receive the sales taxes its retailers generate, the city does receive funding from the state through revenue-sharing programs that distribute funds to poorer communities. That source represents about half of the revenue stream to the Montevideo budget that enables the city to provide public services to its residents and other constituents. One way to enhance the growth of the retail sector would be to widen the current two-lane roads leading to the major highways to four-lane highways. This, with the issue of housing supply, represents the primary assets gap for the further economic development of Montevideo.

Both of these forms of economic diversity were pursued by the community intentionally. Jones explained how the city promulgated some of the growth by funding improvements in the downtown shopping area as well as infrastructure developments that eased access for people to that part of the city. Housing shortages are being addressed by the housing agency, and planning is under way for a new veteran's home that will not only provide needed residences, but create more than two hundred jobs in the process. This is an interesting example of a city that has sought to address two vital issues through a single project. Jones estimates that "a couple hundred homes could be filled immediately, but the costs of purchasing may be too high for the local wage levels. The good news here is that, if you want to work here, you can."

Issues for economic growth	• Workforce shortages
	• Housing shortages
	• Only two-lane rather than four-lane access to major highways
Strategies for economic growth	• Build housing
	• Improve access to interstate highways
Lessons learned	• Have housing in place before attracting attention of employers

Holdrege, Nebraska

One remarkable fact that emerged from the online research into Holdrege, Nebraska, is that the rate of unemployment is 2.5 percent. The national average at the time was over 6 percent. Has Holdrege managed to attract such a sufficient employer base that jobs are plentiful, or is the low rate simply the result of the decline of nearly 6 percent in the population base between 1990 and 2005? This was a question for many of those interviewed in this research, as those trends repeat themselves in several of the locations.

The city's website addresses the economic development assets of Holdrege in great detail. This is, of course, designed to support marketing efforts; however, some of the positive attributes of the city certainly bore further investigation in the interview with the city's leadership. These include low utility rates, the centralized location (presumably in a national sense), a productive workforce (despite an unemployment rate that is lower than "full employment"), designation as the county seat, and a high quality of life.

At present, Holdrege is home to two large manufacturers: BD–Holdrege, which produces medical supplies, notably syringes for patients with diabetes; and, Allmand Brothers, which manufactures and exports construction equipment globally. Additional economic sectors represented in Holdrege include health care, agriculture, and retail.

Strategies identified by city planners for additional growth include securing available land within city limits for an industrial park and arranging packages for prospects to include grants, loans, and attraction incentives. Building the workforce is also identified and bore some further exploration in the interview.

Photo courtesy of Dan Christiansen.

Interview with Robert Rager, City Administrator of Holdrege, Nebraska

Holdrege is located in the south central area of the state of Nebraska. The economy is, and has always been, based primarily on agricultural output. Recent recessions have not hurt the local economy because the demand for and prices of the local crops remained fairly constant throughout. In fact, City Administrator Rager is pleased to point out that sales tax revenues for the city even increased slightly during that time period. The revenues from sales taxes are the primary source of the local budget from which the city provides public services, with property taxes also representing a large component.

Part of the success of the local agriculturally based economy is that back in the 1930s, city elders built an open ditch that funnels water into the city's aquifer. As a result, water for consumption as well as irrigation is plentiful in and around Holdrege. This helps distinguish Holdrege from many of the other isolated small towns in which agriculture is the primary basis of the local economy.

City Administrator Rager was asked about the loss of farming jobs as the local family farms were slowly replaced by large-scale farming that employs technology rather than human beings. He noted that the typical farm in south central Nebraska is between seven thousand and ten thousand acres and seems to employ fewer and fewer individuals.

Fortunately, large-scale farming is not where the best jobs are in Holdrege. As a result, the city has not experienced the same issues with brain drain that other cities in this research have referenced. The two largest employers in town—Allmand

Brothers and BD–Holdrege—employ men and women at all levels of income and across a wide range of skill sets.

Allmand Brothers, a subsidiary of a New Jersey-based firm, manufactures in Holdrege syringes for diabetics. And, BD–Holdrege, which was recently bought by Briggs and Stratton, manufactures light towers and highway light signs in the city. In fact, their greatest issue is their inability to find enough workers to satisfy the needs of the plants.

For the city to attract the necessary workforce, it will need to provide additional housing opportunities for the new workers/residents. The hope is that it will be able to encourage many of the current residents who drive long distances—to Carney or elsewhere—to accept jobs at either Allmand Brothers or BD–Holdrege.

This will have the dual benefit of time and gas savings for the individual and additional revenues for the city of Holdrege. Rager points out that those who work in Carney tend to do their shopping there as well. Carney has a Walmart and a number of other retail options that cannot be found in Holdrege. As a result, the retailers in town suffer and the sales taxes benefit another community.

The result of greater purchasing power being used in Holdrege could also drive demand for some new clothing stores, nice restaurants, and other retail stores that residents need. This is a need but a secondary one to the greater need: housing. The city recently obtained a $100,000 grant from the economic development program of the state of Nebraska. A similar grant was obtained a few years ago that amounted to $450,000. Both grants were used for the purpose of planning for the construction of new housing as well as the cleanup of the existing housing stock, as well as entire neighborhoods in the older and lower-income sections of the city.

Rager's description of Holdrege is greatly different than that of most of the cities included in this research. This city of roughly five thousand residents is home to a YMCA that has about three thousand members. The city also has an arts center and recently allocated $23 million to an addition for the city's hospital. Also, a $17 million bond issue just passed that will enable the city to construct a new grade school. And finally, more than one hundred acres was just purchased by the city as the site for its second industrial park, in the expectation that it will help to attract new employers to Holdrege.

As the city pursues additional employers, it targets businesses that are in the agricultural cluster that logically fit in the community. In this way, it hopes to build a cluster that is interdependent and mutually supportive. A similar effort is targeted at industry segments included in the supply chain for the two major employers already in town, Allmand Brothers and BD–Holdrege. This includes plastics suppliers and others.

An additional strategy relates to programs through the community college that will enable high school students to receive concurrent credit for two-year degrees or certificates. This, Rager believes, will help satisfy some of the demand for welders, plumbers, and electricians.

Rager offers one lesson and gives it great emphasis: "Set priorities for what is best for the community. You can't please everybody; you can only ensure that it is the right fit for the city."

Issues for economic growth	• Lack of housing
	• Lack of retail
Strategies for economic growth	• Build a cluster of businesses to complement existing agriculture-based businesses
	• Increase workforce training
Lessons learned	• Be sure that the businesses attracted fit with the workforce and with the community

Sidney, Nebraska

Over the past ten years, the population of Sidney, Nebraska, has fluctuated between sixty-two and sixty-four hundred residents, more than 90 percent of whom are classified by the Census Bureau as white. The current unemployment rate is roughly half of the national average, which leads to a familiar line of inquiry for the city's leaders.

While the residents do not reflect a great deal of diversity, the local business community does. Once dominated by agriculture, the economy now has strongholds in a variety of business sectors. Federal facilities and installations helped fuel some of the local growth, as did the oil and gas industry. Over time, their impacts on the economy diminished and locally grown businesses have evolved to replace them, including retailers. These are in diverse business sectors such as the hospitality industry and a wide range of construction trades. The city's website trumpets the plans and activities of the community that have facilitated such growth, including the development of hotel rooms, a visitor center, and a conference facility.

The website also provides considerable detail on state and community programs available to help facilitate the attraction, retention, and growth of businesses. But much of what is known about Sidney, Nebraska, can be gleaned from a fascinating, well-researched, and entertaining volume that was coauthored by Loren Avey and the city manager of Sidney, Gary Person. This book characterizes the beginnings of what the newspapers of the day referred to as the "Hardest Hole," the "Toughest Town on the Tracks," "Sinful Sidney," and the "Wickedest Town in the West." However, as the authors point out, "In a positive sense, it was even known as 'The Magical City on the Plains' because growth and prosperity were so prominent" (Avey and Person, 2006).

The city gained that prominence shortly after the Civil War when the westward expansion accelerated. Sidney became a way station and a location for crew changes for the Union Pacific Railroad. In the late 1870s, the discovery of gold in the Black Hills led to business growth in the city to support those who came to seek their fortunes. The monikers with the negative connotations may have been earned during this period. Avey and Person note, "At the peak of the gold rush, historical accounts of the day claimed Sidney had eighty-four licensed businesses selling liquor, including twenty-eight on just one block of Front Street" (Avey and Person, 2006).

This was certainly an interview to which I looked forward with great anticipation.

Photo courtesy of Lori Borchert.

Interview with Gary Person, City Manager of Sidney, Nebraska

In many cases, the city managers and mayors who participated in this research are historians. They can recite the backgrounds of their cities and regions by heart. It illustrates a strong sense of pride in place. Some even did much of the initial research rather than parroting what others have written. Gary Person is at the top of this category of city managers: he did the research, quite literally wrote the book, and knows the history of Sidney, Nebraska, and the region in which it sits as well as anyone.

The year 1867 marked the establishment of both the city of Sidney and the state of Nebraska, and both were the result of the same factor: the railroads were being developed to bring development farther west. Indian tribes in the region fought to forestall the growth that was impinging upon their lands and their lifestyles. A military presence was needed to protect the railroad workers and their families and to smooth the way for the westward push. As the military presence grew into a formal post, the surrounding area needed to be farmed in order to provide sustenance for the soldiers. From this grew the initial economy around Sidney: a military presence and a farming community. Person notes that "locational advantages have always helped us to survive economically."

In the 1870s, gold was discovered in the Black Hills, leading to further expansion of the rail lines and further growth of the city, as well as even greater demand for agricultural output throughout the region: "The town boomed."

Ultimately, however, the gold veins played out and the railroads headed in different directions and what was left was a community that remained in existence solely for the purpose of farming. And it remained as such until World War II represented yet another locational advantage for Sidney as the US Army built a large munitions depot in the area. "A couple thousand people showed up in 1942, literally overnight," said City Manager Person. After the war, oil was discovered near the city, and that helped to sustain the economy for several decades. This was complemented by an additional military presence in the form of Minuteman missile sites during the cold war. However, the oil fields ultimately dried up and the base finally closed around the same time in the late 1960s.

Person described what a difficult time that was for the residents of Sidney and the surrounding county: "The community had to reinvent itself." They turned to two economic development strategies: attract new businesses and grow new companies themselves. The greatest challenge today was that, after forty years of economic decline and job loss, "the local attitudes had soured." Person entered the Sidney scene about that time, first as the editor of the local newspaper and later as the president of the chamber of commerce.

In order to right the local economy, the city invested in infrastructure development (although the approval process took more than a decade) to create a new industrial park proximate to the intersection of major highways in the region. This yielded a lesson: "Embrace business and industry and you will build the reputation that your city will do whatever is needed to bring companies in and provide what they need to be successful." After that, the trend of population decline that had stretched over many years was finally reversed.

The city next invested in new water sources and wastewater treatment facilities as well as a regional power generation plant. After that, four separate referenda were put to vote, and in each case, the issue passed, despite the resultant need to raise tax rates. The first such issue, which was created to provide a building to retain one of the region's largest companies, Cabela's, passed with a 91 percent approval level. Subsequently, the city obtained the necessary funding to redevelop the old Army depot into an office park.

The result: over the last five years, more than $300 million in investments has been realized in Sidney. Today, Sidney has more jobs (eight thousand plus) than residents (about sixty-seven hundred). Thus, the city is the absolute employment center for the entire region. "We have to be," explains Person, "there's nothing anywhere near us except for a few very, very small farming communities."

Over time, the economic base of the city has changed dramatically. As late as the early 1990s, Sidney's economy was largely driven by agriculture. However, just ten or twelve years later, agriculture ranks seventh in the city's economic output listing. City Manager Person notes, "That's a pretty dramatic change for a rural community and is one of the reasons Sidney is thriving and growing." Perhaps more importantly, the economic base in Sidney has become increasingly more diverse.

But, as is generally the case, the growth has also created a problem/opportunity. As the job base grew, the housing inventory has proven to be inadequate to provide places for all of the new people to live. The opportunity comes in the sense that the construction industry will also boom as a consequence. In all of this growth, Person notes, "The city has to be a partner. We know that we are always just one step ahead of objections to the growth so we need to work with everyone and to educate people about the benefits of the development." Nonetheless, the city manager advises, "We are going to grow. You're either growing or you're dying; there is no in between. So, we are going to grow, and it isn't just going to happen on its own."

City Manager Person cites another issue that confronts these isolated small towns more than those that are closer to other urban communities. When the housing is needed, developers prepare plans but the financing institutions are frequently reluctant to finance the developments because it may take a long time to fill the units and the interim period will represent losses for both the banks and the developers.

In the case of Sidney, that reaction found a solution. Cabela's, for whose employees the housing units were most urgently needed, agreed to guarantee the loans and the occupancy. The city's leadership hopes that the success of the project will give lenders greater comfort for later project financing.

All of these projects and developments are important to Sidney, which derives its budgetary resources from a blend of property taxes, sales taxes, and various fees. The objective for the city is to rebuild its economic base and thereby to demonstrate to financiers and companies alike the "stability, trust, continuity, and vision of our city." Says Person, "It's who we are. If you sell what you are to employers, people will see the advantages of a location in your community."

When asked about general lessons for small, rural communities, Person asserts that the rural way of life he knew as a child, and that his parents and grandparents lived before him, is all but gone today from the nation's landscape. Person testified before Congress in May 2014 on this topic. The following is excerpted from his verbal presentation. It is, in large measure, based on these facts that he cited at that time. Eighty of Nebraska's ninety-three counties are considered to be rural; those eighty counties each have less population today than was reported in 1890, and only six have shown any growth since 1950! Sidney is "100 miles from any population base over fifteen thousand residents and 350 miles from the state capital" (Person, 2014).

Person stated that by 1970, most of these jobs disappeared and farming and ranching were about to head into the 1980s crisis mode—jobs left in mass exodus, population declined for forty-five consecutive years, the economy tanked, and the public infrastructure started to erode away (Person, 2014, p. 2).

But, the diversification of the area's economy became a priority focus and agriculture now ranks only seventh as a leading economic sector. States Person, "We have tripled that local economy and valuation base over the past twenty years. We have more jobs per capita than almost any community in America.... We have another $300 million of new projects ... moving forward this spring" (Person, 2014, p. 3).

For Person and the city of Sidney, Nebraska, there was no easy way to this success. "We did it through hard work, one new job at a time, one new business at a time, and one challenge to overcome at a time. We took risks and turned failure into the educational blocks that built successes in the future" (Person, 2014, p. 4). His message is that if we can do it in Sidney, Nebraska, others can do it elsewhere.

Issues for economic growth	• Housing shortages
Strategies for economic growth	• Build housing
	• Build infrastructure
	• Economic diversification
Lessons learned	• Prepare the infrastructure for industry before businesses arrive
	• Interact regularly with local industry
	• Diversify the local economy
	• Realize that cities will either grow or die; there is no in between

Valley City, North Dakota

The unemployment rate of Valley City, North Dakota, at the time of this writing, was exceptionally low, at less than 3 percent. This was an important area to discuss with the city's leadership because it can be the result of either of two possible factors: first, because the population has been dropping consistently over the past two decades, it is possible that the number of job seekers has simply declined; or second, it could be that there has been a surge in the number of jobs available. It is important in small, isolated communities to look beyond the numbers and understand which specific forces are at play.

Given these two trends, there is also a further consideration that served as a topic of discussion. Because the unemployment rate is an indicator of available workers in the community who are interested in employment, how can Valley City attract new employers and be able to offer the employment base it will need? Or, does it not want to grow?

If the city does have intentions to expand the employment base, there are several assets that will support the plan, including the Valley City State University and a business incubator in the Regional Technology Center. Exactly how Valley City might use those assets to support overall business growth is an interesting discussion.

Photo courtesy of George Dutton.

Interview with David Schelkopf, City Manager of Valley City, North Dakota

City Manager Schelkopf related that most of the cities in North Dakota are located where they are due to their proximity either to navigable waterways or to railroad lines. In the case of Valley City, the Sheyenne River was the cause for the initial settlement to be placed in today's location. The city lies approximately sixty miles from Fargo and thirty miles from Jamestown. As the valley derived its fertile soil from the riverbank, the area became home to many farms and ranches. In 1922, the city developed a great deal of infrastructure designed to facilitate the use of the river for these purposes.

However, today farming and ranching have been eclipsed in the Valley City economy by oil extraction as the leading industry. Says Schelkopf, "North Dakota is fundamentally changing" as a result; further, this is leading to growth statewide. John Deere employs about four hundred people in the city and future local growth for the farm equipment company is expected. The company owns about thirty acres of land that is thought to be where the expansion will occur over the next several years, and the city is now preparing it for use by new businesses coming to the area.

The city's budget is stable, as the city owns the electricity generation plant and the resultant fees enable the city to fund such things as "twenty-four/seven police and fire protection, which is unusual for a city of our size." It has also enabled the city to develop the industrial park, which is at present dedicated largely to John

Deere (thirty acres) and the National Guard (eighteen acres). In order to finance the economic development activities of the corporation, the city imposes a seven-tenths of one percent add-on tax to sales in the city. Those proceeds are used to support the local economic development corporation.

The city also manages a large business incubator that, Schelkopf acknowledges, needs more activity. It has, however, launched one very successful business, Eagle Creek, which now employs seventy-five people in the city. "But, it's an opportunity and we need to do more there." As the utility taxes accrue directly to the city budget, Valley City is able to impose one of the lowest rates for electricity in the state of North Dakota. The revenues generated from these activities enable the city to provide public services while keeping the tax rates for businesses and residents low. "We are all very proud of that," says the city manager.

One strategic asset for economic development that has greater potential than its present application is the University of Valley City, which has more than twelve hundred students. "They are great partners. They develop courses that are specific to the needs of our employers, and they allow their meeting space to be used by local businesses."

With recent business growth across the state of North Dakota as well as in Valley City, the population is growing again. Says City Manager Schelkopf, "There were more people here in the 1970s than there are now, but we are growing once again." The result is a need for housing. "We want to grow but the costs of infrastructure development are climbing. We see the growth as a means of providing the necessary resources for infrastructure development and maintenance. Growth helps offset the climbing costs of everything."

The type of housing that Schelkopf favors would be expandable. That would allow young families to buy a home and to build additions over time as their needs and incomes change. In this way, it could be seen as more affordable for young people to buy homes and would help to keep them in Valley City as their families grow. This leads to Schelkopf's first lesson for other communities of similar size and geography: to get the companies, cities need to have the infrastructure already in place to attract and handle growth.

A second lesson offered is that a vital economic development program is critical. "Growth doesn't just happen. Those who understand the value of growth need to stay active in the planning and the process. A long-range plan for land use must be in place so that when a company comes to your city, you can tell them where they can locate and what you can do for them. From there, you need to be flexible so you can work with any additional requirements. The city has to be ready to say, 'Here's what we are willing to do.'"

Finally, in small cities and towns, "everything is right there. Everything can be seen so you have to create a place that is livable. We have built bike trails and walking paths. We're going to use the river again. There's not a place in June and

July that is more wonderful than North Dakota. It's beautiful. The opportunities are tremendous for our town."

Issues for economic growth	• Business incubator needs more tenants
	• Housing shortages
	• Need for infrastructure despite rising costs
Strategies for economic growth	• Build housing
	• Build infrastructure
Lessons learned	• Growth pays for the ever-increasing costs of infrastructure
	• Build the infrastructure before businesses arrive

Great Lakes

Carmi, Illinois

Carmi, Illinois, is located along the banks of the Little Wabash River. The river setting has driven the local economy from the very beginning of the city's existence, when the initial business in the area was a mill that drew its power from the river's currents. Today, the river's impact is felt most prominently because the soil in the area is quite fertile, allowing a variety of agribusinesses to be very successful in and around Carmi.

Today, nearly 450 farms in the city and the surrounding area produce grain, corn, wheat, soybeans, and more. But, an agriculture-related cluster has grown in the area as well. This includes grain elevators, fertilizer companies, seed dealers, and more. One item of discussion for the city's leadership was whether that cluster was planned and pursued or whether it grew of its own accord. Another area of inquiry was whether the local leadership feels that this represents a sufficient degree of diversification in Carmi's economic base. The surrounding county, White County, is the third largest oil producer in the state of Illinois. The city's website outlines the potential for a cluster around the industry that would include equipment supply and maintenance, soil treatments, drilling and casing, inspection services, and more. Is there a plan in place yet to attract or develop those businesses in Carmi?

Oil is one possible industry sector for growth and economic diversification in Carmi.

The city was severely affected by flooding in the 2011 and the US Department of Commerce's Economic Development Administration responded by granting Carmi $1 million to build new sewer lines and other infrastructure to the city's new industrial park. This will yield nearly twenty-three hundred feet of reinforced roadway for heavy vehicles and nearly twelve hundred feet of sanitary sewer lines to the park. The interview covered any plans that are in place to market the park actively for business relocation (US Department of Commerce, 2013).

Photo courtesy of Todd Atteberry.

Interview with Sandra Irvine, City Administrator of Carmi, Illinois

The city administrator of Carmi, Illinois, Sandra Irvine, notes that the local economy is difficult to revitalize because the city has no four-lane access to the major highways that pass through the region. This serves to isolate Carmi to an even greater extent than some of the other communities throughout southern Illinois. Additionally, she points out, because the economy has declined, the population has also declined over recent years.

Today, agriculture remains the staple of the city's economy, although Irvine noted that the practice of high-volume fracking could open up some new jobs for the mid-range future. This practice however, awaits decision making in the state legislature where the issue is quite contentious. In the meantime, a serious brain drain has caused the younger workforce to depart for places unknown, leaving behind a much more senior group in the local population and in the labor pool. The city and the potential employers are awaiting a decision from the legislature that will hopefully enable the extraction industry to grow and add employment opportunities and incomes for the residents as well as tax revenues for the city.

The city of Carmi has now passed a bill that adds an additional three-quarters of one percent to the local sales tax. This provides a little more funding for local public services and diversifies the tax base away from overdependence on real estate tax generation. That also makes business attraction efforts focus on retail a little more, although City Administrator Irvine notes that retail has been a great need anyway. Local residents typically drive forty miles to Evansville, Indiana, for nice restaurants, clothes shopping, and even grocery shopping. Irvine maintains that if the city could capture even 10 percent of those lost sales taxes, the city could make a lot of improvements that have been postponed for some time.

On the other hand, there is some good news on the retail front. The movie theater that has been boarded up for a long time and an older strip mall with several vacant storefronts are being looked at by private interests for revitalization. A new hardware store has recently opened. This type of store is really important to the residents of small towns, maintains City Administrator Irvine. She still feels the city needs to find a few key retailers to come to Carmi to satisfy such basics needs as a ladies' clothing store and a shoe store.

There are some assets in the community that will be attractive for the business community. Several small campuses of colleges that have their main bases elsewhere are located in and around Carmi, and can provide tailored training for local employers. The city plans to use their representatives in discussions with economic development prospects as they discuss the benefits of a location in Carmi.

The proximity to the border with the state of Indiana creates a challenge for the city of Carmi and the rest of the region. Stores and business locations must compete with those in the Hoosier state. Illinois' tax policies and reputation for not being business-friendly make such competition for a border community much more difficult than it might be for others. For Carmi, the real issue is that employers—both potential and existing—can also simply drive over the state line to take advantage of opportunities within a lower-tax environment. The sense throughout the balance of the state seems to be that in Illinois, legislative policies are set in a manner that primarily supports Chicago and its environs, and are not always beneficial to smaller communities, especially those as far away from the state capital as Carmi.

City Administrator Irvine concurred with many of the other local leaders in this study when it comes to attempts to attract large employers to the community.

Issues for economic growth	• Fracking legislation is stalled in state legislature
	• Brain drain
	• Shortage of retail
	• Shortage of restaurants
	• State tax policies (located near Indiana border)
Strategies for economic growth	• Attract retailers and restaurants to reverse revenue leakage to other areas
Lessons learned	• Grow local small businesses as well as attracting others

"Grow your own small businesses and encourage them to grow in their home communities. Help them get started and then encourage them, support them. We don't look for hundreds of jobs at once. If we can get fifty jobs, we're thrilled!"

Kingsford, Michigan

The onset of the era of the mass production of automobiles provided the genesis for the city of Kingsford, as it did for so many other small towns throughout the northern part of the Great Lakes region. The production facilities that grew in Kingsford were later used during the Second World War to produce gliders for the military. Later, many of those facilities were either upgraded or torn down. From the latter, another spin-off was created. The charcoal briquette company that bears the name of the city was started simply in order to sell off some of the lumber that was scrap from the rebuilt wooden automobile manufacturing facilities in and around the city.

Additional industries have grown in and around Kingsford and now constitute a different kind of industrial base in the region. The city's population in recent years has held fairly steady at just under fifty-five hundred residents. One question posed to the city's leadership related to the demographics of that population and the ability of the area to support the job workforce needs of new businesses that might consider Kingsford as a location.

Photo courtesy of Theresa Peterson Proudfit of the *Iron Mountain Daily News.*

Interview with Tony Edelbeck, City Manager of Kingsford, Michigan

Kingsford, Michigan, has a fascinating history and Edelbeck relates it with obvious pride. His origins, while not in Kingsford, are within the region, and he has served the city for nearly thirty years, the first twenty-five of which were as its director of public works.

Kingsford and a neighboring municipality, Iron Mountain, are sister cities and have, for thirty or forty years, worked very collaboratively to advance the region and enhance the quality of services for their residents. The region first became more than timberland in the late 1800s. At some point in time, a relative of Henry Ford, Edward Kingsford, persuaded the businessman to buy up large areas of acreage in the Upper Peninsula in order to have access to its timber. One industry facility and one industry segment led to others, and at one point in time, Ford workers numbered more than eight thousand in the region. Most of the timber operations used parts of the wood for various processes, but consideration was also given to what uses could be made of the waste. One such use for the wood ultimately led to the development of a new product: Kingsford Charcoal Briquettes. The company stayed in the city until 1964, when it relocated the operational facility to Kentucky and the headquarters to California.

The economy had already begun to slow following the 1950 departure of much of the Ford businesses and suppliers in and around Kingsford. Several local businessmen took ownership of various parts of the facility with the objective of creating and attracting new business operations to operate in the plant. The result was that companies moved in began to create jobs, including such firms as Load-All, a garbage truck manufacturing business, and Northwood Metal Fabrication.

Other businesses also thrived in Kingsford. The Grady Foundry, a large, existing company, had been established in 1947. More recently, Oldenburg built an $8 million plant. At the same time, businesses began to grow in the neighboring city of Iron Mountain, initially in the area of mineral extraction, as the name implies. Today, more than 130 firms conduct business operations within the city limits of Kingsford.

All of this commercial activity benefits the city and its residents in more ways than simply job creation. The city's budget is based primarily on property taxes, with sales taxes also contributing. Of course, the growth of new businesses, particularly those that generate sales tax revenues for large-ticket items (e.g., garbage trucks), pay substantial property taxes, thereby enabling the city to provide high-quality public services to its residents. The governor of Michigan has implemented policies that return as much of the locally generated funds as feasible back to the communities around the state, and the Michigan Economic Vitality Incentive Program (EVIP) encourages regional collaboration and cooperation in the provision of public services.

Ultimately, such programs enable municipalities like Kingsford and Iron Mountain to realize budgetary savings through shared and more efficient facilities. For these two cities—Kingsford and Iron Mountain—this has meant joint facilities for wastewater and sewage treatment and clean water provision. Following on these successes, regional approaches to the provision of municipal services have begun to be implemented in various forms of local planning.

City Manager Edelbeck notes that such practices are not new to Kingsford and Iron Mountain, which have done so "for thirty or forty years. You have to. We are so close by and have all the same needs. Out here, we need to collaborate anyway due to the distances to other places." Indeed, this is a refrain repeated by other leaders in this research. In short, relative isolation is recognized and induces communities to work together in a collaborative spirit to realize great efficiencies in the provision of basic infrastructure for their residents.

Industry growth in both cities leads to visitors coming to the area for a variety of purposes. That has, in turn, yielded the growth of retail establishments and a growing hospitality industry. In turn, job growth in those industries has led to growth in the residential home building sector. The growth of those businesses then created a demand for new training opportunities, particularly as manufacturing functions have become more computerized and technical. The region has responded by establishing a center for technical training to prepare new employees for local businesses as well as to retrain the current workforce. This increasing diversity in the business base throughout the region has "definitely helped us in the current economic downturn," advised City Manager Edelbeck.

Many of those interviewed noted that they needed to be cautious about both business and residential growth because they did not want the city or the region to get too big, thereby changing the quality of life currently enjoyed by all. This is not the case with Edelbeck, who noted that Kingsford has developed the streets and other infrastructure to accommodate new residents and new residential developments. The city has also developed a $2.5 million tool and die facility to encourage additional economic development. "We have come from having all our eggs in one basket to a diverse and healthy economy here in Kingsford," noted Edelbeck.

Issues for economic growth	• Concerns about growth altering the quality of life
Strategies for economic growth	• Economic diversification
	• Regionalism
Lessons learned	• Diversify the local economy
	• Pursue regional cooperation

Ashland, Wisconsin

Ashland, Wisconsin, is a port location on Lake Superior and much of its economy is related to the juxtaposition of the community to the lake. Originally established as a settlement in the mid-1850s, the early residents of Ashland enjoyed a friendly and collaborative relationship with the local Ojibwe Indians. By 1872, the first sawmill was operating in the area, and five years later, the first rail line from Ashland to Chicago became fully operational.

In recent years, the population base of Ashland has declined but only marginally. Unemployment was hovering just under the national average at the time of this writing, implying an economy that is stable but for which some additional growth might be welcome (the national average for unemployment is nearly 9 percent). This was a topic for discussion with the city's leadership during the interview.

Photo courtesy of Ed Monroe.

Interview with the Honorable Bill Whalen, Mayor of Ashland, Wisconsin

Ashland, Wisconsin, sits on the edge of Lake Superior, and much of the historic economy was driven by that position. Today, some of the economy is still a result of the city's geography, but not entirely, and not in the same ways as in the past. Because much of the recent economic growth has been tourism based, the city sees its fortunes as being tied very closely to those of the state of Wisconsin. "As it goes up," said Whalen, "we go up. Right now, fortunately, tourism is on the rise." This is an especially important consideration in Ashland, which collects 40 percent of its general fund revenues (in a $17 million city budget) from the state of Wisconsin through a formulaic revenue-sharing program that is overseen by the state government.

Tourism is more important now to the Ashland economy than ever before. For many generations, forestry and the extraction and transshipment of iron ore were the staples of the region's economy. However, the forestry industry is less productive now, and the last shipments of iron ore departed as far back as the late 1960s. The iron dock is still in place and holds potential value for the future economic growth of the city and the region.

The iron dock is nineteen hundred feet long and is the longest such dock in the world, according to Mayor Whalen. He feels it could be developed into a maintenance facility for tankers and could accommodate as many as four 1000-foot ships simultaneously.

The mayor, however, sees the transition from an extraction economy to other industries as tough. Many of the people in the community remember times when the economic drivers once thought to be solid for many years to come began their decline. "It's hard for them to forget those times." For the newer residents of Ashland, such difficulties are not a barrier to trying new things. The tourism trade is one of those new things, but it needs constant nurturing from the city's leadership.

One of the more interesting attractions for visitors to Lake Superior is the ice caves. When the lake freezes sufficiently, dramatic caves and ice "sculptures" are created naturally. As this is the first winter in five years that has occurred, the tourism trade for that reason alone has been brisk. Indeed, when one observes pictures of these natural formations, there is no disappointment, as the results of the winter cold and winds are unusual and quite spectacular. Further, although many of these have been formed over centuries, each occurrence is formed by greatly differing conditions and each winter can make changes, so the results are always unique. This year, there have been ninety thousand visitors to the caves. They spend money for gasoline, meals, and hotels while in town.

Another quite interesting and definitely unique attraction is the historic murals of Ashland County. These are a series of murals on the sides of buildings in Ashland and throughout the county (also named Ashland) that depict the history of the area. They are, separately, quality works of art; collectively, it is a tourism experience that Mayor Whalen feels is unparalleled anywhere.

While some of the area's largest employers are the local hospital, schools, and the public sector, the largest employer (450 jobs) manufactures paper-folding machines. Still, tourism is already significant and presents significant growth potential as well. To enhance the growth of the tourism industry, Ashland and the region seek to provide the services that make peoples' visits more enjoyable, thereby encouraging them to stay in the area for longer visits and to return more often.

For example, the mayor notes that the city dedicated substantial funds to the improvement of the road leading to and entering Ashland. This has become a "welcoming gateway" to the city. The $6 million plus expenditure has created a "wow factor for the city as you approach it," according to Mayor Whalen. US Route 2 passes by Ashland and brings with it traffic entering and leaving Canada. Of course, this contributes to the growth of the area's hotels, gas stations, restaurants, and retail establishments, but importantly, it also helps generate sales taxes that enable the city to provide public services to residents and visitors alike.

Two local colleges—one a two-year and the other a four-year institution—also attract visitors to the area who buy gasoline, stay in hotels, and visit the local attractions. There is also a program involving the colleges through which they have begun to purchase as much of their food as feasible from local sources, thereby helping the agricultural employers in the region. The goal of this program is to reach the level of 85 percent of all such purchases coming from local producers.

The regional airport is also an economic engine, but it serves a different purpose for Mayor Whalen than might be found in the other cities in this research. The mayor is a flying enthusiast who starts many of his days having his morning coffee at the airport. In this way, he meets people coming and going and believes he has made some very valuable future connections for the city in the process. As a lesson, Mayor Whalen said that a small city must be "welcoming and have that kind of feel." The city has a revolving loan fund that makes loans to residents to fix up their homes. The repayment is not due until they sell their homes. "This is really important; many of the homes are picturesque, but old. We want to create—and, we want to present—a welcoming, entrepreneurial community in Ashland. This will take time. It won't happen overnight. There is no silver bullet. It has to come from within. But, we can and we will make it happen. This is such a great little town."

Issues for economic growth	• The hard times left an indelible impression and a risk-averse attitude
Strategies for economic growth	• Beautify the city
Lessons learned	• Improve services for tourists to enhance their visit
	• Beautify the city

Rice Lake, Wisconsin

The city of Rice Lake, Wisconsin, proved to be the source of an interesting interview. Unlike many of the cities in this study, Rice Lake has a steadily growing population that is reflected in the upgrade of numerous public facilities. Two new schools have been built and major renovations have taken place at the local university (the University of Wisconsin, Barron County) as well as at the local technical college (Wisconsin Indianhead Technical College). Additional improvements in local infrastructure include a new airport and a new hospital. Discussion with the city's leadership focused on the reasons for, and the sources of funding for, this type of growth. Is the city experiencing sufficient growth that supports the demand for these new and improved assets, or is it building them as attractions in anticipation of attracting new businesses and residents?

Photo courtesy of Curt Snyder.

Interview with Curt Snyder, City Administrator of Rice Lake, Wisconsin

Many years ago, the logging interests around what is today's Rice Lake, Wisconsin, had, for unknown reasons, pressed for incorporation. Long afterward, the city remains but the timber companies had long since departed. Today, much of the city's economic opportunity derives from its central location: a one-hour drive to Eau Claire, Wisconsin, and about a ninety-minute drive to Duluth, Minnesota. As such, Rice Lake serves as the hub for the entire region's service providers with a catchment area of around eighty thousand people. It is thus essential that residents of the region are able to find the services they require without having to travel extraordinary distances to larger urban areas. This is an issue that this research has shown to be common in small, isolated cities and towns, and especially vital as the degree of isolation increases.

In addition to the services businesses in Rice Lake, the city also boasts more than two thousand manufacturing employees as well as several sizable agricultural enterprises, although the latter, according to City Administrator Snyder, tend to be much smaller than one typically finds in cities of this size and degree of isolation. This has been largely reflected in dairy outputs over the past several decades.

Snyder noted how many similarly sized cities have a tendency to chase the big employer in hopes of the "game-winning home run." That is, they want to try to solve all of their employment needs with a single business attraction. Snyder and Rice Lake have taken a more strategic and gradual approach to economic growth; they prefer to make efforts to "garden" their own new, small businesses.

To accelerate this type of growth, Rice Lake has created three tax increment financing (TIF) districts in which small businesses can grow while being permitted to pay reduced taxes and fees. He describes the types of companies in the districts as largely "value-add" businesses, meaning that they assemble items from other sources and add value as they work. These districts have been successful in growing several diverse small business operations.

A couple of examples are the production of bulk heads for long-haul trucks that are manufactured by F and G Products, and the production of refrigerated bodies that can be attached to various types of trucks. The latter are manufactured by Johnson Trucks. To support these companies, the local technical college works closely with the industry to provide their future workforce and to upgrade the skills of the existing workforce. Due to the role played by the local technical college, an interview was also conducted with Craig Fowler, the president of Wisconsin Indianhead Technical College (WITC).

One very practical reason for this approach is that if a large company were to announce that it was locating in Rice Lake, "we would not have the workforce to support them. We like the idea of growing our own small businesses that will expand over time."

In many communities, economic development targets for attraction reflect the nature of the local budgets. That is, if sales taxes or real estate taxes are the prime generator of the local tax base from which public services are provided, the economic development plan focuses on businesses that help expand the relevant tax base. The city of Rice Lake, while not overly dependent upon sales taxes, does benefit from them.

However, the Wisconsin sales tax allocation policies changed in the mid-nineties to the detriment of the city. At that time, the state legislature froze the shared revenues from sales taxes to local municipalities, which in effect capped the levels of revenues at then-present totals. Any growth beyond that no longer goes to the state's budget. Prior to that change, the city was realizing as much as 5 percent growth each year in that stream of revenue.

As a consequence, the city had to reduce its own workforce by as much as 10 percent on two separate occasions even though the area was experiencing significant growth in the local economy. Today, property taxes are the dominant revenue stream for the Rice Lake general fund. That has had the effect of shifting the burden of public service costs to the homeowner and away from those who purchase goods and services. This is further complicated, according to City Administrator Snyder, by the fact that many of the land users in small towns like Rice Lake are exempt from paying property taxes. These entities can often represent significant land holdings in a small town, and may include churches, hospitals, universities, and other organizations that have an exempt status.

In terms of lessons learned in Rice Lake that may be transferable to other similarly sized and placed communities, City Administrator Snyder notes that small towns do not fit common molds: "There is no one-size-fits-all solution. All cities of eight thousand in population are different. States cannot deal with them in a single, structured policy. Small towns contribute a lot to a state's economic development but don't get nearly the credit they deserve. States need policies that reflect the differences and importance of their small towns."

Issues for economic growth	• Workforce issues
	• State legislation froze local revenue-sharing limits
	• Public institutions (e.g., hospitals, universities) do not pay taxes but do use infrastructure
Strategies for economic growth	• Help grow local businesses
Lessons learned	• Grow your own small businesses as well as attracting new ones
	• State policies need to treat all small towns differently rather than with a one-size-fits-all approach

Northeast

Caribou, Maine

Incorporated on the eve of the Civil War and located at the northernmost tip of the state of Maine, Caribou has a population that has leveled out in recent years at just over eight thousand. For much of its early existence, agriculture and the shipment of agricultural products were the basis of the local economy. This was complemented in the post–World War II era by the development of Loring Air Force Base nearby, but its closure after the conclusion of America's involvement in Southeast Asia created serious economic hardships for many in the small, isolated city of Caribou.

A question for the city's leadership when interviewed was about the city's population. The city's website stresses repeatedly that Caribou is "economically, culturally, and socially inviting," and that it is a community that "welcomes, supports, and responds to a diversity of new people and new ideas."

However, the data tells a different story. The 2010 census reports indicate that the population was, at that time, more than 96 percent white. Given these statistics, one point of discussion was about how Caribou plans to be "a community that celebrates the values and lessons of a multi-cultural heritage that serves as its strength and as its foundation in a progressive, modern world."

Significant transportation connections would seem to provide Caribou with potential assets for a new wave of economic growth. These include numerous state and interstate highways, including Routes 1 and 95, as well a municipal airport. Local attractions emphasize snow activities such as skiing, snowboarding, ice skating, and more.

Yet, according to the city's website, one in seven of its residents is below the poverty level (13.9 percent between 2007 and 2011). What are the plans to attract or create enough employment opportunities of the type that can help elevate the living standards of its residents? Numerous federal and state programs are in place to help attract and incentivize employers to locate in the area or to specific zones in the region in which special tax benefits apply. What are the recent successes in bringing businesses to those zones and to develop the city's economy further?

Photo courtesy of Paul Cyr.

Interview with Austin Bleess, City Manager of Caribou, Maine

Caribou, Maine, has a history that extends back in time more than 150 years. Founded in 1859 to support a sawmill and lumber yard, the city later developed a strong economic component around agriculture, primarily potato growing. Today, Aroostook County, in which Caribou resides, ranks first in output in the United States for potato farming.

Much of the economy had been driven for some time by the presence of Loring Air Force Base in the community. With twelve thousand people on base, the local economy sprouted support industries for the base and its families. However, following the dissolution of the Soviet Union and a variety of other geopolitical decisions and events, the base was closed in 1994. "The community lost twenty thousand people and ten thousand jobs overnight," said Bleess. "Caribou has been trying to recover ever since."

There have been successes over the years. One company grew out of a garage and into a building that the city provided as an incentive. They grew to three hundred employees before being sold to another company and relocated to Georgia. The building that housed the company is now being marketed by the city to start-ups as incubator space. Then, the Great Recession occurred and, according to city Manager Bleess, "really hit the county very hard." At the same time, publicly sponsored revenue-sharing programs began to decline in the level of contributions to cities like Caribou. All of these impacts came on the heels of one another and Caribou has been trying to recover from the losses since that time.

In order to continue public services without the loss of critical programs, Caribou had to increase the tax rate. This coupled with the fact that "Maine is a hard state in which to do business" has resulted in additional decline in the area's economy. In the southern part of the state of Maine, businesses can escape the state's onerous permitting and other processes required to start a business simply by jumping over the state line into Vermont. In Caribou, that is not an option. In this sense, its isolation can be regarded as serving a competitive advantage. On the other hand, southern Maine resides on a different power grid than the northern part of the state. Thus, businesses and residents in Caribou pay higher rates for their power than in southern Maine, thereby creating a competitive disadvantage.

But Mainers, according to Bleess, are a tough lot. "People here believe we can work through tough times and recover." Agriculture again became the dominant component in the region's economic base. Today, 40 to 50 percent of the sixty-seven square miles of the city of Caribou is used to raise either potatoes or broccoli.

Caribou does have a regional airport that permits easy access to Boston and New York, but for those who prefer to drive, times are seven to eight hours to Boston and even longer to New York. Most things produced in Caribou must be trucked out because the rail lines are not in good repair and are not efficient to use. Trucking, however, adds additional costs for items that are manufactured in Caribou. This is especially true for larger or heavier items.

Canada is more proximate and does benefit the economy of Caribou because there are four points of entry into the United States from Canada into Maine, and all of those roads converge in Caribou. This provides significant numbers of customers for retailers in the area. Many Canadians even come into Caribou to purchase groceries and clothing items that are cheaper than can be found over the border.

Looking forward to new economic growth, the city's planners have identified agriculture and manufacturing as key targets. The city has developed what may be a thoroughly unique approach to business attraction. This entails engaging a business broker under contract to the city to buy and move businesses from elsewhere into Caribou. Local residents would buy the companies and would be supported by a loan from the city. The loans will ultimately be repaid and the city will receive additional tax revenues.

To provide public services to the citizens of Caribou, the productive use of real property must expand. Between 50 and 60 percent of the city's tax base is derived from real estate taxes. By expanding the commercial side of that tax base, residential rates can be kept as low as possible. Thus, economic development program efforts are directed at filling the existing buildings so there will be a demand for the new buildings that will contribute marginal increases to the city's tax base.

The economic growth of Caribou also benefits from the colleges and universities that are nearby. Within a fifteen-mile radius of the city, there are two universities and a community college. If the circle is expanded to forty-five miles, another two are included. These assets have been useful in support of local planning, the conducting of studies to assess the economic viability of certain industries for the city and the region, and by helping develop business plans.

The community college has developed training programs that are responsive to the specific needs of the area's employers. To date, this has included customized training in such areas as sheet metal fabrication and machining. Bleess notes that community colleges are gaining importance for local economic development and are becoming increasingly popular as a result. "They're quick and responsive, and their training relates directly to the jobs that are available in the community today."

In terms of the regional collaboration that has been characterized by other communities in this study, Bleess says that it has just begun in his region. His previous experience was in the state of Minnesota, where such collaboration is *de rigueur* for small, isolated cities and towns. "I think Maine is a little behind the curve on this. But, Caribou and Presque Isle have begun discussions" about sharing the costs of

Issues for economic growth	• Loss of military base caused loss of residents, revenues, and tax base all at once
	• Revenue sharing has declined
	• State policies chase companies to other states
	• Cost of power
	• Rail lines in disrepair
	• Remoteness of city's location
Strategies for economic growth	• Market retail across the border into Canada
	• Fill existing buildings to create demand for new construction
Lessons learned	• Business growth helps to pay for public services

police and fire dispatching and various areas of public works in search of budgetary efficiencies. "Some things may work and some things may not. We are very rural, so being remote is a challenge for us."

Titusville, Pennsylvania

The city of Titusville, Pennsylvania, owes its establishment to the oil that is in its soil. Today, due to the efforts of the local redevelopment authority, Titusville markets a two-hundred-plus-acre industrial park for business attraction that includes about 670,000 square feet of existing industrial space. All environmental questions were remediated under the guidance of the Pennsylvania Department of Environmental Protection, rendering the site immediately available for occupancy by prospective business clients. The website reports that, today, more than two hundred jobs have been created by twenty-five businesses located in the park while more are still considering locating there.

Population declines over the past fifteen years have been considerable, implying the loss of jobs, perhaps all within the context of one or a few incidents. If that is indeed the case, the lower-than-national-average rate of unemployment in Titusville is more likely to be reflective of the diminished population base than the replacement of the jobs that were lost. This was one topic of conversation for the city manager.

Photo courtesy of Diana Durstine.

Interview with Larry Manross, City Manager of Titusville, Pennsylvania

In my previous research for this series, *The Economic Viability of Micropolitan America* (New York: CRC Press, 2013), mayors of micropolitan cities across the

United States replied overwhelmingly that they had been born and raised in the city of which they were now mayor.

Larry Manross, the city manager of Titusville, however, was born in the city hospital and was raised within five miles of the city. For twenty-eight years, he owned and operated an automobile parts and service store in the city. When he sold that enterprise, he was selected to serve as city manager. This is not too surprising, given the nature of the city's finances and budgetary issues being faced at the time. There was an evident realization that the new leadership needed to have the kind of business acumen that could be applied to the municipality as well as a thriving business. This proved to be a wise choice as the city entered the ensuing budget season with a projected shortfall of $150,000 on a total municipal budget of slightly more than $3 million. However, various changes enabled the city to end the year in the black.

City Manager Manross recites the city's history easily, from the discovery of oil in the area in 1859 to the growth of mill jobs to the loss of it all. At one time, the steel mill in Titusville employed between twelve hundred and thirteen hundred people. The loss of those jobs not only meant people who were unemployed, but also spelled the loss of significant revenues for the city budget from which public services are provided. It also meant that there would be many buildings that would be out of use and simply sitting empty in place.

The city responded by acquiring twenty-six buildings that were renovated and re-leased. Today, they house numerous new businesses and several hundred jobs. Manross learned in that process that small town businesses need primarily to be in the business of producing and selling consumable products. "Significant demand beyond consumables simply doesn't exist."

One of the actions taken to reduce the financial problems was to cease the city's practice of borrowing, on average, about $1 million each year until the tax revenues were received to repay those loans. By borrowing only what was absolutely needed and developing better timing for city expenditures and the revenue stream, Titusville was able to reduce the amount it has to borrow annually to only about $300,000. "The difference in the interest payments alone helped to balance our budget."

Another example of changes in past practice that realized immediate positive results relates to the use of the city's grants under the Community Development Block Grant (CDBG) program. In the past, such funds were used for expenditures related to the sewer system despite the fact that the sewer fund was able to do so. Once those funds were used, the CDBG monies were available to purchase a new fire truck.

City Manager Manross notes that the shale industry is a primary economic development attraction target for Titusville. Given the city's history, the people are knowledgeable about, and interested in, attracting the drilling to their area. To promote the outreach, the city's redevelopment agency used grant funding to refurbish a four-story building for use by the shale industry. The city has suffered significant job losses in recent years (the mill closed down completely in 1991) and is hoping to create an industry base that will bring the sons and daughters of Titusville back home. "It's beginning," says Manross, "some things are beginning to come back into the downtown now and people no longer worry about the city just closing down. Seeing is believing!"

City Manager Manross answered a question about how the state of Pennsylvania, with its reputation for being less than business-friendly, affects the city's ability to attract and retain businesses. He said that the new governor of Pennsylvania seems to have a better grip on those issues than others have. "We cannot overtax the shale drilling industry. We want them to come and we have to cultivate them. They are the future of the state of Pennsylvania."

Another way in which the state has affected its cities relates to the pension plans to which municipalities must contribute on behalf of their employees. At present, the city must pay an annual contribution to the state's pension fund of $500,000 from a total general fund expenditure of just over $3 million. The sense is that the state needs to look for ways to help grow the economy.

Issues for economic growth	• City is still recovering from massive job losses that occurred all at once
Strategies for economic growth	• Support growth of shale industry
Lessons learned	• Small town businesses need to make consumable products because they bring revenues in

Southeast

Arab, Alabama

Little information is available online about Arab, Alabama. What is known about the city's population growth is interesting; the population grew between 1990 and 2000 by more than 13 percent and again through 2005 by another 4.5 percent. Still, the unemployment rate remained lower than the national average at the time of this writing. This implies not only growth but also an economic base able to support the new residents and their requirements.

Photo courtesy of Kim Johnson.

Interview with the Honorable Bob Joslin, Mayor of Arab, Alabama

Mayor Joslin is fluent in the language of the businesses in his community. Arab, unlike many of the cities in this research, has a thriving and highly diverse economic base. This is due, to a large extent, to the relative proximity to both the Redstone Arsenal and the aerospace companies located in and around Huntsville. Both cities are relatively close and have helped to foster the growth of a diverse manufacturing base in Arab. This complements the cotton-growing component of the local economy.

Current employers include a medical tools manufacturer that produces items ranging from heart catheterization equipment to contact lenses to various tools used in hip and knee replacement surgeries to the micro-cameras employed in neurosurgery. Other manufacturers in Arab produce automobile brake apparatus, coatings for drugs, and hydraulic cylinders for large vehicles. This is a level of diversity in the business base that other communities envy.

Because of the relative proximity to the Redstone Arsenal and the NASA–Huntsville facility, engineering and other technical skills—at all levels—are abundant in and around Arab. And, while those skill sets are in demand and could help the city grow more quickly, and although Mayor Joslin would like to see Arab grow further, he wants to be sure that the city can maintain its "small town atmosphere." Arab is fortunate to have the choice to grow further or not, whereas other cities and towns in this study may not have the option to curtail growth in order to retain their communities' small town feel.

As well, to grow the city of Arab further, there are some challenges that must first be overcome. The city needs a few high-end restaurants to keep residents spending their money in town rather than traveling to Huntsville for a nice meal. But Mayor Joslin worries that there may not be sufficient demand to make upscale restaurant owners consider a location in Arab. An additional challenge to further growth is that while there is rail in the region, it is ten miles from Arab, and that presents a difficult challenge for businesses that rely on shipping their products to markets or middlemen outside of the region.

The city's budget is dependent upon sales tax revenues, so the economic development targets naturally include those that will generate sales. The city does have an ad valorem tax, but it is intentionally kept low in order to attract more businesses to the community; in fact, it is the lowest in the state of Alabama. It also means that a very important strategy for Mayor Joslin is to encourage residents to do their shopping in Arab rather than in Huntsville, where so many local residents commute to work each day.

The city provides public services on the strength of a 9 percent sales tax; however, of those 9 percentile points, 4 go to the state of Alabama, 1.5 go to the schools, and 1 goes to support and maintain the city's infrastructure. This leaves just the remaining 2.5 of the 9 percent for the provision of city services.

New sales taxes are therefore critical to the city's growth. To offset some of the pressures on the city's general fund, Mayor Joslin is working with the mayors of the other three cities in the region to plan for the sharing of the costs of common public services, including, potentially, the handling of hazardous materials, the maintenance of jails, and more. His feeling is that the state legislature is more forthcoming with financial support for regional efforts that seek to reduce redundant local costs.

For economic development purposes, Mayor Joslin feels that job creation can be more easily accomplished in small towns by growing new, small businesses rather than attempting to attract large existing employers from elsewhere. Another strategy the mayor is pursuing relates to working with the local public schools and community colleges to ensure that their course offerings reflect the needs of the business community. Mayor Joslin notes that the Arab public schools have been rated the second highest public system in the state of Alabama on an assessment of a wide-ranging series of factors. The school system understands that there are numerous available positions for tradesmen, and that those positions require two-year certificates or on-the-job training rather than a four-year college degree. "The jobs are there and the pay is good. We are going to focus more on providing this part of our workforce as well as the high-end engineering and other workers." Because of the number of employers in the region and the relative proximity to Huntsville, the city has not experienced the brain drain referenced by other leaders in this study. In fact, the opposite problem is greater: there are not enough people to fill all of the jobs of the local employers.

The communication between the mayor and city council is the hallmark of Joslin's administration. "We have to stay in touch with our businesses all the time. We need to know what they want and need. We stay in communication with our residents; we talk things out. We have a great council, great businesses, and great people. We want to grow it while keeping our small town feel and we can do that!"

Issues for economic growth	• Shortage of nice restaurants
	• Rail is ten miles away
Strategies for economic growth	• Grow businesses locally
	• Pursue regionalism
	• Increase workforce training programs
	• Business retention
	• Develop a "shop locally" program
Lessons learned	• Grow your own small businesses as well as attracting new ones
	• Communications are vital
	• Collaborate with businesses constantly

Hamilton, Alabama

Hamilton is located in the northwestern corner of the state of Alabama, in an area originally settled by the Chickasaw Indian tribe. Later history saw the area grow as it served as a tollgate town for the turnpike that passed by the region.

Today, the city boasts two industrial parks, a branch of the North Mississippi Medical Center, and the Bevil State Community College. It is unclear how those assets contribute to the economic development of this small, isolated city. Those were topics of discussion with the city's leadership.

The city's population base has been inconsistent over the past generation, first growing by more than 17 percent between 1990 and 2000, but then declining by more than 4 percent over the ensuing five-year period. The causes of these changes will also be discussed. The present unemployment rate is high relative to the national average (at the time of this writing) of 8.6 percent. The rate in Hamilton at the same time approaches 10 percent.

Photo courtesy of Harold Parker.

Interview with the Honorable Wade Williams, Mayor of Hamilton, Alabama

Hamilton, Alabama, was once home to a thriving ball bearing manufacturing plant as well as three mobile home manufacturers. Today, the ball bearing company's workforce has declined from about six hundred to around two hundred, and there is only one of the three mobile home producers left in Hamilton.

How does a small town continue after such job loss? Mayor Williams noted, "We are keeping our heads above water. People's attitudes stayed pretty positive overall, but it has been a constant struggle because we have to compete for business locations with larger cities that can offer more … more college-educated workers … more existing buildings. The competition is really very tough."

Mayor Williams noted that small towns have to take maximum advantage of any competitive advantages they may have. And, they usually have to offer companies incentives to come to Hamilton rather than going to places that are closer to larger urban areas and have more to offer. One means by which Hamilton can incentivize businesses to come to town is through an abatement of the city's sales tax. The total sales tax is 9 percent, 3 percentile points of which come to the city's coffers. The city can agree to an abatement of some or all of those tax payments for a new company to come to town for a period of up to seven years. The abatement scales down over time, but it can help an employer cover its costs of relocation or construction. On the other hand, it reduces the revenues to the city's general fund and makes the provision of public services more difficult.

One company that is presently interested in a possible Hamilton location as a result of this incentive capability is a manufacturer of log cabin homes. The other reason Hamilton is appealing to this particular company is that there is already a facility available that suits its needs. The building in question was city owned. Hamilton sold it to the company at a much-below-market rate. In this way, the sales tax abatement was not necessary and the city's revenue stream from businesses was enhanced rather than diminished. In addition to the sales tax revenues, the city's budget is also based on revenue from an "occupation tax," which represents one percent of all the salaries in the city.

Isolation is a considerable problem for the city of Hamilton in terms of growing the economic base. Situated forty-five miles from Tupelo, Mississippi, and one hundred miles from Birmingham, Alabama, it is difficult to attract manufacturers who then need to ship their product. However, the city is well situated in terms of access to a major highway. The city has four exits off of Interstate 22, which runs from Memphis to Birmingham. Targets for economic development focus, in part, on that intersection. They include warehousing and distribution, restaurants, service stations, and truck stops. "A lot of taxes come from that area," said Mayor Williams.

Hamilton is home to two industrial parks that are owned by the city and that are ready for companies to locate and build quickly. The necessary infrastructure is already in place. Both parks have at least two hundred acres and considerable land and buildings still available. Mayor Williams noted that companies won't come if the site will take a lot of time to be prepared. Thus, such preparations represent investments for a city like Hamilton. The return comes when the companies come to town and begin to pay taxes.

Lessons from Mayor Williams include two prominent considerations. First, a professional economic development manager is important. "Mayors in small towns can't do everything. Having a professional economic development person represent us full-time is really important." In this case, three neighboring counties share a person and the relevant costs. The counties include Marion, which is home to the city of Hamilton, as well as neighboring Lamar and Franklin Counties.

Mayor Williams also recommends that "small towns should not be afraid to ask for help. You can't do it all yourself. Borrow money if you have to and view it as an investment. We needed to borrow money to prepare the industrial parks for new companies. We built two spec buildings, too. It took two years to fill them, but now we are getting the revenues from that investment. One loan was for a million dollars."

Finally, there is one challenge that is faced by many small, isolated cities and that affects Hamilton as well: the brain drain. There are no jobs available that keep the brightest kids in town. The brain drain is something Mayor Williams wants to reverse. "We want to bring in the jobs that will keep our kids here in Hamilton."

Issues for economic growth	• Still recovering from massive job losses all at once
	• Unable to compete with larger cities that can offer more
	• Isolation of the city
Strategies for economic growth	• Offer incentives to attract businesses (e.g., the city sales tax)
	• Build infrastructure in the local office park
Lessons learned	• Incentives are a must for small towns
	• Prepare the infrastructure before businesses are attracted

Thomaston, Georgia

Thomaston is in an area of Georgia that was initially established by the Creek Indians. Due to the presence of numerous waterways, the area was at one time filled with mills that used the waterpower to grind flour and cotton gins. Later economic sectors of strength in the region included textiles; however, as much of that business went to lower-cost areas of the world, the city replaced it with manufacturing, including a B.F. Goodrich plant that manufactured tire cord. Much, though not all, of that industry is gone from the area now as well.

Despite the loss of various industries and industry segments from Thomaston, the population over the past generation has remained relatively unchanged. Unemployment is in excess of a relatively high national standard and, at the time of this writing, is at more than 11 percent.

An effort is being made by the city to attract and support the growth of services businesses in the city and has elicited the support of the local Southern Crescent Technical College. The manner in which this occurs was part of the discussion with the city's leadership.

Photo courtesy of King Davis.

Interview with the Honorable Hays Arnold, Mayor, and Patrick Comiskey, City Manager of Thomaston, Georgia

Mayor Hays Arnold is the fourth in his lineage to serve as the mayor of Thomaston, Georgia. This is more than an interesting fact because it suggests the length of time that community leaders and their families often remain in America's small and isolated cities and towns. For them, the future of their city is due to far more than simply their homes and jobs. It is part of their personal histories and, often, those of not only the preceding but the successive generations as well. Many an interviewee in this study attributed their service to the community to the fact that "I live here, my parents lived here, and I want my children to live here." This, of course, means that there must be a continuous means of supporting one's families in these small and isolated cities and towns.

The economic base of Thomaston was generally agrarian through the 1900s. At some unrecorded date, a group of local leaders recognized that cotton was not stable enough as a crop to base the future fortunes of the city and the region. To complement the planting and production of cotton, related companies were developed to provide an economic degree of diversity to the city's business community.

The first such effort was the creation of Thomaston Mills, which became the region's largest employer before several iterations of downsizing of its workforce.

The Mills ultimately went out of business in 2001 as the result of competition from overseas markets that could provide much lower labor costs. Again, this is a comment that was repeated throughout the interviews with small cities and towns.

Following the closure of Thomaston Mills, the city was able to sell off parts of the plant and the remaining machinery to several small businesses. Those enterprises then began to grow and even further diversify the economic base of the city. This was a critically important effort because the city had lost nearly seven thousand employment opportunities—both direct and indirect—over a relatively brief period of time. Sadly, many leaders in other cities in this study have indicated that with such staggering job losses, the citizens simply either left or demonstrated very negative reactions and a sense of discouragement that had the effect of forestalling new economic development attraction and job creation.

That was not the case in Thomaston, however. Mayor Arnold noted, "The community's resilience was amazing!" Part of that resilience was due to a very active chamber of commerce in the city and a very engaged business community generally. But, the mayor noted, "Much of the positive energy came from the people of Thomaston themselves."

Perhaps surprisingly, the people of the city convinced themselves that the newly empty commercial buildings and homes should be viewed not as losses or liabilities, but rather as assets for business attraction. "People can buy homes and businesses can buy buildings here very cheaply now. Those are opportunities."

And fortunately, the approach was effective. Standard Textiles, a company based in Cincinnati, Ohio, that produces high-end sheets and hospital textiles, decided to buy some of the space in the abandoned mill and has been expanding "quite rapidly ever since." When queried about the potential for losing yet another textile manufacturer from the city and from the United States, the mayor expressed that the belief in Thomaston is that their products are sufficiently high end that they will keep the production processes here in the United States rather than moving overseas because the quality and expertise of the workforce in Thomaston exceeds the importance and value of the production costs to the company.

Another example of this type of reuse in Thomaston has been the Yamaha Music manufacturing company, which closed its doors due to competition from China. The large complex has been purchased by the Animal Health Services Company, which has grown over time, although at a much slower than expected rate due to the recent loss of one of the company's more significant contracts.

In addition to regarding vacant commercial space as attractive assets for business attraction, Mayor Arnold also sees an unemployment rate that exceeds 11 percent as an asset for new businesses. "Those are people who are ready to work." Although there may be as much hope in that assessment as there is realistic assessment, there is an inherent enthusiasm and general outlook that is hard not to appreciate.

As has been the case in other cities in this study, the loss of businesses has meant the loss of the middle managers who ran them. They are the most employable elsewhere and they take with them the brightest young students as well. This is a great concern for the leadership of Thomaston, as it is elsewhere in small, isolated cities across the United States. Thomaston has the advantage of not being quite as isolated as some of the other cities in this study. As a consequence, residents can commute to Macon or Atlanta for employment and remain in their home communities, but they would, of course, prefer job options closer to home, which perhaps explains the 11 percent rate of unemployment. Still, those who would work closer to home if they could, plus those who are seeking employment, create an available labor pool that the city expects to serve as a marketing attraction for Thomaston.

The asset gap for the city that most consistently stands as a barrier to further economic growth is the significant distances from Thomaston to major highways. US Highway 19 is a four-lane highway that passes through the city on a north-south route. The great need now is for a transportation corridor that would support east-west freight traffic. Without such an additional arterial the mayor believes that manufacturers will not regard Thomaston in the absolute best light possible as a location.

Thomaston builds its city budget largely on the basis of sales tax revenues. There is a 1 percent add-on to the state sales taxes that accrue to localities in Georgia; however, while most of the supporting infrastructure and needs are in the city, a disproportionate share of the revenues generated by the one-cent tax goes to the surrounding counties instead. This is a refrain heard in many of the cities in this study and points to serious barrier to growth for many small, isolated cities and towns across the country. A local utility generates fee revenues, of which $1 million annually is transferred to the city and enables leadership to minimize the tax burden on the residents of Thomaston to some extent. The mayor stated that the city is, as a result, very interested in attracting retailers, and cites as possibilities Wendy's, a tractor supply store, Electric City, and others who will create both jobs and revenues to support city services through electrical fees and sales taxes.

Mayor Arnold and City Manager Comiskey offer a few lessons for economic growth in small, isolated cities. The first is that small cities of this description cannot afford to put all of their eggs in one basket. Thomaston Mills taught them that lesson, as did the closing of a B.F. Goodrich tire plant that once provided 3000 jobs, and the closing of a Carter's Enterprises (children's clothing) with the loss to the city of 450 jobs. "Textiles were much too important to us. A large printer came to town and that helped to diversify our economy here. We couldn't rely just on textiles. Never let yourself be put into that position," warns the mayor.

As another lesson, the mayor asserts that small towns cannot "always try to hit home runs … an auto plant, for example. Try to hit four singles and see how much better that is."

City Manager Comiskey added that cities need to be prepared for the day that a company is ready to consider one's city. Thomaston built a large reservoir after a recent drought. "We knew that we have to be ready for businesses to come here, and that means that the infrastructure has to be in place." Mayor Arnold added that federal stimulus money has been employed to maintain and add a lot of infrastructure in the city, which meant that rather than working on a few streets each year, the city was able to address the needs of entire neighborhoods.

In sum, "We've got a great story to tell. It's been a struggle. It's not been an easy path in any sense. But, we'll prevail!"

Issues for economic growth	• Still recovering from massive job losses all at once
	• Brain drain
	• Loss of middle management
	• Vacant buildings
	• High unemployment rate
	• Companies locate in county for lower taxes while the city has to pay for the infrastructure and services
Strategies for economic growth	• Present unemployed workforce as an asset
	• Present empty commercial space as an asset
	• Attract retailers
	• Pursue smaller businesses for expansion
Lessons learned	• Diversify the local economy

Kosciusko, Mississippi

Named for the Polish general who supported American efforts in the Revolutionary War, Kosciusko is located along the Natchez Trace, which is a 440-mile path that area natives created from what is today Natchez, Mississippi, to Nashville, Tennessee, thereby connecting three major rivers, the Cumberland, Tennessee, and Mississippi.

While the population of Kosciusko has held relatively constant over the last decade or more, the unemployment rate in the city and surrounding Attala County, of which it is the county seat, is quite high. At the time of this writing, the unemployment rate was over 12 percent at a time when the national average rate was slightly under 9 percent. One discussion had with the city's leadership is why residents have remained in the city and the region despite job availability being so scarce.

Photo courtesy of Mayor Jimmy Cockroft.

Interview with the Honorable Jimmy Cockroft, Mayor of Kosciusko, Mississippi

Jimmy Cockroft has served as mayor of his city far more than the norm in small cities. At the time of this writing, he had been mayor of Kosciusko for seventeen years. And, he believes this is a positive situation. "You just can't get much done in four years. You need time to plan things and see them happen." As a retailer by trade, Mayor Cockroft believes in a customer service orientation for the city as well. "It's part of our quality of life."

Located in the geographic center of the state of Mississippi, Kosciusko proudly offers much of which other cities in this study decry as being absent in their small towns: great schools and a great medical community, including ten family doctors and four nurse practitioners for a community of fewer than seventy-five hundred.

Over time, the city has grown and contracted like the others; however, it has one significant advantage: it is the birthplace of Oprah Winfrey. Mayor Cockroft related how Kosciusko has benefitted from her support of projects in the community, including a Boys Club and a Girls Club. While atypical, it is indicative of the sense of belonging that remains throughout the lives of those who come from small, isolated cities, even those whose careers have taken them to places far beyond their origins.

Local businesses in Kosciusko have come and gone over the years. Superior Coach once manufactured school buses in Kosciusko, but that plant was closed in the late seventies. It was followed by several others, each of which left behind not only employment needs but also serious shortfalls in the tax from which the city provides public services to its residents, businesses, and visitors. As was the case in other cities and towns of varying sizes, the NAFTA Treaty hurt the local economy in Kosciusko as different types of jobs departed for markets with substantially lower labor rates.

The resolution of some of those needs has come in the form of new, locally generated small businesses. These have included dairy operations, a plant that makes large air conditioning and heating components, and numerous small manufacturers of various items around the city. These small businesses are likely to be the future of the local economy because Kosciusko has a few assets that are barriers for the larger manufacturing operations. For example, there is no four-lane highway and there are no rail lines that would facilitate the transshipment of product. That means that manufacturers in the areas would have to use a lot of trucks traveling significant distances and making poor time to deliver their products to market. Larger manufacturers have better options in that regard. Mayor Cockroft refers to this type of situation as being "not biz-friendly," which says it all.

Still, the city enjoys a geographic position in the middle of the state, and the mayor believes that enhances his constituents' quality of life because, although Kosciusko is indeed somewhat isolated, its residents can easily reach any of several larger urban areas within an hour or hour and a half. This provides access to additional shopping, recreation, and more.

The city's budget is doing reasonably well, which may explain Mayor Cockroft's pride in describing the quality of the public schools and other public services in the city. The sales tax revenues that accrue to the local budget surpassed $2 million this year for the first time. Sales tax revenues represent about three-fifths of the local general fund from which public services are financed. A percentage of the (state) sales taxes generated returns to the city, thus making sales tax-generating businesses likely targets for economic development attraction programs.

The mayor, however, cites the economic development need for the community most succinctly: "Jobs … we just need jobs." Further, the mayor feels, "We can make that happen. We all have to work together in a small town. The public and the

Issues for economic growth	• No four-lane highway
	• No rail access
	• NAFTA has caused loss of employers
Strategies for economic growth	• Work to grow local businesses
Lessons learned	• Collaborate with the business community regularly

private [sectors] ... we're all partners. We all know one another. Small town residents want people to be in leadership positions to whom they can relate. We see each other in church, at the store, on the golf course. We have to be partners in this."

Brevard, North Carolina

Brevard, North Carolina, has seen some significant shifts in its population base over the past two decades. From 1990 to 2000, the city grew by a substantial 26 percent. However, over the ensuing five years, the base saw a decline of more than 2 percent. The causes of such a turnaround were a subject for the interview with the city's leadership.

The city is home to several assets that would seem to be drivers for economic growth. Local leadership discussed the extent to which the city and its business community take advantage of the Brevard College and the Blue Ridge Community College to stimulate and support growth. Additionally, they reviewed how the city has used its proximity to the entrance of the Pisgah National Forest to generate jobs in services industries.

Photo courtesy of Transylvania County Tourism, visitwaterfalls.com.

Interview with Joe Moore, City Manager of Brevard, North Carolina

According to the city manager of Brevard, North Carolina, Joe Moore, the city "understands what we are good at." It is why the economic base of Brevard is stable and vital. That base is also fairly diverse and includes timbering, agricultural businesses, tanning operations, paper production, and tourism.

The noteworthy connection between all of these industries lies in an expression used repeatedly during the interview by City Manager Moore: "woods and water." The city is surrounded by a national forest, a state forest, and numerous parks, as well as the French Broad River, so named as it represented the demarcation between English and French land holdings prior to and during the Revolutionary period. This is what Moore meant by "understanding what we are good at." The woods and the water resources are at the core of all economic activity in the city. The businesses that work within this notion of woods and water are small, and they range from timbering to herb production. City Manager Moore hastens to note that the largest employer in the city that is not related to woods and water is a polymer production plant for threading machines. Interestingly, even its location in Brevard relates to the woods and water theme: the CEO wanted to live near the woods and water, and found the lifestyle of Brevard and the region to his liking.

City Manage Moore sees the purpose of the city's leadership most clearly; he asserts that his mission is the provision of a friendly, small town environment. "We're a walkable community with community centers where people can gather and meet." When asked about whether there was an economic development strategic plan for the city of Brevard, Moore stated, "We aren't really that overt about our outreach. It's really more of a theme that we present: woods and water. People come here because of our natural gifts." He offers as evidence the Oskar Blues Brewery, a Colorado business that sought an East Coast location. They selected Brevard because the executive making the selection decision is a cycling enthusiast who found the allure of the woods and water in the area appealing.

Still, while companies and executives rate the local quality of life in communities a critical factor in their site location decision-making processes, they must be pursued in today's very competitive practice of economic development. Many communities have a desirable quality of life. For Brevard, this means that companies are targeted that will provide both jobs and tax base support for the city.

Because the tax base is driven in large measure by real property tax revenues, the city is interested in companies coming to town that will use land and generate the tax base necessary to provide public services to residents while not burdening them with the full costs of those services. Additionally, more targeted programs for the retention of the city's existing business base is presently in planning as well.

When asked how being small and isolated has affected the city and its economy, City Manager Moore responded that being small and isolated isn't necessarily a bad thing. "We are part of a larger region and a much larger mega-region. Brevard can be either a home base while people work elsewhere or a base camp from which to enjoy the wood and the water." He also noted, however, that for that approach to be fully realized and to be successful, the city has one outstanding need: a greatly enhanced broadband capacity. "Today's businesses consider this an absolute requirement."

As a lesson for other, similar cities to emulate, City Manager Moore suggests that communities "know who you are. Individuals come and go and families change, but the natural setting—the resources—stay the same." Related to that lesson is that communities cannot try to be what they are not. Cities have to "compete on their strengths, which forces you to understand what you do well and to build on that."

As a final thought, Moore noted that small towns in general are "great laboratories for this nation. They are places for us to regain what we all have lost. Here, people work together to move the community forward."

Issues for economic growth	• Inadequate broadband capacity
Strategies for economic growth	• Build on the area's natural assets
	• Increase broadband capacity
	• Business retention
Lessons learned	• Use the natural resources that are nearby
	• Business retention needs to be managed well and regularly

Roxboro, North Carolina

Roxboro, North Carolina, has experienced slow but steady growth in the population base over the past decade. At the same time, the city has managed to keep its rate of unemployment about 25 percent below the national average. Large employers appear to be in the energy sector and include Duke Power and Capital Power.

This is complemented by Certainteed Gypsum, the Eaton Corporation, Georgia Pacific, and a variety of other companies in substantially diversified industries. This variation in the economic base of the city and the region implies stability in the local economy. This was a primary topic of conversation with the city's leadership, as it represents a key concern for other cities of like size and relative geographic isolation.

Roxboro, which is located midway across the northern border of the state of North Carolina, is closer to much of Virginia than it is the rest of its home state. Its most significant geographic asset is the relatively short distance (approximately thirty miles) to the Durham–Chapel Hill conurbation and the universities of that region. It was interesting to explore in the interview the extent to which those institutions of higher learning are engaged in the economic development of the city of Roxboro.

Photo courtesy of Abby Gentry.

Interview with Stephen Steese, City Manager of Roxboro, North Carolina

Roxboro's city manager describes his city as "a typical small city as far as this research goes. It is just far enough away from other cities to be a stand-alone community." The economy has experienced decline and growth and has learned lessons throughout both experiences.

The Collins and Aikman Corporation had at one time as many as four plants in the area. It manufactured automobile interiors but elected to leave that business line and closed its Roxboro and Person County plants. This caused the loss of 1240 jobs all at once and left the area's economy decimated. Steese said that residents did not leave town as a result but did have to commute significant distances to find new work. It is approximately forty-five minutes by car to Research Triangle Park.

City Manager Steese noted that the company employed about half of the city's workforce and used a significant share of the city's water, from which the city derives revenues for the budgeted services it provides to its residents. Media proclaimed that the loss of revenues from this one company alone could result in the need to increase the tax rate in the future.

Steese noted that the city learned a lesson in that large companies are not only hard to attract but also hard to lose. He is interested in either attracting or growing smaller, sustainable operations that "will hire fifty, one hundred, or a couple hundred people." Much of this has been coming through corporate expansions rather than the attraction of new businesses to Roxboro. Following the 2008–2009 economic slowdown, the economy came back and employers began to hire additional people. Some of these expansions came from within the automotive sector and have included Eaton, which manufactures various parts and expanded just three years ago; GKN Drive Trains, which expanded two years ago; and Spun Tech, an Israeli company that produces nonwoven sheets and has added seventy new jobs to the existing base of about one hundred. As well, Merck is manufacturing from a local business park. Indeed, of the recent job growth, there is only one source new to the area, a company that produces candles and which came to Roxboro recently and is already expanding.

Given the recovery of the community from the large job losses, the question of employer attraction outreach was raised. Steese stated that earlier efforts were less vigorous than the current programs. Prior to two years earlier, the entire effort was conducted by volunteers. In partnership with Person County officials, Roxboro's leadership concluded that the effort needed to be more regional in scope and professional and consistent in nature. This collaborative effort is sensible for Person County, whose only city is Roxboro.

Two full-time positions have been created, one of which will work on traditional economic development business attraction and the other on the issues of growing commerce in the downtown area of Roxboro. To support the effort, several systems and databases are being established to help companies when they become interested in Roxboro. These include building inventories, GIS capabilities, utility rates, and more. The state of North Carolina's economic development program, which is now in the process of evolving from a purely public agency to a public–private partnership, also supports the new efforts.

Targets for the two new positions will be somewhat different. The traditional economic development outreach will focus on plants that use land and generate the property taxes that today constitute about 49 percent of the city's budget, while the downtown focus will work to increase travel into the city and its retailers because sales tax represents an additional 14 percent of the city's budget.

In order to further accelerate the growth of Roxboro's economy, and that of Person County, Steese would like to have greater access to major highways. The first phase of widening Highway 501 into Virginia is under way, but phases II and III have not yet been funded. When completed, Roxboro will be able to boast of a four-lane uninterrupted highway through the city and reaching from Durham to Richmond. This is a critical need, as the city is at least thirty miles from an interstate highway.

Steese offered two lessons to the leadership of cities of similar size and settings. First, "you must have buy-in from partners. A full team working toward common goals is very important because growth like this requires a lot of different skills sets. The city and county working together, along with other institutions in the community, is critical here." Steese also offered that "we need to be prepared for the requests from prospects when they do come in. We now have the data ready and can answer questions about timing, infrastructure, utilities, and more. We can give businesses a fast turnaround."

Roxboro has not yet recovered all the jobs lost, but its city manager believes that "we are getting there. We're really trying hard. We've acquired a large site for future growth, including large employment-based operations. We're going to do very well in Roxboro."

Issues for economic growth	• Greater access needed to highways and interstate
Strategies for economic growth	• Grow businesses locally
	• Attract small businesses
	• Professionalize the economic development program
Lessons learned	• Pursue smaller companies that will cause less dislocation if they leave than a larger business
	• Professionalize the economic development program
	• Regional approaches to economic development are essential
	• Teamwork is important for economic development and must include all elements of the community

Covington, Tennessee

Covington, Tennessee, has experienced slow but steady population growth over the past fifteen years. However, at the time of this writing, the city's unemployment rate exceeds the national average and stands at 9.3 percent. One area of inquiry for the interview with the city's leadership was the extent to which these two facts are related. In other words, has the unemployment rate been inflated by the influx of new residents, or are there other reasons, such as job losses, that have driven up the unemployment rate?

The city seems to have a substantial number of assets for further economic growth. It is situated forty miles from Memphis, the city's website boasts the presence of three industrial parks, and Covington is the county seat of Tipton County. This latter fact means that there is county-based employment in the city to complement the local government and private sector jobs. Its proximity to the Mississippi River may also generate some economic development opportunities, and that too was addressed with the city's leadership.

Transportation access also appears to be an asset for further growth in Covington. The Memphis and Paducah Railroad began operations in the late 1800s, and US Highway 51 runs through Covington en route to Memphis and other locations.

Photo courtesy of Harvey Wilson.

Interview with the Honorable David Gordon, Mayor of Covington, Tennessee

The county of which Covington is the county seat was at one time much larger than it is today. The area was originally inhabited nearly two hundred years ago; however, as it was bisected by the Mississippi River, the area was ultimately divided into two separate counties. Mayor Gordon explained that much of the residential growth is on the south side of the city, as people have chosen to live in Covington and drive for employment and other pursuits to Memphis, which is about forty-five to sixty minutes away by automobile.

The drive over such distances for employment opportunities has been necessitated by the loss of the many small family farms that were once prevalent in the area, and by the advent of a few large agribusinesses that have replaced them and that require little in the way of direct employment due to the many relatively recent advances in farming technology. Similar trends can be observed over time in the dairy business as well. In the late sixties and early seventies, Covington was home to more than twenty dairies; today, there are none. The same tale can be told of the local hog production industry, now entirely gone from the economic scene in and around Covington.

Still, the local economy remained relatively stable for a while. The most critical blow to the local economy came when a manufacturing plant that produced television sets and stereos, and employed twenty-five hundred people in town, shut down. Those jobs all went to Asian communities, which were able to offer the businesses significantly lower labor costs. As the production processes involved were highly labor-intensive, there was little debate as to the outcome of the site location decisions. Mayor Gordon noted, "We learned a good lesson then: don't put all your eggs in one basket!"

The city planners responded by seeking employers to come to Covington at the same time they began efforts to grow new small businesses in the community and supporting their growth over the initial start-up phase. While this has proven to be a reasonably successful strategy, business attraction has also contributed to local growth. Mayor Gordon believes that both are important growth objectives and that they complement each other.

One business attraction success relates to a Unilever plant that located in the area and now employs more than one thousand people in what is believed to be the world's largest ice cream production plant. Another lesson was learned from this experience: the region's water supply was both abundant and of very high quality, and this represented a very important economic development asset for companies in the food production business. The city now seeks other food manufacturing operations as one of its two primary economic development targets.

The second economic development target for Covington, Tennessee, is automotive parts production. This is in keeping with the proximity of the region to automotive manufacturers in Tennessee and elsewhere in the southeastern United States.

Mayor Gordon also emphasizes the importance of regional approaches to economic development attraction for small cities in rural areas. A neighboring county has a "mega-site" for corporate relocations, and all six communities in the region market the site collectively. This normally is a productive approach for small, isolated cities if—and only if—the city is not overly dependent on the real estate tax base for the local general fund and the provision of public services. Interestingly, Mayor Gordon answered an inquiry by observing that the regional effort for economic development was not a continuation of a trend in regional cooperation. Rather, it was the first substantial effort of this magnitude. And, it was an idea that was conceived and implemented over a single lunch among regional peers! Further, it has since led to other regional considerations, notably in the area of workforce training and development.

Workforce development is an economic development challenge for Covington and its regional partners. The mayor notes that the current workforce is both available and reliable, but it does not yet possess many of the skills sets that today's companies require. The Tennessee College of Technology and a branch of the Dyersburg Community College provide training that is tailored to the specific needs of the employers presently located in town, as well as offer to do so for new businesses as well.

Under the heading of lessons that could be offered to other small, isolated communities, Mayor Gordon posits that a vibrant downtown is an essential requirement because it not only shows off the community, but also illustrates its pride and vitality. A decade ago, Covington spent $3.5 million to renovate the downtown. At the time, there were between fifteen and twenty storefronts that were vacant. Today, there are only two such options available in Covington. By Mayor Gordon's reckoning, the city holds events and festivals on about one-third of the weekends, year-round. This brings people to town and they support local merchants and restaurants.

Festivals and special events are critical to the economic success of the city because the sales tax base constitutes the majority of revenues in the city's general fund. Fortunately, since the recession year of 2008, the city has had only one year in which the sales tax revenues were flat. Every other year has brought growth in the sales tax base. But, even in the area of retail, Mayor Gordon notes that communities need to understand which retailers will be interested in the community and focus on those. Too often, he believes, cities and towns want to go after retailers for which they are "just not right. It's just a dream."

One final lesson from Mayor Gordon: "Don't be afraid to try something different. We built a unique plant—as far as we know, it is the only one like it—to gasify woody waste and sewer sludge. We used to have to pay for it to be hauled away, and now PHG Energy converts it to gas that we use right here in town. And, some of the revenues go to fund our parks master plan." People from all over the world come to see it. And, we're very proud to show it to them."

Issues for economic growth	• Loss of small family farms
	• Loss of agriculture
Strategies for economic growth	• Grow local small businesses
	• Create regional efforts for economic development
	• Revitalize the downtown
	• Create festivals and events
Lessons learned	• Diversify the local economy
	• Regionalism for economic development is an effective approach
	• A vibrant and attractive downtown is important for business attraction

Lexington, Tennessee

The population of Lexington, Tennessee, has been increasing steadily over time, which is somewhat atypical for the cities in this study. From 1990 to 2005, the city grew from just over fifty-eight hundred residents to just under seventy-six hundred, an increase of nearly one-third over a fifteen-year period. This was a point of inquiry for the discussion with the city's leadership. Why has the growth occurred, do they want more, and how are they growing the economic base to accommodate the increases in the residential numbers?

The city's website notes the economic advantages of having a regional airport located nearby, and this served as the basis for another avenue of inquiry with the city's leadership. How is the airport contributing now to the city's economic performance, and how would its further growth—if feasible—enable additional growth?

Finally, the website of the Henderson County Chamber of Commerce lists 10,667 (2008) jobs in the county in which Lexington is located. Manufacturing jobs account for more that twenty-one hundred of those jobs, and retail another twenty-three hundred or so. The broad category of services accounts for about thirty-seven hundred; that needs to be understood in terms of what the actual jobs are and how they can be expanded to support further economic development. More than half of the establishments are classified on that same website as white collar, and that should also be a productive area of inquiry about the future economic base of Lexington and its environs.

Photo courtesy of Greg Bird, City of Lexington building inspector.

Interview with the Honorable David Jowers, Mayor of Lexington, Tennessee

As is the case with several of the mayors included in this study, Jowers, a lifelong resident of Lexington, has just begun his second stint as its mayor. His first tenure as mayor ran from 1987 to 1999, at which point he needed to earn enough money to support himself, and that was not going to happen with the part-time salary as mayor. Now, following various private sector positions, David Jowers is once again the mayor of Lexington, Tennessee.

Unlike many of the small towns included in this study, Lexington established a pay rate for its mayor. The city began to pay its mayor in 1992, though "small towns like this just can't pay much." But, he feels that this is an important decision for small towns to make. "A full-time mayor is critical to success in a small town like Lexington." This is an area that was examined with other mayors in subsequent interviews.

Lexington, Tennessee, had enjoyed economic development successes in the nineties by attracting several manufacturing operations. When the economy declined nationally in the late 1990s, Lexington began to suffer through significant job losses, but it was really in the 2007–2008 time frame that the city and the region began to experience the serious economic decline from which they are still feeling the ill effects today. Lexington's unemployment rate today exceeds 10 percent, while that of the entire state of Tennessee is around 9.5 percent. This is an especially uncomfortable situation for the people and officials of Lexington because there was a time when jobs were plentiful in the city, a time when the city could boast as many as fourteen thousand jobs for around seven thousand residents and neighbors.

Thereafter, however, Johnson Controls and other employers with substantial workforces in the area departed, and the city and region saw the economic picture decline. That, of course, meant that the city also had increasing difficulties in providing public services to its constituents. The state of Tennessee does not collect an income tax. There is, however, a state sales tax of 7 percent to which the local governments in the state are allowed to add as much as 2¾ percent for local services. To this, local governments can add various utility fees as well. Cities also collect property taxes.

The conundrum for Lexington has been that when the jobs left, property values declined, thus yielding less taxes at a time when sales of large-ticket items also declined. This was particularly felt in the area of public safety, which today receives about $2 million of the city's $7 million budget. This is another area to be considered in future revenues: What is the first thing cut in the municipal budget when revenues decline, and what is the first thing increased when the economy grows and the tax base increases again? Is there any constant across the various cities in the study?

Then came what Mayor Jowers referred to as "the knockout punch": federal revenue sharing stopped for small towns. At some point, the federal revenue-sharing program continued for cities larger than fifty thousand residents, while smaller cities and towns like Lexington had to apply for their federal funding through Community Development Block Grants (CDBGs). To a large extent, these are not formulaic allocations but competitive.

Regrettably for cities like Lexington, this did not curtail the practice of unfunded mandates from state and federal agencies. One example Mayor Jowers cited was the federal requirement to build ramps into city sidewalks to accommodate individuals in wheelchairs. While this was seen as a worthwhile endeavor, the federal government provided no funding to Lexington for the projects, and the city could not afford to pay for the construction on its own. This resulted in several letters to the mayor and council from federal officials that were critical of the city's lack of compliance.

Mayor Jowers is a veteran mayor who has the experience base from which to offer some observations that may be instructive to other cities of like size and geography with similar concerns. First, he notes that there is a lot of competition for business attraction. To be successful, local leaders need to learn what the companies are looking for; "You need to be ready for them." For instance, the city realized that if it were to develop land to be used as an industrial park but a prospective employer would have to wait up to two years to get the necessary infrastructure to the site, it could not be successfully marketed. Thus, when the city did develop an area for manufacturing businesses to locate, it was built out to be fully prepared at the outset. This meant that the thirty-acre site has the utility lines in place and the environmental and archaeological studies already prepared and approved. "We're ready to receive businesses at that site," notes the mayor.

With a 10 percent unemployment rate, the workforce is ready to go as well. Further, for the specific types of training an employer requires, the local community college, which has an enrollment of about five hundred students, is prepared to serve as the training arm for companies. A local vocational-technical school can also contribute to preparing the necessary labor force once a company discloses its workforce needs.

There are, of course, some gaps in what the city can offer prospective new employers. Lexington could probably grow faster, advised the mayor, if it had better connections to the interstate highways in the region. Interstate 40 runs nearby, but the roads leading to it from Lexington are in need of widening and maintenance. The mayor notes that the city has been working to obtain a bypass for nearly twenty years.

Tourism is another area that Mayor Jowers believes could be an economic development opportunity for Lexington and the region in which it sits. The city has seven lakes within ten miles of the location of the city hall, and a system that connects many of them was built in the 1960s. A state park in the region presents another opportunity to bring people into the area. The mayor recognizes that those visitors will buy gasoline and help to support the local merchants while they are in town.

To facilitate the attraction of visitors, the nearby regional airport is vitally important. Funded in the late nineties by the federal government (90 percent), the state of Tennessee (5 percent), and the two local governments (5 percent jointly), the airport has six thousand feet of runways.

These lakes and outdoor activities are also attractive assets for business executives considering locations. Mayor Jowers told of one executive who brought a facility to the city because he saw the lake and decided that he wanted to live by it. "You never know what will do it, but first impressions are really important."

Is the mayor bullish about the city's economic future? Despite the current situation and the historic trends and experiences, Mayor Jowers remains enthusiastic. "We're going to get some more jobs here. It's going to happen!"

Issues for economic growth	• Still recovering from massive job losses
	• Declining property values
	• Declining city budget
	• Unfunded state and federal mandates
	• Inadequate connections to interstate highways
Strategies for economic growth	• Prepare infrastructure in the business park prior to interest from businesses
	• Increase tourism marketing
Lessons learned	• Prepare the infrastructure for businesses before they arrive

McKenzie, Tennessee

Another small city in Tennessee has a similar story to tell, although the trajectory to recovery seems to be a little further along. The population of McKenzie has been fairly level for some time at slightly over five thousand, and forecasts indicate little change is expected. The unemployment rate has been running over the national average in recent years, and that served as the focus of discussion with the city's elected and appointed leadership.

The city's website cites the fact that its mayor is serving in her hometown, which is not at all unusual in smaller cities and has previously been cited in this research as an important contributing factor to the ability to accomplish plans in towns of this size. Mayor Holland was asked whether she agrees.

Another area of inquiry addressed the past—and future—ability of the city and its employers to maximize their location—roughly midway between Memphis and the state capital in Nashville. In fact, the city's origins lie in its desirability as a location for a railroad station between the two and that would allow ease of access to the state's primary urban areas.

Both Bethel College and the Tennessee Technology Center are in the city's limits, with other institutions of higher learning also located nearby. Noteworthy is the extent to which future growth plans rely upon these institutions as strategic partners.

The city's website provides a listing of the occupations held by the city's working residents. This indicates an emphasis on the following: education and training, 9.45 percent; health and health technologies, 11.4 percent; production, 11.61 percent; and transportation and moving, 9.01 percent. Nearly 53 percent are classified a working in white-collar positions. This will lead to inquiries about the nature and salary levels of current employment in McKenzie, as well as future employment opportunities for the city and its residents.

Photo courtesy of Gary Chandler.

Interview with the Honorable Jill Holland, Mayor of McKenzie, Tennessee

McKenzie is a city of more than fifty-three hundred residents in a region of about eleven thousand people in the northwestern corner of Tennessee. It is located midway between Nashville and Memphis and is home to Bethel University. Its location along the Mississippi River is part of its charm, but not necessarily a substantial part of its economic growth, according to Mayor Holland. The railroads were at one time in the city's history an economic driver, but the lines were destroyed repeatedly by both sides in the Civil War.

The delta region, in which McKenzie is located, is one of the most poverty-stricken areas of the state. Industry and retail establishments in the city had fared well for many years and were able to provide much of what city residents needed. Thus, revenues stayed in town and the tax base was fairly constant. That ended when a Walmart came to McKenzie. The revenues from sales at the Walmart stayed neither in McKenzie nor in the state of Tennessee. Further, when it came to the city, many of the locally owned and operated stores and other establishments found they could no longer be competitive and went out of business.

When, just before Christmas of 2013, the Walmart also closed, the city also took a big hit—so much so that the mayor froze all but emergency hiring for city positions. This is a concern expressed by many small town leaders. One large loss can have a dramatic impact on everything in the city. Of course, one large gain could be equally impactful for residents as well as the tax base, but the story of a single, impactful—potentially, devastating—loss was more commonplace in these interviews.

As local governments in Tennessee do not have an income tax levy from which to finance public services, they are heavily reliant on sales taxes and property taxes. Both sources were destroyed with the loss of Walmart. Thus, that single loss "started the slide." Another unfortunate result of the closing of the Walmart was that the area's Amish community—about five hundred strong—no longer had the ability to do their shopping because they do not drive and could no longer reach the sales centers. This had an impact on their families, but on their livelihoods as well because they could not reach the remaining places available to buy feed and grain.

McKenzie has good news as well. Mayor Holland cites the growth of Bethel University as the fastest for institutions of higher education in the state of Tennessee and the third fastest in the nation. The university is a full partner in the city's economic development efforts, as well as the redevelopment of some of the older sections of McKenzie.

One of the challenges of the city for economic development that the mayor cited is the quality of the potential labor force. There is an apparent reluctance on the part of some residents of McKenzie to seek employment while unemployment insurance benefits are still available to them as an alternative. There are some who have drug use or criminal activities on their records and are thus less marketable to new or prospective businesses.

The university can help fill positions with employers who are seeking qualified and energetic employees. Students are being trained in technology areas and provided as interns to nearby industry. Even the city uses some of the students as interns in the economic development campaign. Once trained, they help make cold calls to help identify potential business prospects. In the end, they receive academic credit, work experience, and something to put on their resume when seeking full-time employment.

The university, the city, and the business community have also formed a partnership to plan for economic development and to identify the most appropriate targets for McKenzie. Mayor Holland notes that for small cities, every key sector must pitch in. The state also contributes through the provision of industry incentives for training and the expedition of capital equipment acquisition. The university has also become a much greater generator of demand for sales in McKenzie, enabling the growth of a new restaurant and a game store. "Students do spend money," the mayor noted.

In terms of the attraction of new businesses to McKenzie, the mayor advised that it is not an activity that can be conducted from one's office. "You have to get in front of the companies. You have to go to them." In fact, Mayor Holland even joins the teams that travel to make calls—paying out of her own pocket for the expenses—to support the city and its economic development efforts. "We have to be competitive. There are a lot of cities out there like McKenzie, and they all want the same things. We need to distinguish ourselves." Toward that end, the city has created a new downtown master plan that includes walking areas, recreational areas, and restaurants with outdoor dining.

When asked about whether she feels that small cities are making a general resurgence in terms of their attractiveness to people and to families, Mayor Holland agreed. Smaller cities are generally regarded as safer, and many have very good K through 12 educational offerings. She returned to McKenzie—where she was raised—from Tampa and she believes that, as a result, her children received better educations in McKenzie. Further, with the university being in the community, as well as a performing arts facility, there are numerous cultural opportunities to attract visitors, make sales, drive tax benefits to the city's budget, and enhance the community's quality of life for residents, businesses, and visitors alike.

To attract greater levels of visitation and spending, the city, in 2013, held its first-ever Southern Fried Food and Sweet Tea Festival, which was very well attended and served to remind people of the quality of life small towns can offer. "We wanted to bring folks back to McKenzie and reconnect them with others. It really is a wonderful place."

Issues for economic growth	• Poverty
	• Walmart drove out local retailers
	• Walmart revenues do not stay in the areas
	• Walmart closed and left the city short of retail
Strategies for economic growth	• Form a partnership for economic development with the university and the business community
	• Create a downtown master plan with streets, parks, and restaurants
	• Create a festival
Lessons learned	• Collaborate regularly with local businesses, universities, and other institutions in the community

Galax, Virginia

The city of Galax is located in the Virginia range of the Appalachian chain. Much of its renown today finds its origins in the culture of that background. For example, the Old Fiddler's Convention is a major annual attraction for aficionados of bluegrass music. A fifty-seven-mile park that ranges through several counties along the New River also gives Galax a strong tourism asset and helps to support retailers in the community. Hunting, fishing, and other outdoor activities complement the outdoor festivals and help to support the retailers and the hospitality industry in Galax.

The Commonwealth of Virginia and the successive administrations of its governors have, for many years, been diligent in providing support to bolster the economies of small cities and towns across the state. Galax has received significant attention from Richmond to create and sustain growth. This too was an area of discussion with the city manager of this small, isolated city in southwest Virginia.

Photo courtesy of Ray Kohl.

Interview with Keith Barker, City Manager of Galax, Virginia

A basic land venture provided the impetus for the founding of Galax, Virginia, but the city languished for years as a rural outpost and really began to grow only after the Norfolk and Southern Railroad agreed to add a rail spur to the fledgling community. By the mid-1950s, Galax had emerged as an area sizable and prominent enough to seek and receive status as a city from the Commonwealth of Virginia.

For many years, the textile and furniture manufacturing industries were sufficient both to grow and to diversify the local economy of Galax, but by the mid-1960s, those industries had largely gone overseas as a result of the substantially lower labor rates and were no longer adequate for employing the city's and the region's residents. At the time of the demise of these industries in this area, Hanes employed 350 textile workers, and other large employers also had large workforces in and around Galax.

Over a very short period of time, most of these businesses departed for global regions that could offer lower production costs, and a large number of jobs were lost to Galax all at once. It was the fact that everything seemed to happen at once that created the greatest problems for the city. There was simply not enough time to recover from one loss before the next one was announced. City Manager Barker noted that the unemployment rate jumped from 3 to 4 percent one year to 12 percent the next. Webb Furniture Enterprises closed two plants and cut six hundred jobs in the area. Soon thereafter, Bassett Furniture closed two of its plants and reduced its operations in Galax from manufacturing to exporting, and reduced its workforce from one thousand to about thirty overnight. All of this happened in rapid succession. At first, it generated difficulties, but soon the situation was a full-blown disaster.

Like other cities in this research that also went through this kind of rapid economic decline, the population reacted variously. Some people left town, while others remained in Galax and sought different means of earning a living while remaining in place. Some took advantage of locally provided training in entrepreneurial skills to start their own businesses. This program resulted in about 250 new business start-ups over a five-year period.

An incubator facility, aptly named Crossroads, was established at that time to help new businesses share costs and experiences as they began to grow. A sense of camaraderie developed that encouraged all of the tenants of Crossroads to persevere through the challenges faced by all small businesses as they start out.

Still other displaced workers in Galax simply commuted daily to those areas where jobs did exist. City Manager Barker notes many people simply became more mobile. "My finance director drives about thirty miles to work but, out here, it only takes her about thirty minutes to drive from her home to the office." That people stayed in Galax and looked for alternative employment opportunities points to the kind of quality of life that so many other small and isolated cities promote. They offer safe neighborhoods, lower taxes, less expensive costs of living, good schools, and a general sense of community that one might not expect to find in larger urban areas.

Companies are attracted to Galax, according to its city manager, by these same elements of an overall quality of life, but also find it attractive because there is a large workforce that is readily available in the city as well as throughout the larger region. The city then adds to the mix a simple and responsive process of approval for construction plans, permitting, and other development functions that are critical to business attraction and retention.

Barker explains that when the Albany Furniture Company, which is based in Mississippi, located a manufacturing plant in Galax a few years ago, thus creating 175 jobs over time, it indicated that the personal service offered them in getting settled was critical to their decision and their satisfaction. Said Barker, "They have my cell phone number and can call me any time they need something." Several other small cities and towns in this research have also made this point: in a small town, there is time to be responsive and a sense that all parties are partners in progress and economic growth and thus must work together.

As the largest community in this region of Virginia, Galax must be the site of all the various public services that people and families generally require. It is the site of the only hospital for miles around. Similarly, it serves as a hub for shopping, recreation, culture, and a variety of other types of services. If the city's budget was based largely on sales tax revenues, this would be an even greater advantage; however, sales taxes represent only about 14 percent of the total in the general fund of the Galax city budget. Another 16 percent is derived from the real estate tax base, and another 13 percent from a transient occupancy tax. Fees and other sources account for the remainder of revenues. The diversity of sources, Barker believes, helps keep the public services for which the city is responsible fairly constant throughout economic peaks and valleys.

City Manager Barker proudly notes that Galax works very closely with companies new to town to help them get settled. An example was provided of a Sheetz store that located in Galax, bringing six full-time and thirty part-time jobs and a $6 million investment. The city provided the sewer connections to the site at its expense but in turn not only received the initial investment and construction job, but also generated the ongoing tax revenues. Barker believes the return will ultimately exceed the city's expenses. In this way, the initial outlay can be viewed as an investment rather than purely as a cost.

In another example, the city worked closely with Consolidated Glass and Mirrors to acquire a grant from the Virginia Tobacco Commission, which enabled the company to purchase the necessary equipment to manufacture solar mirrors in Galax. This created sixty jobs for people who will then spend their salaries in the local stores, gas stations, and elsewhere. Barker notes that he strongly encourages residents to make their purchases from Galax merchants whenever possible. In this way, people help each other.

In terms of asset gaps that would enable Galax officials to market the community more effectively for economic development, City Manager Barker has at the top of his list greater fiber broadband to the city and the region. Many efforts to do so are under way. One beneficiary to date has been the local hospital, whose patients can now access certain medical tests over the broadband and no longer have to leave Galax and often drive considerable distances to receive such examinations and their analyses. The need for greater broadband capacity in small cities and towns has been a recurring theme in this research. Further, there appears to be a direct relationship between the degree of need for greater broadband capacity and the extent to which the cities are isolated from larger urban areas.

Another item on the city manager's wish list is a natural gas line. Such a line does not presently exist because its ten-mile path to Galax would have to pass through another county. At present, electricity must be used, and those rates are potentially higher at various times than natural gas might be. Lower utility rates are a clear asset when marketing communities to manufacturers for which those costs are very prominent items in their operating budgets.

The final item Barker would like to have in the city's economic development arsenal is to have the local community college—Wytheville Community College—offer more than two-year degrees. "An employer who wants to hire thirty welders right away doesn't necessarily care if the welders they hire have passed history or science classes, especially if he has to wait two years for them to be available. We are working with the community college now to help develop some opportunities for more certificate courses in the skill areas that are currently in demand."

As a lesson to leaders in other small, isolated cities, Barker offers, "The personal touch is vital. I'm on a first-name basis with all of the plant managers here." Barker added that if one can't find those kinds of relationships and partnerships in small towns, progress will be hampered. This repeats the notion mentioned by other interviewees in this research that there is a sense in these communities that "we are all in this together" that is not as typical in larger cities and towns.

Issues for economic growth	• Still recovering from massive loss of jobs all at once
	• Residents must drive long distances for jobs
	• Inadequate broadband capacity
Strategies for economic growth	• Increase workforce training programs
Lessons learned	• Collaborate with local businesses on a regular basis

South Boston, Virginia

The origins of South Boston, Virginia, can be traced as far back as 1796, when the location was first populated by white settlers. By the pre–Civil War era, the city had grown and commerce had been advanced by the arrival of the Richmond and Danville Railroad, which was intended to connect the tobacco growers of the region to various markets and distribution points to the south and, from that point, northward and even westward.

Today, the economy of South Boston is still dominated by agribusiness, although tobacco farming is less evident and has been replaced by corn, wheat, oats, hay, dairy, and livestock. This has also generated an abundance of farm and animal waste that enabled the construction of a $178 million biomass plant that converts waste into energy for transshipment and sale.

This is complemented in the local economy by small advanced manufacturing specialties as well as several logistics and distribution operations. Still, the unemployment rate among the residents of South Boston is around 9 percent at the time of this writing, and the population, which had grown by more than 21 percent (http://www.usbeacon.com) between 1990 and 2000, then declined by more than 4 percent over the subsequent five-year time frame. This was a point of discussion with the city's leadership. Are there strategies in place to reverse those trends? And, does the city have the capacity to accommodate new residents, as well as new employers, should they achieve success through those strategies?

Photo courtesy of Drew Morris.

Interview with the Honorable Ed Owens, Mayor of South Boston, Virginia

South Boston is a small town located on the Dan River in southern Virginia. Its mayor, Ed Owens, described it as "once the largest tobacco producing and processing markets in the United States." For years, the community considered itself fortunate to host a series of industry sectors. When the tobacco business declined, it was replaced by textile manufacturers. These included such well-known companies as Burlington, West Point/Pepperell, and others. People felt fortunate to have one industry grow as the other was declining.

However, Mayor Owens very astutely pointed out that the industries involved came with weaknesses. "Everyone was employed, but it was in low-paying jobs with little or no educational requirements. We had no … we have … no culture of education. When those industries went offshore, we were left without a well-trained workforce to help attract new employers."

The community learned its lesson. Mayor Owens and other key leaders in the city and the surrounding Halifax County gathered together to "redefine our economy." They knew that greater educational attainment would be at the heart of the future growth for the city and the county. The group created the Southern Virginia Education Center to address the need. Starting in a trailer with about one thousand square feet of space, the program has now grown into more than eighty thousand square feet. The mayor proudly notes, "Today, in this area, you can go from GED to Ph.D., and never leave home." The mayor notes, "We are changing the culture of education here and people are starting to see its value because they are able to get better jobs after the training."

The training is also directly responsive to the demands of local employers. There is now a precision welding center, a Center for Nursing Excellence, and more. The mayor sees this training as the first part of what people will come to know as "lifelong learning." "We are trying to teach 'stackable skills' so they can learn skills now and then add to them later."

Another significant need for future economic growth in and around South Boston has been broadband access. Today, there is about ninety miles in the city as well as the network operating center. Because existing carriers would not allow the city to tap into their existing lines, the city needed to start from scratch and raise about $210 million to support the effort, nearly half of which came from Virginia's Tobacco Commission. "This is state-of-the-art broadband that we have."

There is a strategic plan for the economic growth of the city and county that was developed by the chamber of commerce. Vision 2020 takes the "long-term view with a very fluid approach to growth. We need to be able to change over time as the economy changes. We are still a year or two out because we need to train the workforce first." And, like many small cities and towns, South Boston would like to reverse the process of the brain drain, and bring back some of the kids who have left to find jobs. "We need the jobs and we need to have things for the young people to do that will bring them and their families home." The Tobacco Commission started a program called Back to Your Roots to help in that effort. This program contacts people who have moved away to let them know when there are new employment opportunities available back home in South Boston.

As lessons for other city leaders, the mayor offers that a small core group of individuals must work together as a team. And, we must get the young people involved in this. "You must have as much diversity involved in planning for the future as possible: old and young, black and white, male and female. We all must be a part of it."

Mayor Owens concludes that South Boston would be greatly impacted if one hundred jobs came in a once. "It would be transformative for the community. But, we will also benefit from companies with ten or fifty jobs. We are coming back. We are putting things in place. We must be patient."

Issues for economic growth	• Undereducated workforce
	• No culture of education
	• Brain drain
Strategies for economic growth	• Increase workforce training programs
	• Create a culture of education
	• Increase broadband capacity
Lessons learned	• All parts of the community must work together regularly to attract new businesses
	• Put things in place before businesses arrive

Elkins, West Virginia

Elkins, West Virginia, is blessed with a number of strong assets on which economic development has been, and can be, based and even accelerated. These include an excellent institution of higher education, Davis and Elkins College, the Tygart Valley River, and significant lumber that can be harvested, as well as the rail lines on which to ship it and other products.

From the census year of 1950 to the present time, the population of Elkins has declined steadily, starting at more than nine thousand and reaching a 2010 level of just over seven thousand. Still, the city's transportation infrastructure appears from the outside to be sufficient to support further economic growth and business attraction. This includes access to numerous major highways and an airport with significant additional operational capacity. Questions for the city's leadership addressed how the present economic development plan seeks to employ those assets for further growth in the city and the region.

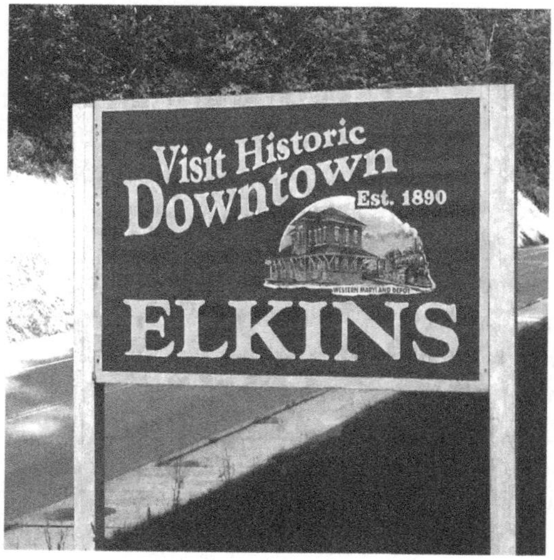

Photo courtesy of Van T. Broughton.

Interview with the Honorable Van Broughton, Mayor of Elkins, West Virginia

Following four terms on the Elkins City Council, and a four-year hiatus from office, Van Broughton became the mayor of Elkins eleven months prior to this interview. Having moved to the city as a child, he has been a resident for nearly fifty years. Among the interviewees in this study, this seems to be fairly typical of the mayors included and fairly atypical of the professional city managers who have been involved. The latter group tends to serve in one community for a number of years and then move on to another assignment.

What is a constant among these professional administrators is that their breadth of previous experiences has been either in lower-level positions in larger urban areas or in similar positions in similarly sized cities elsewhere. For some, their career experiences have been within a state or a larger region, but that is not a constant factor for all in this profession, many of whom have moved from small cities on the East Coast to small cities in the Midwest or Southwest. In short, the constant for them is not the geography as much as it is the size of community to be managed. This seems to imply that the issues and challenges confronting small cities and towns are similar despite the general location.

The city of Elkins, West Virginia, was initially established as the result of the discovery of coal deposits in the larger area. That led to the establishment of a rail yard to accommodate the shipments of coal, which in turn enabled the growth of the timber industry and the development of even more jobs. All of this meant that the area was rather prosperous until other sources of energy began to replace the coal that Elkins could provide. Mayor Broughton indicated that there may now be some possible interest in reopening some of the mines. And, natural gas deposits add to the potential for growth in Elkins. However, to return to production in those mines, there are a number of challenges yet to be overcome.

The population of the city has declined rather dramatically over the past fifteen years and the economic comeback has been slow. One of the city's largest employers is Armstrong Floors, which benefits from the tremendous supplies of high-quality timber that is readily available. Still, the city's economy remains largely dependent upon its proximity to several renowned tourist attractions. "These attractions bring people to town, they buy gas and meals, and they stay in our hotels. Snowshoe is one such resort." Mayor Broughton further notes that winter skiing is now complemented by summer activities such as mountain biking competitions, hiking, and golf. Such activities have helped these attractions to smooth out revenue peaks and troughs. In turn, that has enabled the city to sustain employment levels somewhat on a year-round basis.

More consistent year-round revenue streams also help the city plan its expenditures. To complement that positive trend, Elkins has also developed several events—in fact, "almost a different event every weekend"—that bring people into town over the entire course of the year. This helps support the city's budget as well as the local retailers.

Supporting the local merchants is important to Elkins, which receives some of it general fund revenues from sales taxes. Most of the budgetary resources for city services, however, are drawn from the business and occupation tax—known as the B&O tax, which is charged to all business owners. Mayor Broughton feels that the city has begun to see the reversal of the long trend of job losses. "We had a terrible domino effect here. First, we lost the coal mines, which led to the loss of the railroad yard. When operations in the railroad yard ended, there were fewer people spending money in the shops and no one was buying houses. That hurt the stores and other local employers and the town lost tax revenues."

To help offset those losses and to bring people back to Elkins, the city established a plan that permits new employers to have the first two years of business operations in Elkins free of any payments of the B&O tax. "Many businesses have taken advantage of that and it really helps them."

Another way in which the mayor and the city are working to provide what businesses need is to attempt to arrange better cell phone and Internet service in and around Elkins. This is a common theme among the small city leaders in this study. If one location cannot provide it, the jobs will simply go elsewhere.

Another area of focus the mayor believes will help improve the local economy has been the subject of numerous discussions over a lengthy period of time: increasing the interstate highway to four lanes. Once finished, "that would mean a four-lane road from Elkins all the way through West Virginia and, of course, more visitors and more commerce for our city."

In part as a result of the various actions being taken by the city, Mayor Broughton related that "some of the shops are starting to open up again and some of the For Sale signs are starting to come down." And, people who missed the small town atmosphere are starting to come back to the region. Davis and Elkins College is constructing new buildings and beginning to attract more international students.

The mayor sees all of these things as signs of a new day for the city. Still, his primary lesson is an echo of one offered by his peers in other cities: "I know everyone in town. I know their faces; I know most of their names. I walk through the town every day. They're all my neighbors and friends. And, I'll never forget where I came from. I *was* that stock clerk at Kroger. I *was* that merchant downtown."

Then, at the end of the interview, the mayor became the questioner: "Do you want to know what this town is like? Not long ago, there was a terrible incident here. A home burned and five people died: three of them were children. I was out there at three in the morning and so were a lot of other people. We all felt so bad! In just three weeks, this town raised $110,000 for the funerals. This was through bake sales and car washes and such. That is Elkins. It's a caring, loving community." It is a sentiment that was expressed repeatedly in these interviews. Life in small towns is different because people depend on and are there for one another.

Issues for economic growth	• Population decline
	• Massive loss of jobs
	• Decline in city tax revenues
	• Better cellular coverage needed
	• Need better access to interstate highways
Strategies for economic growth	• Create events and festivals
	• Improve cellular service
	• Create incentives to attract employers
	• Improve access to the interstate highway
Lessons learned	• Collaborate with the business community on a regular basis

South Central

Pocahontas, Arkansas

The city of Pocahontas, Arkansas, is located along the banks of the Black River in the northeastern corner of the Natural State. The region's history has seen several nations claim rights to the area, including, in order, France, Spain, the Confederate States of America, and the United States of America. Additionally, its location has placed it, over time, within the borders of either Arkansas or Missouri.

As the county seat of Randolph County, Pocahontas is the most prominent city in the area. With a population slowly on the rise over the past two decades, Pocahontas now comprises roughly 55 percent of the county's total population base. A point of discussion with the city's leadership had to do with why they believe the city's population is growing despite an unemployment rate that, at just under 10 percent, exceeds the national average by more than 1 percentile point. Another topic was how the city's economy benefits from being the hub of services for the larger region, and how it plans to enhance that position through its economic development strategic plan.

Photo courtesy of Randolph County Chamber of Commerce, Pocahontas, Arkansas.

Interview with the Honorable Frank Bigger, Mayor of Pocahontas, Arkansas

Pocahontas, Arkansas, lies in a favorable geographic location for economic development. To the west of the city lie the Ozark Mountains and to the east lies the delta region, in which the soil is very conducive to a variety of farming pursuits. The area is also attractive for water sports and other outdoor activities.

Pocahontas was initially founded as a trading post in the late 1700s and later was subsumed as part of the Louisiana Purchase in the administration of President Thomas Jefferson. Its location along the banks of the Black River made the city "rural but accessible," according to Mayor Bigger.

The timber industry was the dominant economic activity for many years, but after the forests had been cut down, the land was cleared and planted primarily for cotton. As a result of planting cotton crops, the area needed slaves for the planting and the harvests. Thus, when the Civil War began, Pocahontas joined the southern camp. As a result of the Civil War and the area's choice of sides, the cotton planters not only lost their free workforce, but also saw much of the fields damaged throughout the conflict.

A series of early 1900s recessions further hurt the area's economic base. Finally, following the Second World War, the southeastern region's relatively inexpensive labor began to attract manufacturers from the Rust Belt down to southern states. Arkansas benefitted from that trend until, beginning in the early 1970s, the same manufacturers left Arkansas and went overseas in search of more advantageous labor rates.

The cycles of business growth for Pocahontas have shifted in positive directions more recently, however. Within just the past few years, peanut growers in Texas concluded that their future was no longer in the Lone Star State because the water tables could no longer support the crop. Pocahontas, however, not only has plenty of water, but also the type of soil that is best for the growth of the crops. This is now a thriving business sector for the city.

Additionally, the poultry business has become well established in Pocahontas, as the Pico Corporation opened a plant in the city and, in the process, invested what Mayor Bigger believes to be the largest single capital investment in the history of the state of Arkansas: $160 million. Mayor Bigger was quick to point out one of the great benefits of this line of commerce.

In a statement reflecting a sensitivity that reaches far beyond Pocahontas, Mayor Bigger noted, "I now know how Indiana and other states of the Rust Belt felt when their businesses left and came down here because I have now seen some of our businesses close down and go overseas." He also noted that, whereas the shoe factory closed because overseas labor was less expensive, the chicken slaughtering and packaging plants will not be likely to go outside of the area. As that represents a lot of jobs, this is a positive for Pocahontas and provides a sense of security for the employers, the workforce, and the city, which relies on the tax revenues generated by those operations.

Today, the city is home to twelve hundred to fifteen hundred manufacturing jobs. Those employers are supported by the Black River Technical College, whose fifteen hundred students are trained for the specific needs of the local businesses. And, the resources of the institution are often offered as part of incentive packages for companies considering locations in the region. Partnerships between all elements of the community are critical in Mayor Bigger's view: "In a town like this, you have to lean on each other." This is a consistently echoed sentiment throughout all of the interviews included in this research.

The city faces a common challenge for small towns that have lost their largest or most prominent employers. The loss of the best young minds is not a surprise; the brain drain is well documented and has been cited by numerous leaders in this research as a key concern. However, there is more to consider: after an area's youth have departed, the demographics of a small, isolated town can change substantially. In the case of Pocahontas, the remaining residents are, on average, much older. The mayor notes that today, 25 to 30 percent of the residents are over the age of sixty, meaning that they will need different types of housing and different types of services from the city over time.

In terms of lessons learned that he would pass on to peers in similar situations across the country, Mayor Bigger notes, "The small cities that survive will be those in which there are a variety of jobs and a variety of institutions and a variety of people. They will also be places where people just will not give up, where they keep pushing and pushing to succeed and retain a positive attitude that they can, and then they will."

In 2011 and 2014, the city suffered devastating floods. A great deal of city equipment, as well as personal and business property, was either completely lost or seriously damaged. The city's insurance, provided through the Arkansas Municipal League, covered everything but water damage. Keeping a positive attitude and a drive to rebuild and succeed has sustained the community through these kinds of disasters. Without that kind of determination, Mayor Bigger believes that the Pocahontas of today would be a far different place.

Issues for economic growth	• Jobs have gone overseas
	• Brain drain
	• Aging of the city's population is creating budget pressures
Strategies for economic growth	• Economic diversification
Lessons learned	• Collaborate with the business community on a regular basis
	• Involve the older residents and the youth
	• Diversify the local economy

Colby, Kansas

Established in the late 1880s, Colby, Kansas, calls itself the "Oasis on the Prairie." Around the city is a significant supply of lumber for home building, and that was indeed the original business in town, as the timber was required to build homes for the people arriving on the new Union Pacific and Rock Island Railroad lines. Today, those transportation assets have been complemented by Interstate 70, off of which Colby has one exit.

In recent years, the city's population has declined significantly. Between 2000 and 2005, nearly 8 percent of the people in Colby relocated. With an unemployment rate of less than 4 percent at the time of this writing, there are two possible explanations for this trend. Either the decline in population reduced the job applicant pool and thereby also reduced the unemployment rate, or people have ceased their job search until a later time due to the absence of opportunities, and are thereby registered as underemployed instead. This was a topic of discussion for the interview with the city's leadership.

The notion of underemployment is a difficult one for small towns because it defies accurate measurement. Often, individuals who are unable to find work accept either part-time work or lower-paying jobs or simply stop trying. If they accept lower pay or a part-time job, they are reported as employed and benefits that accrue to the city on formula bases are diminished. If they stop seeking employment, they may not be counted in the workforce at all. That results in a lower-than-realistic unemployment rate.

Photo courtesy of the Colby Visitor Center.

Interview with Tyson McGreer, City Manager, and Christy Preston, Director of Economic Development, Colby, Kansas

In some ways, Colby, Kansas, is a city on the rebound from some rather significant declines in the local economy. The positive news is that there are a number of trends that indicate growth as well as a number of plans in the works that will help to accelerate the pace of change. There are also some substantial barriers to further growth in and around Colby that will need to be overcome in the near future.

One of the positive trends of the past year or two is that the city's budget records reflect near-record levels of sales taxes generated within the city limits. This is important for Colby because the city's general fund is based largely on sales taxes and a mill levy, or real estate tax. However, when asked whether their economic development targets focus primarily on businesses that will generate additional sales tax revenues, thereby bolstering the city's revenue base, the answer was rather emphatic. While that is indeed a consideration for the Colby economic development program, there is also a considerable focus on attracting other jobs. In that sense, the real emphasis is being placed on attracting jobs that will encourage the young people who left to return to their home community in search of more and better employment opportunities.

City Manager McGreer noted that bringing the kids back to Colby is vital for the city's future growth. A large proportion of the city's population has been lost in recent years, and many of the state's smaller communities are forecasted to lose as much as 30 percent of their current population bases over the next several years.

Bringing people back to Colby echoes one of the key issues cited by the leadership in many of the other cities involved in the research for this book. How, then, does Colby propose to accomplish this? One approach is to emphasize entrepreneurialism and to support those who make the effort to start new companies. While there is no local college or university, and the local community college is not yet engaged in the entrepreneurial process, the city is reaching out to it to initiate such a program. Part of the concept involves the notion that individuals can learn to start a business and use the Internet to market it. They can thereby return to their hometown and be productive over the web.

Other strategies include supporting the existing business sectors: agriculture, which has always been a strong element of the local economy; the local hospital, which is the city's largest employer; and the trades that are still in demand, including electricians and plumbers.

When making the pitch to potential employers or business owners, Colby's officials offer a strong school system, a relatively low cost of living, and proximity to the interstate highway. Further, Colby's representatives, like all the small town leaders who were interviewed, noted that in a small town—especially an isolated one—people must, and do, pull together. As an example, the local hospital has been expanded three times in recent years. For the most recent expansion, the community helped provide the necessary funding through fund-raisers and individual donations. In a similar process, the city's water park was built, including a pool and hiking trails, which were also built with community contributions totaling, in this case, more than $100,000 of the $400,000 total expense. The feeling is that these types of amenities will both attract tourism and draw support for local shops, restaurants, and more.

As has also been expressed by much of the leadership in other cities, the downtown retailers compete, to some extent, with a Walmart that is located on the edge of town, near the interstate highway. Because the Walmart is near the highway and attracts much of the pass-through traffic, downtown realtors have to find their own niche in order to survive. Clearly, they will not be successful in attempting to compete with a major chain operation. City Manager McGreer points out that the city needs to keep a positive relationship with Walmart: "If they leave town, they will simply go somewhere else, and then we will lose their business and the convenience of having them in the city. People here think nothing of driving one hundred miles to buy what they need."

With the objective of bringing people back to Colby to live and to provide jobs that have been lost, that success could also cause problems. "If too many people come back to town all at once, we won't have enough places for them to live," said McGreer. "We are working to build places where employers can come to Colby and find shovel-ready areas in which to build, complete with the necessary infrastructure already in place. If we don't have that to offer, they will just go someplace else. As the city manager, that is my primary challenge." The city would like to attract or create businesses with five or ten jobs at a time. "If five hundred jobs come all at once, we would have no place for them all to live."

However, one cannot be incautious. McGreer notes that he has seen other communities that built development parks and then were unable to market them successfully, leading to budget issues and irate citizens. "It's a chicken-and-egg situation. Sometimes, you have to take a risk. By its nature, economic development is a risky business. But you also have to be prudent."

The leaders from Colby, Kansas, offer a few key lessons for other cities of like size and location to consider. The first is that citizens need to understand the city's plans. They must be educated about what is happening and why. It can create a kind of buy-in or, at least, an acceptance. Second, the city cannot do things alone. The citizens need to be involved, as does the business community, and others. In Colby, city-county relations are very strong, and that helps make things happen. This in turn may argue for a stronger program of creating new companies organically rather than an attraction program that could draw larger, existing employers to Colby.

Issues for economic growth	• Brain drain
	• Population losses
	• Local retailers cannot compete with Walmart
	• Housing shortages
Strategies for economic growth	• Encourage entrepreneurialism
	• Encourage businesses to sell off the Internet
	• Increase tourism marketing
	• Prepare shovel-ready sites
Lessons learned	• Prepare the infrastructure before businesses arrive
	• Communicate plans to residents regularly
	• Interact with businesses on a regular basis

Fort Scott, Kansas

With a relatively stable population base since the 1990 census reports, and a lower-than-national average rate of unemployment, Fort Scott, Kansas, is different than many of the cities in this study. The fort, named for General Winfield Scott, was originally established as a US Army post on what was, at the time, the Indian frontier. This region of Kansas also experienced a great deal of turmoil and bloodshed during the Civil War. Those disruptions were ultimately followed by the city's initial growth and the establishment of a base economy, largely agricultural in nature, complemented by various small industrial establishments. Those are still the economic staples of the economy in the city and throughout the region.

Fort Scott is located eight miles from Kansas City and eighty miles from Joplin. Do those distances represent an economic development asset or a barrier to growth? North of the city is a two-hundred-acre industrial park with rail and highway access, which was a topic of discussion for the interview with the city's leadership. Has it worked or not? Why? How? The numerous economic development tax incentives listed on the city's website were also subjects to discuss. What has been effective and what has been the experience with the companies' return on the city's investments? Additional areas of inquiry included the outcomes from the city's two-hundred-acre industrial park and the extent to which Fort Scott Community College is engaged in the city's economic development efforts.

Photo courtesy of Kenny Felt.

Interview with Dave Martin, City Manager of Fort Scott, Kansas

City Manager Dave Martin noted that Fort Scott, Kansas, had as many as twelve to fifteen thousand residents as recently as the eighties. Subsequently, however, several of the city's larger corporations were bought by distant concerns and the local operations were shut down. The result was the loss not only of much employment, but also of many families who had called Fort Scott home for years or even generations.

In 2005, a fire swept through the historic downtown, destroying several of the oldest and finest homes. On the back of the substantial job losses, there grew "a growing malaise in Fort Scott and the town got put on hold. No one knew what to do. Everyone was just in shock." Many small cities and towns are overly dependent on one or a few employers. Their losses can be damaging to the local psyche, but that can often be overcome and people can be impressively resilient. Similar reactions to a devastating event, such as a major fire or flood, can also cause negative reactions generally, but again can often be overcome. To have these events occur back-to-back and in rather quick succession, people can often simply become overwhelmed and unable to respond.

Martin added a note that others in this research have also made: "My family is from here and I love this town. My wife is from here and my four daughters are from Fort Scott. I managed a warehouse for a corporation in the city for many years. About five years ago, the city just took a deep breath and started over." His business experience was of great value in this process: "With thirty years of corporate management and human resources experience, I had learned to manage budgets and make hard decisions. I thought that was a plus for the city so I became the city manager. We first needed to rebuild the trust of the citizens in the city's government. With the help of a lot of good people, we began to turn things around."

In economic development terms, the emphasis on recovery was placed not on attempts to attract large manufacturers or other employers, but rather on retaining the existing businesses in town and working with them, to grow. Programs were put into place to work with city residents to support any new entrepreneurial efforts. We weren't looking for hundreds of jobs. Fifty or sixty jobs from four or five companies can really help in a small town!"

After some time, Blue Cross/Blue Shield built a call center in Fort Scott and added 150 higher-paying jobs to the economy. That really got the ball rolling. The community was then able to focus on its key amenities. A pool that had been closed was purchased by the city and converted into an aquatics center, and the local country club, which had been abandoned by the departing business executives, was also purchased by the city and converted into a municipal golf course. Additional amenities were also constructed to make the city more attractive to potential employers and workers. Bike and hiking trails were opened and a new park was laid out and developed.

At the same time, it was clear that the brain drain had hurt Fort Scott. One of the key concerns of businesses seeking locations relates to the workforce, and Fort Scott's was not adequate as an attraction asset. Programs were begun to bring back the young men and women and families who had left to find employment opportunities elsewhere. The pitch was that they could live and raise their families in Fort Scott while working in Kansas City, about one hour away. The highway access to

Kansas City also serves as an attraction for businesses. Interstate 44 runs right past the city's two-hundred-acre industrial park. Ultimately, it is hoped that they will also want to work in Fort Scott rather than commuting to larger areas.

For families, Fort Scott offers a strong public education system, which engages the community in a variety of partnerships. In one such arrangement, fifteen corporate executives come into the schools regularly to mentor young men and women about career choices. The local community college works with businesses in the area to tailor its courses to the specific needs of local employers, which benefits the companies in town but also makes its graduates more immediately employable in the local economy. Other courses offer the "soft business skills that employers have told us they need more and more"; these include resume writing, timeliness, behavior on the job, and more.

What City Manager Martin finds most important in his role is transparency. "People may not agree with us and what we ultimately decide needs to be done, but they must be able to have input into decisions, and we must ensure that they understand why we are doing these things." But, even more critical is this: "If you aren't passionate about where you are the city manager, you're doing a disservice to the community. I love this town."

Issues for economic growth	• Recovery slow from the loss of many jobs all at once
	• A catastrophic incident
	• Loss of population
	• A community-wide malaise
	• Brain drain
Strategies for economic growth	• Business retention
	• Encourage entrepreneurialism
Lessons learned	• Employers want to locate in an attractive community
	• Communicate plans to residents regularly

Charleston, Missouri

Charleston, Missouri, at the time of this writing, was suffering a rate of unemployment that exceeded the national average: 9.6 versus 8.6 percent. Population in the city has fluctuated over time, although not broadly. Relatively marginal gains and losses may not reflect the state of the local economy. The question of that relationship was a matter of discussion in the interviews with the city's leadership.

Photo courtesy of Richard Goode.

Interview with Richard Goode, City Manager of Charleston, Missouri

Charleston, Missouri, and its surrounding jurisdiction, Mississippi County, are at the top of the "boot heel" of the state. According to City Manager Goode, this is the poorest part of the state of Missouri. The poverty is in part driven by the predominance of agricultural activities in the region. At one time, that sector provided a great deal of job growth, wealth, and revenues for the city's tax base, but farming in the region today tends to be large automated enterprises that require relatively little manpower. This represents a very serious problem for the city of Charleston and Mississippi County. City Manager Goode estimates that 92 percent of the land area in Mississippi County is farmland and is not likely to be sold for development, as it is a very valuable commodity in that part of the state. The result is a fairly limited amount of land that remains for development or other uses.

Accompanying the poverty levels in the city and the county are low levels of educational achievement, a brain drain of those with the more marketable skills sets, and no rail service. City Manager Goode estimates that three-fourths of all the manufacturing prospects they discuss with communities statewide require rail service to the sites. Charleston is "immediately discounted from any further consideration." Small cities with so few assets to market have difficulties in attracting companies to locate. This is especially the case when the city is also isolated from larger urban areas.

The state of Missouri has created additional challenges for Charleston. The state enacted a law that places a ceiling on the tax rates that cities are authorized to apply within their boundaries. The so-called Hancock Amendment "hamstrings communities in terms of how they can increase local tax revenues. In Charleston, we have maxed out on the allowed rate for property taxes. That leaves sales taxes as our largest revenue source, and we simply can't control the sales tax revenues." This is a common problem for jurisdictions whose tax base is overly dependent on sales tax revenues because they are very sensitive to local, state, regional, national, and even global economic forces that are far beyond their influence. As such, when retailers have good times and bad times, the city's tax base can mirror those increases and declines. And, then the city services can be supported or not, depending on the current levels of the sales and sales tax revenues.

The agricultural businesses in the region surrounding Charleston do generate some taxes and some jobs in such businesses as farm equipment sales and repair, but they are very small businesses that do not produce much revenue or many sales. Similarly, there are also a few cluster-related services companies, including crop insurers, but again, there are few jobs associated with their operations and relatively little generated in the sales taxes that benefit the city's budget and enable the provision of public schools, public safety, infrastructure, human services, and more.

To find work, many of the residents of Charleston drive to Cape Girardeau, which is a forty-five-minute drive. Goode notes that, in that part of the country, a forty-five-minute drive is considered burdensome. The result: "We have a fair number of people who won't make that effort and, as a result, are on welfare. The state tries to help us but, simply put, we are a small rural community with no qualified labor force."

Despite the challenges and the poverty, the city is making efforts to turn its problems around. It is hoping to attract a vocational-technical school to Charleston. The idea is both to train local residents and to serve as a magnet for the attraction of new people to the city who will take classes, and then remain in the city as they start businesses and create jobs and incomes for residents in the city and taxes for the general fund. As this plan, if successful, would also provide educational opportunities for the current residents of Charleston, the city too will benefit. Presently, only one in four of the graduates from Charleston High School move on to higher education or further training of any kind.

Following a lengthy interview, during which the challenges of growing the local economic base in Charleston, Missouri, seemed to become increasingly bleak, a pregnant question remained: Can Charleston, Missouri, survive? Most people would hope for an immediate, assertive, and at least somewhat hopeful response.

City Manager Goode was briefly silent and then thoughtfully replied, "That is yet to be determined, but it is in question. We talk a lot about what Charleston should be like in twenty years, but who knows?" He gives the example of Cairo, Illinois, an hour's drive across the border. "In the fifties and sixties, Cairo was a thriving city. Its downtown was booming. Today, it is almost a ghost town. We have that as a close-by example of what can happen when a small town loses jobs and can't bring them back, and it frightens people." Even federal aid can no longer be counted on, intones Goode. "The feds have no more money for things like street repair or sidewalk construction. The money has evaporated."

Given the thoughtfulness of Goode's response to my earlier question, there appeared to be an opening to ask a really tough question: *Should* Charleston, Missouri, survive? "It's a fair question," said Goode. "Companies go out of business. Are communities any different? The mechanics are the same for communities that are no longer viable." To support his stated concerns, Goode notes that the young families and the fresh talent that a community needs are gone. "We have lost the fresh ideas and the energy of the youth."

In the context of lessons learned that might be useful to other small, isolated cities, City Manager Goode said that small businesses need to be the focus of economic development efforts. "It's foolish to look for one big company to be the economic development savior for this town. And, when there is one company in play, all communities compete for it and then it becomes and incentivizes war." For Charleston, the emphasis needs to be placed on what the community can do to support the growth of small businesses from within the community. Additionally, cities have to be good places for people to live and for families to want to locate: "A cornerstone of economic development in small communities needs to be in making the community an attractive place to raise a family. People—and companies—expect that."

Issues for economic growth	• Poverty
	• Loss of jobs in farming due to technological advances
	• Brain drain
	• No rail service
	• State legislature capped property tax rates
	• Loss of federal aid
Strategies for economic growth	• Attract a vocational-technical school
	• Encourage entrepreneurialism
	• Invest in new facilities
	• Improve the quality of life
Lessons learned	• Grow your own small businesses as well as attracting others
	• Employers want an attractive location

Chillicothe, Missouri

At the crossroads of two US interstate highways, 36 and 65, Chillicothe, Missouri, is situated some seventy-five miles from St. Joseph, Missouri. On what was once Shawnee Indian lands, the area initially based its economy primarily on agricultural pursuits but has today diversified it to include a range of business operations.

The city's industrial park, with more than 175 acres of land, now houses employers from a wide range of sectors. These include government facilities, manufacturing functions, warehousing and distribution operations, cold storage, and more. The industrial park has been designated in its entirety as a foreign trade zone (FTZ), which enables either storage or value-added work to be done without incurring duties until shipped out of the zone en route to their ultimate market destinations. In discussions with the city's leadership, the issue of capacity within the existing park for further growth and development was covered, as well as the extent to which the FTZ could be used to create additional growth.

Photo courtesy of the city of Chillicothe, Missouri.

Interview with Ike Holland, City Administrator of Chillicothe, Missouri

Holland notes that the unchanging size of the city's population base over time is unusual in his experience. Small towns like Chillicothe tend to either grow or contract for various reasons. This has not been the case in Chillicothe. He attributes this, in part, to the extent of his city's isolation. The closest larger urban area is Kansas City, which is more than a 1.5-hour drive from the center of Chillicothe.

Another significant gap in the economic development offerings of Chillicothe is that there are no institutions of higher learning within at least a one-hour drive. City Administrator Holland poses my next question without prompting: "What supports the stability of this Missouri community?" The city's economy is focused on its industrial park. In that single location, employers include a plastics manufacturer, the largest glove maker in the United States (there were as many as four of those in the city sixty years ago), a producer of air filters for engines, and one of the country's largest producers of wire rope for cables.

"The city has had its ups and downs, economically," said Holland. "It goes back to the forties when there was a large stenography school in the city. The United States Army used to send all of its stenographers here for training. Of course, that went the way of stenography itself." Over time, industries came and left. "The city has had to continually reinvent itself."

Today, in addition to the employers who are located in the industrial park, two of the largest employers include the local school district and a nearby women's penitentiary that employs about five hundred people and also makes substantial purchases of food and other items in the surrounding community. This is an important footnote. In small as well as large cities, primary employers, through their local spending patterns, spin off additional jobs in the primary and secondary economy. Employees earn money and buy homes and cars and groceries and clothes, all of which support jobs for the construction trades, retailers, educators, and others. Although the exact ratio depends on a range of factors, a general rule of thumb that can be assumed is that for every job in the primary economy, there are another two to three that are thereby supported in the secondary and tertiary economies.

City Administrator Holland further noted that for a city to be attractive to employers—for both attraction and retention purposes—there must be the range and quality of amenities that companies and their employees need and expect. This sometimes requires city leaders to be creative in the means by which they can make things happen.

In Chillicothe, the city owns the local hospital, which needed to be replaced. The city put a referendum on the ballot that the voters rejected. Thus, in order to build the hospital, a varied package, based largely on bond financing, was assembled that supported the $14 million land purchase and the $27 million construction costs for the hospital building and a related medical services building. Much of the arrangement included a strong public–private partnership that produced contributions of about $5 million. "Now, we have a modern facility that will serve the community. It includes the latest technology for teleconferencing and telemedicine so people can get things done here by people in Chillicothe and don't have to go all the way to Kansas City for their appointments." Holland points out another advantage of such a facility: as people age, they will be able to remain in their homes here in Chillicothe because they will be able to access regularly the medical treatments and evaluations they need.

Another example of the city turning a problem into an economic opportunity relates to the renovation of the municipal swimming pool. As a pool for residents, it was losing money, so the city turned it into a water park and recreational facility, with water slides, rock-climbing walls, and more, at a cost of more than $4 million. Today, the park attracts between four hundred and six hundred people daily in the high season and employs as many as thirty young people as lifeguards. Holland's conclusion from this experience is that cities have to invest in new facilities when times are difficult or they won't be the beneficiaries of the turnaround when it does come. "You don't get the option of building something employers need after they get here because they simply won't come."

A final example offered by Holland is the football stadium for the local high school, which was built at the cost of $2 million, none of which came from the city's budget or other public sources. The entire expense was paid from private contributions. City Administrator Holland proudly notes, "I have never before in my career seen people be as generous as they have been in this community."

Chillicothe is also fortunate to be located at the intersection of two major highways. Several retailers and hotels have located at that junction, thereby serving the local residents as well as those passing through the area. Another asset is a cold storage facility, which Holland describes as "the size of five football fields." The facility currently houses a Tyson Foods operation, and the city is interested in attracting other users for this facility.

The city's budget has a large component that is derived from sales tax revenues. However, when asked if, as a result, the attraction targets for economic development are businesses that would be expected to generate additional sales tax revenues for the city, Holland said that was not necessarily the case. "We don't want just any jobs. If we can bring in more industry, that will generate the demand for retail. Retail follows industry."

Issues for economic growth	• No local institutions of higher education
Strategies for economic growth	• Improve the quality of life
	• Invest in new facilities
Lessons learned	• Retailers will follow development and industry

Perryville, Missouri

Perryville, Missouri, is located about fourteen miles from the Mississippi River, immediately across from the state of Illinois. Its location near the river would seem to imply an economic development asset, and this represented a topic of discussion for the mayor of Perryville.

The city is also sufficiently distant from other urban areas—for example, St. Louis is about eighty miles away—that it must be as self-sufficient as possible in terms of providing services and amenities for its residents, employers, and visitors. This too will need to be covered.

Most, though not all, of the leadership in the cities included as case studies in this research indicated that their isolation from larger urban areas did indeed imply the need for greater regional cooperation. The interesting stories are those from the areas in which such collaboration is *not* the case. The mayor indicated into which of those categories Perryville falls and how this has impacted its economic growth and revitalization.

INCORPORATED 1831

THE CITY OF
PERRYVILLE
MISSOURI

Plant your family here.

Courtesy of the Wright Group.

Interview with the Honorable Deborah Gahan, Mayor, Brent Buerke, City Manager, and Scott Sattler, Director of Economic Development, Perryville, Missouri

Mayor Gahan was joined in the discussion by Brent Buerke, the city administrator, and Scott Sattler, the economic development director. The mayor described Perryville as a community in which religious orientations have helped to form the city and even its demographic distribution. On one side of town, the Catholic community is very strong, and on the other side of town, the Lutheran community is predominant. She hastens to point out, however, that there have never been disputes or difficulties that arose from the distinction. To the contrary, she says,

"This is a very family-oriented town. When we redesigned the city's logo recently, we asked a lot of people what they thought was important to represent. The most important component was family and the second was the natural environment." The mayor characterizes Perryville as a town in which families stay and to which the children return.

While that sounds great, it works in practice only if there is an employment base that is attractive enough to make it possible for the children to return and raise their families in the community. But, the unemployment rate is relatively low in Perryville, and the forecasts for job growth at the time of this writing exceed the national averages rather significantly. That would imply that Perryville is indeed primed for further growth. To this point, the history of Perryville's economy has been one of growth, loss, and regrowth. Along the way, the city's leadership has learned some lessons about what to do that may be instructive to others.

For many years a predominantly agricultural-based economy, manufacturing made an entry into the region and helped to stimulate its growth for some time. However, in the late 1980s, a couple of key industry losses hit the area pretty hard. A local chicken factory closed, and shortly after that, two shoe factories also closed their doors. One of the two shoe companies—International Shoe—was a significant employer and its departure cost the area a lot of jobs. That occurrence also had a dampening effect for a time on the general demeanor of the residents toward trying to rebuild the economy. To reverse both the trend and the attitudes of the residents about their collective economic future, action needed to be taken.

The facilities in which these companies were located were purchased by a group of local residents in the form of the city's newly minted Industrial Development Authority (IDA). This enabled local officials to pursue the attraction of new businesses. Mayor Gahan notes that once profits became available, the owners elected not to take them out, but rather to use them to finance the development of an industrial park that further enabled growth in Perryville.

As a result, Perryville is home to a factory for Gilster-Mary Lee, a diverse food services company with four thousand total employees, about sixteen hundred of whom are housed in the Perryville plant. A Toyota parts manufacturer added another fourteen hundred jobs to the region. An electric company and others have not only enhanced the employment base and the tax base, but also brought significant diversity to the economic base of the city.

For the mayor, that experience epitomized the nature of Perryville, and perhaps small, isolated towns in general. "There were no egos involved. The question everyone asked was 'What can we do for us all?'" She acknowledges that the role of mayor is one of constant relationship building for the common good. When asked whether this degree of cooperation is, in part, due to the fact that Perryville is so isolated from larger areas, the mayor concurred. "We are a do-it-yourself community."

In addition to the strength of collaboration, Perryville is not without physical assets for economic development. The bridge across the Mississippi River to Illinois brings people through town in a relatively constant stream and generates a consistent level of customers for the local retailers. An educational center was developed to help local youth prepare for college or jobs. Nearby ports and a regional airport help to round out the asset base that can be offered to businesses that consider locations in Perryville.

Regional collaboration is regarded as a must for Perryville by Mayor Gahan, who notes that this includes not just municipalities but also the school systems, the hospital system, and others in the community. A cooperative relationship in marketing for economic development even exists between Perryville and Chester, Illinois, on the other side of the bridge. The term *region*, for this small town, has a practical meaning that involves interactions that do not always stop at the state line. To what does the mayor attribute this effective though larger level of community? "Maybe it's because we're midwesterners. We take care of our neighbors."

There are also, of course, gaps in the array of assets the city can offer to business prospects. What is needed to promote further economic development includes a rail spur and the ability to offer two-year degrees as well as four-year degrees right in the region. "Community colleges are becoming increasingly important in our area, but we need them to focus entirely on positions for which our employers are hiring." There is also an opportunity to enhance the city's economy by attracting more tourists to the city and the region. One of the unusual attractions in Perryville is an old, now unused seminary where the city used to house a copy of the Gutenburg Bible and a Fabergé egg.

Festivals have added an additional new component to the economic activity of Perryville. The local Optimists Club built baseball diamonds and soccer fields that can be used to attract regional tournaments. Those tournaments will in turn attract people who will shop, eat lunch, and buy gasoline. The eleven fields were built privately by selling the naming rights for them. Coupled with $120 million of investment and 630 new jobs attracted over the past three years, there is much to celebrate in the city. On the whole, Perryville enjoys "an energy not seen in years."

Issues for economic growth	• Still recovering from massive job losses all at once
Strategies for economic growth	• Financed the development of an industrial park
	• Regionalism
	• Create festivals and attract tournaments
Lessons learned	• Regional efforts for economic development can be very effective

Breckenridge, Texas

Like many cities of the Southwest, Breckenridge was founded as a station stop along the railroad lines, in this case, the Wichita Falls and Southern lines. After 1969, however, the lines were no longer used and their impact on the economy of the city and the surrounding area was gone. In recent decades, the city's population has hovered around fifty-six hundred, neither expanding nor contracting appreciably.

In the 1916–1917 time frame, Breckenridge, as well as other cities in the region, experienced dramatic booms due to the discovery of oil. The city's website states that the population of Breckenridge grew twentyfold in just one year, from fifteen hundred residents to more than thirty thousand. This boom precipitated a need for the amenities that the city provided its residents, including paved streets, public schools, a fire department, churches, and a YMCA that was built in 1923 and is still in place at the time of this writing. Without being encouraged by the city, providers of business and personal services also came to town, such as lawyers, doctors, and businessmen.

The cause for the boom is evident in the press, which, as cited on the city's website, noted that in 1920 alone, 175 new wells were dug and every one of them came in. Oil still has a place in the city's economy, although other sectors are able to contribute significantly as well. For example, some limited economic impact today can be drawn from the city's designation as the seat of Stephen's County. The dominant economic opportunity appears to lie in the field of raising cattle. An area of inquiry for the city's leadership was about interest in a more diversified economic base and the sustainability of the city's economy in the absence of such diversity.

Photo courtesy of Andy McCuistion.

Interview with Andy McCuistion, City Manager of Breckenridge, Texas

McCuistion identifies the city's greatest economic development needs as more and higher levels of retail and restaurants to accommodate the population base in and around the city. He also notes that manufacturing would be an attractive addition to the economic base, but realizes that all of the cities around his have similar objectives, although Breckenridge may have a head start on manufacturing generally because it is home to Bold Ideas, a subsidiary of Colt Competition, which makes rifles in a local 135,000-square-foot facility. This enables Breckenridge to demonstrate to other employers that they too could be successful in manufacturing there, and that the city and the region have the workforce to support such activities successfully.

McCuistion recognizes the need to attract more businesses to Breckenridge in part because of concerns about the local tax base and the extraordinary demands for budgetary resources. The city constitutes is tax base on two primary sources: an ad valorem tax and a sales tax. The rate for sales tax is 8.5 percent, but only 2 percent of that is returned by the state of Texas for inclusion in the city's operating fund. The state also imposes limits on the property tax rates the city can impose, and that requires the city to reduce the tax on residents by an amount equal to the revenues above certain limits. Thus, it really does not help the city to elevate that revenue stream over the currently established mark, as the net result for the Breckenridge coffers will be zero. What is needed are means of increasing the revenue streams from which the city provides public services to its various constituents.

Although the city wants to expand its business base, there are some barriers that need to be overcome, notably infrastructure issues and the water supply. A recent drought has created great problems for the city and the region, which has had to negotiate for additional rights to river and lake water. The lake, which has been the greatest source of water for the city up to this time, is now at only a 24 percent level. There is an inherent flaw in the purchase of additional rights, however. The mineral content of the targeted new source is much different from that of the existing source and will therefore require reverse osmosis treatment before being potable, and that is a very expensive process. When asked if this concern about water—both present and future—will hamper business attraction (and perhaps even business and residential retention) efforts, McCuistion immediately responded that it must. These problems for west Texas are cyclical. In fact, the concern is greater on the retention side because the attraction piece is less important to the city at this time.

A second barrier to business growth in Breckenridge is the lack of available housing stock in the city and throughout the region. This is not related to the type or costs of housing but simply the availability of any housing for new residents. Further, much of the existing housing stock is substandard and has prompted the city to implement new programs to repair or raze some of the existing stock. While this was a necessary step for the city, it also had the effect of exacerbating the shortage problem.

Houses are being identified in increments of twenty at a time, and the owners are being told to fix them or tear them down. If they do not comply, the city will do so for them. "Breckenridge is old and worn and the city's residents have pride in how things look." This also extends to nearly three hundred junk automobiles that have been identified within the city's limits. Some of those vehicles are being hauled away, and others are being garaged to help improve the city's general appearance.

McCuistion attributes his hiring in Breckenridge to his background in financial management for other municipalities. The costs of beautifying the city, improving its infrastructure, and addressing the water-related needs can be tremendous. Three-fourths of the equipment owned by the city is fully depreciated, implying that it is probably past its normal useful life. The city is now borrowing millions of dollars for new and repaired water lines, sewer lines, and wastewater treatment facilities. But, the city will need to be cautious not to create a longer-term financial crisis in the process.

Having identified the primary issues of concern for economic development in the city of Breckenridge, McCuistion is quick to point out the advantages of living in west Texas. "I like it here. I like the natural area; I like the big sky; but you really have to like it to want to stay here and raise your family here."

Issues for economic growth	• Need more retail and restaurants
	• State has imposed limits on property tax rates
	• Recent drought
	• Lack of housing
	• Old infrastructure
	• City needs beautification
Strategies for economic growth	• Attract additional manufacturers
	• Clear vacant houses and junk cars from the city
	• Increase the water supply and infrastructure
Lessons learned	• Work to retain existing businesses
	• Businesses want to locate in attractive communities

Elsa, Texas

While not a great deal of information can be found online about the city of Elsa, Texas, the data does show that there has been significant and steady population growth in this small town over the past two decades. The information that is available online addresses the critical issue for locations in this part of the United States: water supply. This raises the question of how and for what purposes small, isolated towns like Elsa can attract the attention of businesses seeking locations. How would a business ever learn about such a city and what it has to offer companies?

Photo courtesy of Edith Acua, City of Elsa, Texas.

Interview with Joe Contu, City Manager of Elsa, Texas

Joe Contu is a retired police officer and agent who has extensive service along the Texas-Mexico border. His experiences are chronicled online; readers can find numerous articles about those experiences simply by going to a search engine and entering his name. While those experiences are interesting from a number of perspectives, they are most relevant for this research because they have colored his approach to local government management and the issues that are of greatest importance to the people of Elsa, Texas, today.

"The main problem here," says Contu, "is politics." There are two towns and two school districts. Redundant costs for those two systems, as well as for the localities more broadly, are an issue because the overall costs could be minimized to everyone's benefit through greater collaboration. But, that isn't happening, and City Manager Contu regrets what might be unnecessary, duplicative expenditures.

Elections that often result in new administrations every two years represent another form of political problem. Each newly elected body appoints new managers to various positions, thus resulting in the loss of any possible continuity. Happily for Contu, the "current group just wants what is best for the community. This town is hurting financially and future planning—beyond every two-year cycle—is important. But, Elsa, Texas, can be brought back to good shape, says Contu. "We have a Walmart and we have a CVS and a number of other really good retailers and some restaurants."

One of the city manager's emphases is that city employees be more productive and responsive to residents than ever before. Contu walks the street; he is looking for areas that need to be cleaned up or wires that need to be covered. He is taking down unauthorized signs announcing garage sales and personal services. "We are going to beautify this community; I am taking a list of violations we received from the state of Texas and we are going to clean those areas up and get them checked off the list. We need to present a positive image to visitors from outside the area or they won't want to come here."

When asked about how he hopes to be more successful in attracting new businesses to Elsa within the context of cleanup programs that have not yet been completed, the city manager notes, "We have to take pride in our town and in ourselves. A Walmart recently opened in town. Why can't we ask them to tell the story of Elsa for us? If they're happy being here, they can show others that they would be, too."

The city wants to grow, and it has the room for it. One of the targets for attraction is a distribution-warehousing operation. However, the problem that must be solved for that to happen, notes City Manager Contu, is that Elsa lies nearly nine miles from the highway that runs between Laredo and Brownsville. The city would be much more successful in attracting businesses if they could be assured that it would be easy for them to move their product to where it will be sold.

Another possibility for economic development in Elsa is a large gymnasium complex that would attract people from miles around. Those who would come into town to join the gym would also spend money in town at gas stations, restaurants, and more.

The growth of businesses and facilities is important to this city, which derives most of its budgetary revenues from the ad valorem, or property tax. This source is further supplemented by some sales taxes and various fees, such as for water and sewer. As the greatest contributor to the local budget is the real estate tax, there is an issue of long-range planning for the city. Those taxes are generally paid between October and February, which means that the balance of the year has smaller revenue streams and the income must be spread over the entire fiscal year to support the city's public services.

Contu is interested in building newer homes that are of greater value than the existing stock. That would generate greater tax revenues to support the city's public services. He admits, however, to having a chicken-and-egg situation in that the infrastructure needs to be put into place first in order to build any new homes, whereas the new construction is needed to generate the revenues needed to pay for the infrastructure development.

In a discussion consistent with those of a number of other interviewees in this research, Elsa's city manager is quick to point out that any reported numbers regarding population increases reported for the city of Elsa are misleading. The numbers often include a large influx of illegal aliens who, although they do not always contribute to the tax base, do collect a range of public services, including Section 8 housing and food stamps, as well as the costs of public education and more. This can cause severe budgetary problems for a small town like Elsa.

Issues for economic growth	• Regionalism is needed to eliminate duplicative services
	• Not enough housing
	• Beautification of city is needed
	• Many abandoned buildings
Strategies for economic growth	• Improve city services
	• Beautification of the city and enhancement of local pride
Lessons learned	• Employers want to locate in attractive communities

Pecos, Texas

Pecos, Texas, is one of several towns that were founded along the Texas and Pacific Railroad line in the early 1800s. That line ran between the larger cities of Fort Worth and El Paso. Located along the Pecos River, the region enjoys very fertile soil that has sustained ranching and farming activities for many generations.

In recent years, however, the economic base of Pecos has seemingly deteriorated. The population declined between 1990 and 2005 by about 35 percent. In many cases, when that happens, it has the effect of reducing the unemployment rate, if only by reducing the denominator—the total workforce. However, even with the loss of more than one-third of the population base, reports indicate that the unemployment rate in the city exceeds the national average, and reaches to nearly 10 percent (http://www.usbeacon.com). The mayor of Pecos was asked to discuss these trends and their impacts as well as any plans that may be under way to reverse them.

The city is not without some potential assets for economic development, and their roles in the process going forward were discussed with the city's leadership. The most prominent of these include three institutions of higher learning: the University of Texas, Permian Basin; the Odessa College, Pecos Center; and Sul Ross College.

Photo courtesy of Robby Freeman.

Interview with the Honorable Venetta Seals, Mayor of Pecos, Texas

Venetta Seals, the mayor of Pecos, Texas, was included as an interviewee for this study, although she is an elected official rather than a city manager. City managers are the professionals who manage a city's activities on a day-to-day basis. However, in small cities, not all functions are performed in the same ways. In many cases, the mayor is more or less powerful, while in other cities mayors are actually categorized as weak. A weak mayor may have anything from specific management responsibilities to purely political roles.

City managers are professionals who either work their way up through the city workforce to become city manager or move from one city to several others over the course of their careers. In the case of the managers, their longevity tends to be relatively brief compared to the mayor in small cities, who more often than not have either grown up in the area or moved to the city many years before becoming mayor.

Pecos's mayor came to the city only twelve years prior to the interview, which has not been the trend throughout these interviews. She immediately got involved in the community as a volunteer, spent four years as a member of the city council, and was already finishing her first term as mayor and preparing to run for her second when interviewed. In the interim, she also served two years as the chair of the city's chamber of commerce. The point is not lost on her: "If you want to come to this community, the people will welcome you. We have many events in town, and they are all managed by volunteers. People donate their time in a small town. In a town like this, you always know your neighbor."

The economy of Pecos took a historic turn that can be clearly defined. This is somewhat atypical for some small, isolated cities that typically grow and contract more gradually. However, Pecos, which was originally founded on the Pecos River and enjoyed the consequent ability to irrigate the surrounding farms and ranches, subsequently "lost" that asset. Over the years, the consistent flooding of the town by the Pecos River caused the city to move ten miles to the west. From that point of security, residents could still irrigate the farms and ranches, and agribusinesses flourished. However, the state of New Mexico dammed the river upstream for its own purposes, leaving Pecos and other areas quite literally "high and dry." Fortunately, the city sits atop an aquifer so that although the amount of water for farming became an issue, the supply of drinking water did not.

Today, some farming continues, but the number of businesses and the number of jobs have substantially diminished. This has significantly reduced the number of farms producing the well-known Pecos sweet cantaloupes, leaving only one producer today. Oil and gas is now the region's largest industry sector and largest employer. Pecos enjoys the greatest number of operating oil rigs in the entire state of Texas today: fifty-eight. Their sales generate taxes revenues that help support the public services for those who live or work in Pecos, as well as those who visit.

Mayor Seals, when asked what businesses she would like to see attracted to Pecos, noted that she would like to see more retail in the area. This is a reflection on the *isolated* part of small and isolated cities. Pecos had been a bustling city until the 1980s oil bust that sent residents elsewhere in search of jobs. That was followed closely by the purchase by outside interests of an onion plant and its subsequent relocation, with an attendant loss of eight hundred jobs. As a result, the retail establishments that supported the workers and their families also departed in search of areas with greater and more stable demand.

Today, the residents of Pecos have two options when doing their regular shopping: they can either drive 150 miles to Odessa, or they can pay the higher prices in town that are the result of having a relatively few remaining businesses that are thus "the only game in town." Still, Mayor Seals feels Pecos is experiencing a comeback. Old abandoned buildings—both homes and commercial properties—are being purchased and renovated. Some had sat vacant for as many as thirty years. New homes are also being built to house the workers now coming into town for jobs

Issues for economic growth	• Not enough retail
	• Not enough housing
	• Abandoned buildings
Strategies for economic growth	• Attract retailers
	• Build housing
Lessons learned	• Infrastructure needs to be in place before business will locate

on the oil rigs. That growth produces jobs and income, but it also increases the demand on the public schools and other public services. "It's a double-edged sword. We need the infrastructure to catch up if we are to serve more people and more businesses. It just came on us so fast."

West and Southwest

Winslow, Arizona

The unemployment rate in Winslow, Arizona, at the time of this writing was nearly 14 percent—substantially higher than the US national average—and forecasted job growth was in the negative by more than 3 percent at a time when the US national average was fractionally in the positive range (http://www.bestplaces.net). This was a specific area of inquiry for the city manager in the interview.

Curiously, despite the high level of unemployment and the outlook for job growth, the city's population base grew substantially from 1990 to 2005, and forecasts suggest continued growth, although at slower rates (http://www.usbeacon.com). This too was posed as an area of inquiry during the interview with the city manager.

Photo courtesy of Todd Ruth.

Interview with Stephen Pauken, City Manager of Winslow, Arizona

Winslow, Arizona, city manager Stephen Pauken arrived in town shortly before this interview from his service as the city manager of Bisbee, Arizona, a similarly positioned city of comparable size. His ability to compare these cities and the style and processes of both is further enhanced by his service as an elected official (both city council member and mayor) and city manager in suburban Toledo, Ohio, and communities in Colorado as well. Although his service as a mayor in Ohio is atypical of the city managers in this study, the mobility shown throughout his career is not. Further, as is also typical, his service as a professional city manager has been focused on cities of a similar size.

The two cities in Arizona in which Pauken has served—Bisbee and Winslow—both qualify for inclusion in this research: they have fewer than ten thousand residents, and both are sufficiently isolated from larger urban areas. Thus, both have to provide almost entirely for themselves. Bisbee had initially built its economy on the success of copper mining. When the mines closed, however, the area "practically became a ghost town." Over time, a number of artists moved into the city, attracted by the inexpensive housing, and the entire area has emerged as a tourist destination.

Winslow is a tourist destination in its own right, largely on the basis of the 1970s song by the Eagles in which the following verse appears:

> I was standing on the corner in Winslow, Arizona,
> such a fine sight to see
> It was girl, my Lord,
> in a bright red Ford
> slowing down to take a look at me.
> Taking it easy …

The city, which originally grew as a center for train traffic, has enjoyed the tourism that was generated by that single verse. City Manager Pauken said, "All the time, you see people 'standing on a corner' having their pictures taken."

The railroads are still a prominent industry in the area, and City Manager Pauken notes, "I can hear the trains all the time. I don't mind the sound at all; for Winslow, that's the sound of money." The city's budget totals about $6.5 million, more than $2.5 million of which comes from sales taxes. This prompted the question: Are the economic development attraction programs for the city of Winslow specifically designed to attract businesses that generate sales taxes? In that way, the city's coffers for the provision of public services are enhanced. Not so, said Pauken: "It's all about jobs. If people have jobs, then they will have the money to spend in the stores."

The general populace in Winslow has a positive attitude about growth for another reason. Although the area does have a Walmart, the nearest shopping other than that which they can find in downtown Winslow is fifty-five miles away. The attraction or local creation of additional retail opportunities in

Winslow would both enhance the quality of life and represent additional assets for business attraction.

One of the most positive recent economic events affecting Winslow has been the completion of Interstate Route 40, which passes through the area. Prior to its completion, Route 66 passed right through the heart of the city and served as an attraction to its merchants. Route 66 still passes through the center of Winslow at a pace that enables travelers to look at the city and stop for various reasons. On the other hand, Interstate 40 passes through the city, although not through its center, and the speed at which travelers are moving as they pass through Winslow makes it much more likely that they will do just that—pass through it, rather than stopping and looking around, or even simply buying gasoline or lunch.

This has had a significant impact on the town and its merchant base. The city did very well, said Pauken, to realize that the impacts of Interstate 40 were permanent and that they needed to move on. They planned to improve the city and make it more attractive to visitors and prospective businesses. A one-cent add-on to the local sales tax was approved by voters in a referendum and was dedicated to infrastructure improvements and the rehabilitation of several key buildings in the downtown area.

One example is the rehabbing of a former trading post that is now used as the office of the city's visitors bureau and as it welcome center, as well as meeting space that is available for use by residents or local companies. The marginal funds generated by the additional one-cent sales tax have also been used to improve roads, curbs and gutters, and more. Finally, a local bed tax has been implemented that enables the city to be more aggressive and more creative in marketing its tourism attractions.

In addition to the railroads and the tourism industry, Winslow also boasts of having two hospitals, one for the Native American tribes—Hopi and Navajo—and the other for other residents. Not only do these represent important amenities for a town that is small and isolated, but also they are major employers, with a total employment base of between four hundred and five hundred people with a wide range of skill sets. A local airport, with two 7500-foot runways, also supports business growth as well as passenger traffic.

The relations between the city and the two Indian tribes are very positive. Nearly one in four residents of Winslow is an American Indian. City Manager Pauken points out that there is a plant on Hopi land, "just feet outside of the city limits." The plant encompasses more than one hundred thousand square feet of space and is entirely vacant; the city and the tribe are working in tandem to try to attract a user or users. Pauken also notes, however, that the Hopi tribe owns much of the land around the city of Winslow. There is a note of caution about having the city being entirely surrounded by a single landowner. Such situations can cause problems if there is discord between the neighboring entities, but that is not the case in and around Winslow. Pauken said, "It is clear that we all must work together." This is what Pauken likes about being in Winslow: "We can all get along without disagreeing. I can do my job and the council supports me by staying involved and helping where they can. That relationship is a key ingredient to our success here in Winslow."

Issues for economic growth	• Still recovering from massive job losses all at once
Strategies for economic growth	• Build infrastructure
	• Rehab older buildings
	• Market for tourism
Lessons learned	• Regionalism is an effective economic development strategy

Fort Bragg, California

Located at the mouth of California's Noyo River, the city affords its residents, workers, and visitors spectacular views of the Pacific Ocean. In 1855, an exploration group traveled there representing the Bureau of Indian Affairs to find a site for a reservation and settled on the area now known as Fort Bragg. Following the departure of the military in the late 1860s, the fort was used as the site of a sawmill. Like many of the cities in this study, disaster struck in 1906, this time in the form of an earthquake-induced fire that destroyed much of the city.

In an odd twist of fate, the same fire and the resultant damage it created yielded considerable business for the sawmill and the town boomed all over again. The rebirth of Fort Bragg was completed for the time by the final development of a new rail line that served to accommodate the new workers as well as the first wave of tourism for those who wished to enjoy the area's natural beauty. Much of the city's website is clearly devoted to the promotion and preservation of the area's natural amenities.

In subsequent years, the city benefitted from the lumber industry, fishing, and a wide variety of agricultural pursuits, in addition to the growth of several construction businesses. Today, these assets are well complemented by the city's proximity to US Highway 1. Nonetheless, the rate of unemployment at the time of this writing exceeded both 10 percent and the US national average. This was a point of discussion for the city's leadership during the interview.

Photo courtesy of the city of Fort Bragg.

Interview with Linda Ruffing, City Manager of Fort Bragg, California

Ruffing recited an interesting municipal history to start the discussion. Fort Bragg was established roughly 125 years ago, many years after settlers joined the preexisting Native American tribes in the area, the Pomo and the Mendocino Indians. The small military outpost from which the city derives its name only existed for four or five years.

Given the location and the natural resources nearby, the initial business concerns related to the lumber industry and the fisheries that thrive because the city of Fort Bragg is located right on the Pacific Ocean.

As the demand for lumber in the area increased and those businesses grew, the timber resources were depleted, meaning that many of the local Indians were displaced. What grew in the area's stead was essentially a company town, the company being the Union Lumber Company. Additionally, commercial fishing was supported by the city as a harbor was built along one of the area's two largest rivers to support this growing industry.

Ultimately, highly intensive logging practices led to the depletion of the easily available lumber. The year 2002 saw the closure of the mill, which at one time had employed as many as two thousand employees. While devastating in terms of the job losses, the mill had occupied the entire waterfront exposure of the city of Fort Bragg. This left the city with both a problem and an opportunity to find a more attractive and more productive use of its waterfront. To maximize the use of this property, the city engaged in a visioning process. City Manager Ruffing noted that the lesson from that experience was that "small towns need to be creative and forward looking. We need to seize what opportunities come along and engage our citizenry. I believe a lot in community involvement."

The outcomes of the visioning process included three areas of focus: first, the people of Fort Bragg wanted to regain access to the waterfront that had so long been tied up by the mill; second, there was great interest expressed in attracting an institution to the city that would fit well with the area and around which other activities could be planned; and, third, jobs were needed to replace those that had been lost with the shuttering of the mill.

Following this exercise, the city acquired about one hundred acres along its waterfront to build a park and trails. To do so, the city was able to obtain approximately $12 million through grants from the state of California. Bids for the development of the acreage will be released by the city in the near future. City Manager Ruffing anticipates that this will become a strong asset for tourist attraction, which will in turn support the local hospitality industry and retailers in the city. Supporting the local hospitality industry is of critical importance to the city of Fort Bragg, which derives much of its general fund revenues from transient occupancy taxes (or hotel) and sales taxes.

But the city was not finished with its resurgence. It acquired another eleven acres of land to develop a new marine science center, which will include research and educational components, including a two-thousand-pound skeleton of a whale, and will take the maximum advantage of its primary natural resource, the waterfront. This echoes what other leaders in small and isolated cities have counseled about needing to maximize the value of those assets that are naturally available. An executive director has been hired by the city to manage the marine science center, with the instruction to "spin it off as a private entity within two years."

To address the third need identified in the visioning process, the city identified a portion of the former mill site for future development. To make the site more attractive and competitive, the city is working its way through the array of state-required environmental inspections and certifications and will complete those processes prior to business prospects being shown the sites as potential locations for their operations. This echoes the actions of other small, isolated cities that wish to market their industrial sites more competitively. However, in the case of Fort Bragg, it is even more impressive and important due to the facts that the previous use was industrial, that the state of California is very careful about these requirements, and that the land in question is located on the oceanfront, which means that there are significant additional requirements. A prospective employer, however, will not have to concern itself with many of these requirements. The drawback for the city is that costs for these studies and actions are expected to be quite high.

City Manager Ruffing responded to a question about how the people of Fort Bragg were affected by the heavy job losses, noting, "There was generally a sense that we could solve our problems. The positive outlook was actually infectious." As others have noted, small towns don't have big boom times, and for the same reason, they don't experience big bust times either. It's usually more gradual than that, which may have contributed to the more positive reactions in Fort Bragg than in other cities in this research.

The concerns that were expressed in Fort Bragg were primarily about the future of the city's downtown. There are three primary streets, two of which fared relatively well in terms of business retention, while the third saw one shop after another closed and the space shuttered. As the downtown is "both charming and historic, people wanted to do something about that." "Everyone pulled together," noted City Manager Ruffing, "and now things are starting to happen. Some businesses are starting up again."

The city also is the home to a very large aquatic center that was built by a now-defunct regional park district. A foundation helped defray the costs of construction, but the ongoing operating expenses are quite high, so the city, in order to take the operations over, needed to impose a tax. It was put before the residents in a referendum at the height of the recession and was passed by an overwhelming majority. This adds .5 cent to their annual tax burdens but provides sufficient funding to maintain the facility and operate in perpetuity. Aside from not wanting to have an unused facility of this type and size in their city, planners believed it could be used for local residents, as well as to attract swim meets and other aquatic events to the city that will in turn generate sales and revenues for local merchants.

In terms of lessons she has learned as the city manager, Ruffing noted that the leadership of any small town needs to keep its eye on the future. Second, "Keep people involved. In a small town, they can become involved in a lot of things and in very intimate ways. Together, they can make a big difference."

Issues for economic growth	• Still recovering from massive job losses all at once
Strategies for economic growth	• Planning for reuse of a vacant mill
	• Develop riverfront, including hiking trails and bike paths
Lessons learned	• Take advantage of nearby natural resources
	• Infrastructure needs to be in place before businesses will consider a location

Yreka, California

The city of Yreka (pronounced *Wy-ree-kuh*) is positioned in the Shasta Valley of California and shares twenty-two miles of its state's border with Oregon. While the natural beauty of the area and the nearby Klamath National Forest are primary among the current attractions to the region, the early draw was the California gold rush. For a few years, the city boomed; houses were built and businesses grew up to support the prospectors and the transient trade along the aptly named Miner Street. The city drew its name at the time from the word the local Indians used for Mount Shasta: *Yreka*.

As the gold rush reached its inevitable conclusion, the city's population began to dwindle, and adding insult to injury, much of the remaining city burned to the ground in an 1871 fire. But, unlike many other towns in the region that suffered through similar disasters and declines, the people of Yreka stayed in the area and rebuilt the town. In addition to a great deal of natural scenic beauty, Yreka and the county of Siskiyou also enjoy a tremendous sociocultural history that can be marketed for skiing, other forms of tourism, and research.

Photo courtesy of the Yreka Chamber of Commerce.

Interview with Steve Baker, City Manager of Yreka, California

Yreka was established in response to the 1851 gold strike—the second largest in California history. Prospectors needed services and rooms to rent and supplies. With an estimated five thousand residents at the time, the city became the county seat, thereby attracting further growth and stability. However, a fire eliminated many of the historic sites and the city based its subsequent growth on a combination of cattle ranching and lumber mills. Extensive highway connections helped to accelerate the development of Yreka through the 1970s when one economic decline followed another, leaving the city with just one remaining lumber mill and generally very difficult times.

City Manager Baker explained that small cities in California typically follow the economic trends of the state at large, trailing by as many as three to five years. Today, the highways passing through the area represent the greatest economic development asset for the city of Yreka. Five of the top ten sales tax generators for the city are gas stations. This represents another case of a small town accepting the assets it does possess for economic development and making the most of them. This has been a common theme in the interviews, reflecting a sense that this strategy is basic and provides a basis on which to build other, larger strategic concepts.

For the city of Yreka, sales tax revenues are vital; they represent about one-third ($1.7 million) of the $5.1 million city budget from which public services are provided. The remaining sources include about $1.2 million from property taxes and a significant sum from the transient occupancy tax applied to hotel room users while passing through the area.

The dependence on sales tax revenues prescribes that Yreka's economic development professionals pursue businesses that generate sales taxes. There is also a great emphasis on higher-paying jobs for the residents of Yreka and the surrounding, much smaller, communities. As relates to the latter emphasis, Yreka—with state financial assistance—developed the Northeast Industrial Park. City Manager Baker points out, however, that "there are many vacant industrial parks up and down the length of the state of California." In an effort to make its park distinctive, Yreka completed the necessary environmental analyses for businesses considering locations at the park. This has served to create additional interest in the park; for example, Belcampo, a meat-packing plant, expressed appreciation for the fact that this particular issue had already been resolved.

For a business, such studies and remediation of any resultant issues can translate into significant time delays and substantial sums of money. Resolving such issues in a proactive manner is important for Yreka's efforts to attract companies to the park, and the city's leadership believes that it gives their location an advantage over other industrial parks that are not as prepared for companies to locate. The park once offered the tax advantages of being designated an enterprise zone under California law; however, the state ended that program in December 2013 to capture the potentially lost tax revenues.

Another example of a recent economic development success for Yreka is the plan for a new business to locate on the site of a now-defunct mill in the city. This unit will use the lumber that is not normally part of the wood produced for higher uses to manufacture wooden pallets that will be shipped to the orange growers in southern California, where they will be used for stacking and shipping. This represents yet another example of the community taking best advantage of its natural assets for economic development. As Baker pointed out, "The basic natural resources can help attract businesses."

One lesson Baker offers to other small town leaders is that the highly competitive nature of business attraction and retention requires cities and their business communities to work together and to be as professional and responsive as possible. This extends the welcome to a company in a very important way: "It says we want them and we understand their need for speed in getting up and running." The lifestyle of small towns is another great economic development asset. "There are hunting and fishing and skiing and things to do outdoors."

This unified community approach to prospective businesses is very important. "Businesspeople want to know that the city wants them, but they also want to hear it not just from city leaders, but from other businesses as well. It's not that they don't believe the city, but businesses trust and understand other businesspeople." For the cities involved, this often requires a cultural shift that includes expediting the processing of developmental reviews and documentation, greater responsiveness, and often even a heightened orientation to customer service.

In terms of what is missing from the picture when working with prospective businesses, Baker identified Yreka's asset gaps. The enterprise zone legislation was deactivated six weeks prior to this interview. City Manager Baker would like to have that back, as it was an effective means of attracting the attention of site location decision makers for small cities and towns throughout the entire state.

Baker also would like to have greater resources to train the available workforce for potential employers. This would include everything from basic work skills and behaviors to specific technology and job-related skills sets. The local community college conducts programs in areas such as public safety and nursing (around the state of California's Rural Health Initiative). Training tied to the specific needs of prospective employers can be a positive selling feature for new business attraction.

Another lesson offered by City Manager Baker is that small towns cannot afford to have singly focused economies. "The economy must be balanced with retail, services, industrial and light industrial manufacturing. We cannot have our economic base be focused just on building the local budget."

Issues for economic growth	• State ended the enterprise zone program
	• Workforce training needed
Strategies for economic growth	• Economic diversification
	• Take advantage of the natural assets
	• Increase workforce training
Lessons learned	• Diversify the local economy
	• Work closely with the local business community on economic development

Delta, Colorado

Delta, Colorado, is a growing city. In the twenty-year period between 1990 and 2010, the city's population increased from nearly thirty-eight hundred to nearly eighty-nine hundred. This represents an increase of nearly $2^{1}/_{3}$. At the same time, the unemployment rate is below the national average, so the influx of new residents did not elevate the unemployment situation. Discussions with the city's leadership focused on both the causes of this growth and how the city managed to cope with such dramatic increases in demands for services from the city and the region.

Photo courtesy of the city of Delta staff.

Interview with Justin Clifton, City Manager of Delta, Colorado

For much of its history, Delta's economic story has been one solely of agricultural output and sales. Sugar beets growers and dairy farms dotted the landscape and family farms dominated the landscape of the city and the region. In more recent times, mineral extractions generated substantial employment as well, but the city is left today with only two remaining operating coal mines and a few dairy farms.

The city has suffered through a series of boom and bust cycles that have resulted in widely varying spending patterns and uncertain revenues from which the city can provide public services. Oil shale has contributed to the swings, as the technology improved over time and the pricing changed for the product globally. According to City Manager Clifton, in recent years, the mining of coal has become subject to extreme regulatory oversight, and the subsequent impact on employers' operations has cost the city as many as three hundred jobs.

Clifton believes that family farming can return to Delta and the region, but that it will need to be in value-added areas of farming. This may include production and food preparation as well as actual farming. Wine grapes grow well in the region, as do cherries, apples, apricots, and peaches. Clifton also feels that the local economy can be bolstered by the establishment of creative industries ranging from the arts to furniture design and manufacture. This would give stability to local enterprises and to the city's revenue streams.

There is a great deal of attention being paid to the diversification of the economy in order to repeat the historical impacts of changing fortunes in just one or two industries. In an effort not to experience another boom-bust cycle, the city is also focusing on outdoor activities and tourism. There are three national conservation areas and the Black Mountain National Park near Delta that attract visitors to the area. Many of the orchards are attractions for people who want to pick their own fruit. This will attract more visitors to the area as well. Clifton feels that although the resultant jobs tend to be relatively low paying, tourism does create revenues and cash flow, and many will return to the area.

The tourist trade also helps the city provide public services because it does have a tax that is levied on hotel rooms, although the budget is most heavily dependent upon sales taxes, so manufacturing and farming are particularly productive contributors. Today, sales tax revenues for the city are the second highest level in their recorded history. Still, Clifton would prefer to attract primary industries and believes that there are several sectors that are possibilities for growth, including medical care, which he believes has considerable potential for Delta.

Vital to the attraction and retention of industry in Delta, as well as the growth of new businesses, will be the expansion of broadband service throughout the region. Clifton believes that there are also other asset gaps that Delta needs to address. While water and electricity are plentiful, the city needs to have access to rail for manufacturers. There are two highways that run through the city, but the nearest interstate highway is forty miles away. Such transportation connections are critical for producers of goods who seek the most efficient means of moving their freight to various markets.

Another economic development asset for Delta would be a Small Business Development Center (SBDC). One existed in Delta many years ago, but the state of Colorado moved it to Gunnison, which is a two-hour drive from the city of Delta. These centers work with aspiring business men and women to understand the regulations involved in business start-ups as well as to prepare business plans, financing schedules, and more. Clifton feels that it would be useful to have a Delta location for an SBDC again because "without it, entrepreneurial training and support in Delta are basically nonexistent." Such a program, coupled with broadband in the region, would be greatly beneficial.

But, Delta is fortunate in that it can survive even with a small economy in the city. It is located close enough to several larger cities that residents can enjoy the lifestyle of the smaller rural town and work in nearby, larger urban areas. "Still," notes Clifton, "there is a dairy closing and eliminating thirty-seven jobs. That's a lot of jobs for a small town."

City Manager Clifton notes that a small, rural town has to take the long-term view to economic growth. "Investments are critical. If you build an excellent community, people will want to be there. A vibrant downtown attracts people. We have built a community civic center downtown and parks and trails. We are trying to create a desirable place to be. The focus needs to be on building a great community, and that takes time."

Issues for economic growth	• Technology has replaced jobs in farming
	• Forty miles to the nearest interstate highway
	• Small Business Development Center relocated away from city by the state
Strategies for economic growth	• Bring back value-added family farming
	• Economic diversification increases broadband service
	• Create training programs in entrepreneurial skills
Lessons learned	• Diversify the local economy
	• Take advantage of the nearby natural resources
	• Prepare the infrastructure before businesses arrive
	• Businesses want to locate in attractive cities

Gunnison, Colorado

Gunnison, Colorado, certainly qualifies as being sufficiently isolated to be included in this study. It is not only distant from larger urban areas, but also devoid of the primary land transportation networks that sometimes serve as drivers of economic growth and prosperity for small isolated cities and towns.

While Western State College of Colorado and a pleasant-appearing downtown streetscape are positive features, the mountainous terrain and harsh winters may serve either as assets or as problems for present and future economic development, depending on how they are marketed. This was one area to explore with the city's leadership.

While mining and ranching appear to have driven the economy over the early years of the community, it is not clear that they represent impactful industries in today's Gunnison. This was a topic for the interview with the city manager.

Photo courtesy of Gregg Morin.

Interview with Ken Coleman, City Manager of Gunnison, Colorado

Coleman's accession to the position of city manager in Gunnison, Colorado, followed a long career managing the city's public works department. Given the location of the city and the nature of its key concerns, this was an appropriate background to serve as city manager. He acknowledged that the city has both challenges and positive attributes for businesses and residents alike.

The city's remoteness is the first challenge Coleman cited, but in fact, it colored, even if indirectly, many of his comments. Gunnison is located on Route 50, approximately two hundred miles southwest of Denver. While Route 50 is a good thoroughfare, and does bring some traffic past the city, it is not a major interstate highway, which compounds the city's isolation. Additionally, the railroad, which had been strong through the region for many years, ultimately concluded that there was not sufficient demand to run trains to Gunnison and pulled out the service to the city and the region. While there is a nice airport near the town, the capacity exceeds the demand for flights. Much of the usage of the airport is related to people going past Gunnison to the largest ski slopes in the area. Thus, although the airport is both regular and reliable, it tends to be rather expensive, and thus not a strong asset for economic development.

In addition to the loss of the railroad service, many related jobs were also lost from Gunnison. The mining industries in the city and the region are much smaller in scope than in the past, and the extraction operations that do remain are in the surrounding county, not within the city limits of Gunnison. This industry sector provides many fewer employment opportunities today than it had in the past.

There are numerous federal government jobs in the area, mostly within the Park Service and the Fish and Wildlife Administration. When asked whether there were any concerns about losing any of those jobs due to federal budget crises and the federal sequester, City Manager Coleman acknowledged that he was indeed concerned. Any of those jobs that are cut, he opined, will have a disproportionately great impact on the tax base and on the city's merchants because those jobs typically pay higher salaries than do others in the region.

Another concern related to the federal government's position in the city and in the region is that it owns so much of the surrounding land area: more than eighty percent of the county's land mass is in public lands, and will remain so in perpetuity. This means that there is very little privately held land available for development or for the generation of revenues for the city's budget. Further, much of what is privately held is used for ranching.

Today, one of the largest employers in the region is the Western Colorado State College, which is located within the city limits of Gunnison and which enrolls about two thousand students. Those who are enrolled, as well those who visit, do bring some revenue into the town and help to support the local merchant base in addition to the provision of employment.

But, the main economic engine for Gunnison is tourism. This helps to support the retailers in the community, which include a mix of outside chain retailers, largely in the clothing and general shopping areas, and restaurants, mostly local establishments. These are good employers for a small town in a state like Colorado to have because the primary contributor to the city's tax base is the sales tax generated by these shops, restaurants, and other retailers. When asked if manufacturing would also make sense, as it might generate even greater sales tax revenues than the retailers in the city, City Manager Coleman noted that manufacturers do not want to locate in an area that is not only isolated, but virtually unreachable by surface transportation.

In terms of life in such an isolated small town, Coleman regularly tells his constituents that he considers small towns to be the purest form of democracy: "Anyone can come into my office or to the city council meeting and speak their mind." Coleman related the story of constituents who wanted to build various amenities in the community. His response was to create a group comprised of several people who wanted to establish several different types of programs. As a result, the group came together and put forward a plan. Their proposal received overwhelming approval for a referendum that resulted in the construction of a swimming pool and a hockey rink. The two are used to attract hockey tournaments and swim meets and have been "in the black since day 1!"

"The city lives within its means," says Coleman, "and that's why I'm optimistic. We are responsible in the management of our fiscal resources." That is one thing that Coleman believes businesses in any community want. Another is the effective management and development of infrastructure. "We need to keep our roadways, water and sewer, electricity, and all of our public services in good shape. We have great water rights agreements for Gunnison and we have the second lowest rates for electricity in the state of Colorado." For a city manager, Coleman sounds a lot like the public works director he once was. Perhaps, as is the case with others of the cities in this study, that makes great sense since those are the issues with which they must deal most regularly.

And, as with all small towns, part of what they can offer—to businesses and residents alike—is the general quality of life. "There are reasons people want to be here," said Coleman. "You choose a place like this for its lifestyle. Outdoor activities—summer and winter—are here. We want people to come here, enjoy their visit, and come back and, if they'd like, come back and stay."

Issues for economic growth	• Isolation
	• Rail service has ended
	• Poor service transportation for manufacturers
Strategies for economic growth	• Market for tourism
	• Build recreational facilities
Lessons learned	• Infrastructure must be in place before businesses arrive

Lamar, Colorado

Lamar is located in southeastern Colorado, in the plains, closer to Oklahoma than to most of the rest of Colorado. While it does get snow, the region does not include the mountainous areas or ski resorts for which much of the state is renowned. In recent years, a serious drought has had a significant impact on the farming and cattle ranch industries in the area. This was a focus of the interview with the city's leadership. What is being done to replace the economic impact of those businesses while awaiting rain?

The population of Lamar has not changed appreciably over the past two decades, which suggests that either there are alternatives to ranching and agriculture in these down periods or there are seasonal or part-time opportunities that exist in the city. The local community college offers a wide array of basic academic curricula, but also offers several areas of study related to horsemanship and training, which suggests a demand for these workers in the industries that are related to the mainstays of the Lamar economy.

Photo courtesy of Vincent Gearhart.

Interview with the Honorable Roger Stagner, Mayor of Lamar, Colorado

The issue of what is characterized above as a "serious drought" initiates the conversation. Mayor Stagner advised that the current drought is now in its seventh year. This has caused considerable hardships for local businesses, including that of the mayor's brother, who is a cattle rancher. Individuals and families have been struggling to get through this difficult time, as is the city itself.

The mayor explained that the reduced tax revenues have made it necessary to eliminate positions from the city's payroll. Fortunately, that has been accomplished through attrition rather than layoffs. This has meant, however, that city services have been impacted and that the remaining employees of the city are working well beyond normal expectations. But, Mayor Stagner is proud of not having to lay anyone off and is equally proud that, despite the loss of revenues for the city, there have been no tax increases. In fact, the city has even created a rainy day fund from revenues during this period. Throughout this challenging time, the mayor has been intent upon keeping the citizens of Lamar informed and involved. "We try to be responsive to the citizens. And, they are aware: if we buy a new piece of equipment and they ask why, we had better have a good answer!"

Normally, in a time of economic distress for a community, especially a small, isolated community like Lamar, small merchants also struggle because people have less expendable income and are generally more inclined to saving than spending. In order to support the merchants of downtown Lamar, the city created a program whereby citizens who spent money in the shops downtown can get a refund from the city of 10 percent of the receipts delivered, up to a total of $50 for $500 spent. In this way, residents are being encouraged to shop in Lamar rather than driving to larger areas like Pueblo, which is more than 120 miles away. In turn, of course, this has had the effect of supporting Lamar's downtown merchants. This is also very important to the city, which assesses a 3 percent sales tax and builds the local budget—and provides services to the citizens of Lamar—on the basis of those revenues.

One of the city's critical areas of services is its public school system. Mayor Stagner firmly believes that public schools in small towns are typically very good, and Lamar is no exception. There are none of the problems of big city school systems that can make it necessary to pay for a private education. "In small towns, the teachers know the kids and the parents, and they are involved with the children throughout their school days. And, the entire community gets behind the schools and their programs: sports, plays, concerts. There are no overcrowded classrooms and no kids who don't have constant oversight." As for Mayor Stagner's personal experience: "I moved here when I was 2.5. My daughter graduated from these schools and is about to receive her doctorate."

The city also conducts numerous programs to support its downtown merchants by bringing people into the city, including an Oktoberfest, a Snow Geese Festival, and other events. This has had the further benefit of generating additional community spirit and pride. Another outcome of these activities has been that Lamar has not suffered any of the deterioration of its downtown area during this period that has been noted by other mayors and city managers in the interviews conducted as part of this research.

One consistent viewpoint between the interview with Mayor Stagner and his contemporaries is his focus on attracting small companies to Lamar. "I want fives and tens (numbers of employees), not a hundred. If we lose one hundred jobs at once, it hurts. If you lose five, it's easier to recover."

Mayor Stagner's comments are not dissimilar to those of mayors of many of the larger cities included in previous research. On the one hand, large losses can destroy the economy of smaller cities and towns. On the other hand, a new employee with a large number of jobs can represent dramatic positive impacts for local economies, families, cities' budgets, and the institutions and organizations within the community.

The city also owns and maintains a quality ball park, which attracts baseball and other tournaments that provide business for the merchants in town. "This means hotel rooms get filled, restaurants are used, and gas stations are needed. It's the small things that help a city do well."

The mayor noted two important lessons that have been given voice by other mayors and city managers in these interviews as well: "Talk to people and listen to them. The mayor must be approachable. People not only have real concerns and issues they want to talk about, but sometimes they also have good ideas and suggestions that we may want to study and think about doing."

The second of these lessons is that, in small towns, people stick together. "And, small town mayors have to help make that happen. In rural America, you have to find a way to do it yourself; you're on your own. You can't do things alone, but working together, we just find a way to make things work."

Issues for economic growth	• Lengthy drought is still hurting local cattle ranchers
Strategies for economic growth	• Support "buy locally program" by offering refund on taxes paid
	• Create festivals and tournaments
Lessons learned	• Constant communications throughout the community are critical

Salida, Colorado

Like many of the small, isolated cities in this research, Salida was initially founded to serve as a railroad stop en route to larger markets in the region, in this case, Denver in the late nineteenth century. After the railroads ceased to be a dominant employer for this part of the region, residents of Salida found employment on many of the ranches that had been established in the area. The population of the city has leveled out over recent years around fifty-five hundred. A number of other small towns are situated nearby, but none are significantly larger than Salida, which serves as the county seat of Chaffee County.

Photo courtesy of Wiley Middleton, Middleton Photography.

Interview with the Honorable Jim Dickson, Mayor of Salida, Colorado

Salida (pronounced with a long *i*) was an 1880s railroad stop. Mayor Dickson noted that the city was, in fact, the predominant railroad town in the Rockies before the turn of the century, with 111 buildings in the area that now constitutes Salida's historic downtown. Today's economy in Salida is much different, of course, and much of the recent growth has been facilitated by a program of the state of Colorado called the Certified Creative Industries. When the program was first implemented, two cities, one of which was Salida, were designated as the inaugural districts to serve as test cases.

The goal of the Colorado Creative Districts is to build the administrative structure, funding, and community involvement that will facilitate the growth of the industries defined in the legislation as being creative in nature. The notion is to attract and support the growth of creative, profit-making companies in the designated zones.

As a direct consequence of this program, sales tax revenues in Salida grew from about 4 percent to about 13 percent over a few short years. The new companies that grew in the district include taverns, stores, a boutique hotel, artists' galleries and lofts, and a guitar maker. Because the focus is on designated creative industries, Mayor Dickson cites a "surge of energy" in the zone that has led to a dramatic lowering of the unemployment rate in the city and the surrounding area. This is of particular importance to the city and its ability to provide public services to its residents because Salida collects a 7.9 percent sales tax that enables the city to provide public services to businesses and residents alike.

But, the Salida economic base also derives benefits from a host of outdoor activities and festivals that occur in the broader region. And, as many of the activities span the full calendar, there are year-round revenues generated, not just seasonal revenues. The Arkansas River has white-water runs from level 1 to level 5 and is the site of many of these festivals and activities, one of which is the largest such event in the state of Colorado. Rafting has become so popular that there are now sixty-five rafting companies in and around the city. Another warm-weather activity is bicycling; more than eleven thousand cyclists come through Salida annually, making small purchases that help buoy the local merchants as well as the local tax base. And, during the cold weather, skiing is a popular pastime in the area and the city benefits from the revenues generated by that activity.

When asked about the extent to which Salida could grow, Mayor Dickson replied emphatically, "The population and the job base will not grow greatly. We like it the way it is now. We don't want a big surge. Growth can ruin everything. We want to keep our quality of life the way it is." This is a perspective that only some small cities and towns that are isolated from larger metropolitan areas can afford because they have attractions for tourists who will come to town and leave their money behind. Salida is one such location, and it works well for that city because the revenues are spread across all seasons; there are no "downtimes" for the economy. Other interviews in this research are with cities for which that is not an option because they are so isolated that they feel they absolutely need to grow in order to survive at all.

One of the interesting considerations for this research relates to the men and women who serve in elected positions in the case study cities. Typically, they do not have interest in further elective office, or even in remaining in the one they presently hold for an indefinite period. Mayor Dickson is not from Colorado. He met his wife, who grew up in Salida, and fell in love with the town and its people. A retired aviator and Forest Service official, Mayor Dickson sees his biggest challenge as maintaining the status quo. The city is managed by a strong professional team; he merely needs to sustain the presently high quality of life and keep the area in his charge as pristine as possible. "We like it the way it is." And, they can afford to keep it that way.

Issues for economic growth	• Growth will alter the quality of life
Strategies for economic growth	• Attract creative retailers
	• Promote festivals and outdoor activities
Lessons learned	• Cities must work hard to maintain the quality of life as they grow

Winnemucca, Nevada

Over the past two decades, the population of Winnemucca, Nevada, has grown significantly and consistently. The city, named for a Paiute Indian chief, also boasts an unemployment rate that is well below the national average. Located at the intersection of two major roads—US Highway 95 and Interstate 80—Winnemucca can offer businesses excellent transportation connections, including a railroad with daily departures for Salt Lake, San Francisco, and Chicago.

Economic development assets also include twenty-four-hour gaming and numerous outdoor activities, including numerous bow hunting competitions and other activities. One point of discussion for the city's leadership was the revenue sources from which they build the city's budget. Given the nature of the attractions, sales taxes or transient occupancy taxes could be the most productive. It was interesting to learn how local governments in the state of Nevada constitute their budgets.

Photo courtesy of Eddie Davis.

Interview with Steve West, City Manager of Winnemucca, Nevada

Winnemucca has an economy that has always been, and remains today, based on agriculture and mining. That latter component is presently gaining in relative strength and thus provides significant employment opportunities. Its uncertainty as an economic basis for long-term stability, however, may also be a challenge.

Winnemucca is a hub city for a very large region. It is more isolated even than most of the cities in this study, lying 168 miles from the next largest urban area—Reno, Nevada. This means that city merchants must provide all the retail outlets needed by citizens and businesses as well as recreation, dining, and cultural events.

A small component of the local economy is gaming. Although it is a small piece of the economic picture in Winnemucca, City Manager West notes that the city has tried to create a services industry around it. This includes eleven hundred hotel rooms, a number of service stations and restaurants, and a few warehouse and distribution operations at or near the junction of the nearby Interstate 80 and US Route 95. Also supporting the visitation to the city is a small regional airport and convention facility. This may have limited impact, however, as the passengers have to pass through the airport in Reno to get to Winnemucca and can simply stay there to have access to more and much larger gaming and tourism facilities, as well as shows and other types of attractions. Mostly, people would need to fly to Reno and then drive three hours to Winnemucca, which limits the competitiveness of the city's gaming establishments.

The severe isolation of the city makes economic development attraction a very difficult exercise. "We were able to bring in a manufacturer about fifteen years ago, but our opportunities this far away from things are pretty limited. We have a Walmart Superstore because we are the only place in the whole region to shop. There are about eight thousand people in the city and another seven thousand in the rest of the region."

Retail operations are greatly appreciated by City Manager West because they provide sales tax revenues for the city's budget. Through the late 1970s, Nevada's cities benefitted more fully from property taxes generated on land and buildings in their limits. However, the state of Nevada capped local property tax rates, leaving the cities more dependent on sales tax generation. Nevada has a 6.85 percent sales tax, about one-fourth of which goes to the counties and half to the state. About one-fourth remains with the locality in which it was generated. Sales tax revenues today represent about one-third of the city's budget, from which it provides the full array of municipal public services.

It is a major problem for the city that sales taxes are neither a stable nor reliable source of revenues for Winnemucca. Moreover, the city can neither forecast such revenues nor control the forces that influence them. The forces affecting the city's revenues from mining, for example, are dependent upon national and global demand as well as the availability of supply from alternative sources. All of these factors can affect operations or supply and demand, and thus pricing. Expendable income levels are the direct cause of more or less spending in the gaming operations. At the end of that chain lies the city budget of Winnemucca, Nevada.

In addition to the uncertainty of revenues, the Internet has hurt the local economy of Winnemucca. The rather extreme isolation of the city has meant that people have to buy everything locally. "Now, their options, and even the prices, are better on the Internet. It costs our retailers some sales and the city some sales taxes."

Whenever mining operators are in need of new equipment, sales rise and the city benefits. Mining in the area includes silver and lithium, but is primarily mining for gold. The region suffered through significant layoffs in the mines in the early eighties and again in the early nineties. "It's been a little more stable since then, but we always worry about it."

City Manager West notes, "Economic development incentives are really important for us when we try to attract manufacturers. This is something we have to do. There is a lot of competition from cities that are not so isolated, and there is only so much we can do. We do try to keep the city beautiful so people will want to be here." That includes significant projects in the parks, repairing potholes, and improving the facades in the downtown. "We just have so many cards stacked against us, being so isolated."

The obvious question to be explored is whether, in the case of a mining shutdown in Winnemucca, the city would survive. West feels that it would be able to survive, although the situation might become pretty bleak. "The city has been very conservative in the use of its available resources. We have planned for the worst to happen. We have no city debt and a very strong reserve position." After some reflection, West added, "Still, it could be very difficult for us to survive the loss of mining here if that happens down the road. We are so isolated."

Politics even enters in to the picture for Winnemucca. The Nevada legislature is dominated by the state's two largest population centers, Reno and Las Vegas. Rather than using the revenues from those cities to help the small cities survive, they are now considering the use of the revenues from mining operations from here and around the state to support those primary urban areas. "We'll make it," said City Manager West, "but it will always be difficult because we are so isolated."

Issues for economic growth	• Severe isolation
	• Overdependence on sales taxes
	• Seasonality of commerce
Strategies for economic growth	• Attract hotels, restaurants, and other activities around the casino
	• Use incentives to attract businesses
	• City beautification programs
Lessons learned	• Incentives are a necessary means of attracting businesses to small towns
	• Businesses want to locate in attractive places

Taos, New Mexico

Taos, New Mexico, is a thriving community. In the period from 1990 to 2000, the city's population base grew by more than 10 percent, and in the ensuing five-year period, it grew again by another 9 percent. Yet, the rate of unemployment was marginally lower than the national average at the time of this writing.

Originally an area that was home to several Indian tribes, this part of northeast New Mexico still offers much of this type of history and culture to enjoy. This is complemented by a thriving artists' colony as well as a vital, sustainable economy.

The city's 2013 strategic plan for economic development is quite in depth in its analysis and available online through the city's website. In it, there is a SWOT analysis that outlines the strengths, weaknesses, opportunities, and threats for the city's economic growth into the future. A greatly abbreviated excerpt follows (City of Taos, 2013):

Strengths: Natural surroundings and cultural heritage.
Weaknesses: Traffic congestion, affordable housing.
Opportunities: An arts district, convention facility.
Threats: Vacant buildings, high costs, decreasing state and federal resources, heavy retail leakages.

The plan also lists the economic development attraction targets for the city of Taos. These include organic and nontoxic personal product manufacture; software programming; publishing, editing, and transcription; and gourmet and organic food production. An interesting topic of discussion for the city's leadership focused on those industry segments and the reasons for their selection as targets for the city of Taos.

The University of New Mexico–Taos and the Southern Methodist University branch in the area present themselves as strong economic development assets that can play roles in business attraction and retention. The manner in which that takes places in Taos was a topic for discussion with the city's leadership.

Photo courtesy of the city of Taos.

Interview with Rick Bellis, City Manager of Taos, New Mexico

Like some of the other case study cities in this research, Taos both entered the national recession and emerged from it somewhat after the rest of the country. Town Manager Bellis explained that this is the result of having an economy that benefits from tourist revenues and a city budget that is dependent largely upon hotel tax contributions.

Generally, the town's economic history is best characterized as a series of significant fluctuations. The boom years of the 1990s were followed by several years of decline that were reversed by gains in tourism through about 2006. From that point, the tourist industry in Taos began a slow slide in revenues once again. As a consequence, the construction industry, once quite strong in Taos, left the area completely. Bellis counsels that throughout the course of this recent economic history, reported financial and economic data being reported for Taos tells a different story, and he cautions against relying on the data alone without knowing the backstory. This is not the first time this note of caution has been sounded by municipal leaders in this research.

In the case of the economic reports about Taos, the local economy had been artificially propped up for several years because the county around the town built a new administrative complex, including admin buildings, a jail, and other structures. As a result, job numbers, employment opportunities, and economic impact data all gave a rosy view of growth and spending in and around the city that gave the impression of permanence. However, when the projects were completed, the numbers returned to their normal levels and the information very quickly told the underlying and more permanent story.

Tourism to Taos and the attractions in the surrounding area has increased in recent years; however, the expenditures by visitors to the town of Taos have declined. This has had dramatic impacts for the town's budget and its ability to finance public services. The revenues are inconsistent and much more easily forecasted on a month-to-month basis than on any predictable annual cycles. To fill in the gaps a little, the town has arranged for a popular performer to appear in concert in the town. Ticket sales are expected to boost revenues, even if only on a one-time basis.

One economic boon for Taos has been that the area's ski resorts have had constant levels of snowfall over recent seasons. This, coupled with very poor snow years for the resorts in neighboring Colorado, has benefitted the Taos and New Mexico slopes, which has in turn helped stabilize the municipal budget revenues. This recent, albeit temporary, comparative success taught the region a lesson. City Manager Bellis noted that the region and its attractions, including the many ski resorts, must promote themselves as a regional cluster rather than individually. "It is the only way to compete with places like Vale and Aspen."

The budget of the city of Taos is constituted largely from hotel tax revenues, with additional revenues coming from sales taxes. Property taxes are received by the county and represent its primary source for the provision of its public services. In a refrain repeated in several other case study interviews, Bellis notes that the county receives the property tax revenues—a much more stable and consistent revenue source—while the town is required to pay the bill for infrastructure, airport operations, libraries, recreational facilities, the landfill operations, and more.

This has caused Bellis to become an avid proponent of a regional approach to the provision of what are now redundant public services across numerous municipal entities. "We can't afford to have multiple facilities or multiple staff doing the same jobs. The big one will have to be airport operations. Marketing and tourism can be done jointly for the whole region. And then, economic development may be next."

Because Taos has, for generations, had a reputation as an artist's colony, Town Manager Bellis was asked about the stability of that renown as an underpinning of a sustainable local economy. Surprisingly, that reputation, as well as the reality of arts and related tourism as an economic generator for Taos, was described as "misleading." In fact, Bellis advised that only about 2 percent of the town's economy comes from the artists and the galleries.

That scene has changed dramatically over recent years, owing mostly to the advent of commercial sales over the Internet. "The galleries have had their worst year this year, and many of them may be closing within the year." For a long time, the tourists used to be middle-aged buyers who came to the galleries to make their purchases and stayed in town while they did so. Today, "brokers and the Internet make it easier for buyers to acquire what they want without coming into Taos."

Bellis instructs: "Today we have a different visitor profile. They're eighteen to thirty and they want things to do … things outdoors. They want things they can experience. They don't want to buy pottery; they want to make pottery themselves." Bellis believes that the town needs to understand who the new visitors are and provide them with what they want. Some of the possibilities in response to those interests have been free concerts, restoration of the downtown plaza and its buildings (all of which are on the National Register of Historic Places), and events that focus on the unique natural and human history of the region.

Town Manager Bellis offers an important lesson. It is one that has been repeated in other interviews: "You must have a full-time and professional economic development program. In our case, it must be regional, but it cannot be part-time or done by someone without experience in the business of economic development. It's too important."

At present, there is no such person or organization in Taos or who represents the region. Individual efforts to attract tourism dominate—and compete with each other. There is no well-thought-out economic development plan, with industry targets or strategies for attraction and retention. There is no inventory of existing buildings or available land. Bellis has a clear understanding of what economic development is and how to make it happen more efficiently, but it simply does not exist at the present time. "People just thought that tourists would always come here and that we wouldn't have to worry about it, and that is no longer so. We are just getting started on this but it has to be done."

One of the key components of the economic development program envisioned by Bellis is that it must be nonpolitical. It can be neither partisan nor dependent upon political masters. His experience in other locations has been that political oversight of such programs can result in a misdirection of efforts for purposes other than the growth of the economy and the improvement of the community. "If you can get rid of the politics, egos, personal interests, you can do bigger things regionally. Small towns must band together. Consolidation isn't just nice; it's necessary."

When asked whether he thought Taos could survive, Bellis expressed that it would, but only if the right things are done. The area benefits from consistent snowfalls and a "reasonable proximity" to Santa Fe, but it must promote itself to travelers. "We need to build workforce housing and reestablish the secondary home building industry here in Taos. We need to build a more diverse economy in the town and in the region. We are trying to cultivate our image as a cool place, and to do that, we need to get our film festival back again. We need to upgrade the existing hotels in town. We will need to spend money on some things. We are surviving but we will have to work hard at it."

Bellis feels that too many small towns still "have their hands out" to state and federal government agencies and programs. "We can't depend on government alone; those who do are going to die over time. We should act like businesses. Then, we can survive."

Issues for economic growth	• Seasonality of commerce
	• Seasonality of tax base
	• Need for regional cooperation
	• State tax policies for municipalities
Strategies for economic growth	• Create attractions for off-seasons
	• Create activities for younger visitors
	• Depoliticize and professionalize the economic development program
Lessons learned	• For small, isolated cities, economic development must be regional
	• The economic development function must be full-time and professional

Vernal, Utah

Although small enough and sufficiently isolated to qualify for this research, Vernal, Utah, is the largest city in northeastern Utah. Unlike many of the cities in this study, Vernal has seen its population grow in the past decade or two. Although the area was originally established as a Uintah Indian reservation, Vernal's population today is approximately 92 percent white (http://www.usbeacon.com). The unemployment rate (3.8 percent) (http://www.bestplaces.net) in Vernal at the time of this writing also distinguishes it from the other communities in this research. The dual distinctions of an increasing population and a very low unemployment rate were topics for the interview with the city's leadership.

Much of what can be found online regarding the economic base of Vernal relates to tourism activity. The Dinosaur National Monument is a large area that has been protected since 1915 and encompasses more than 210,000 acres in which prehistoric animal and plant fossils from the late Jurassic period have been well-preserved. Other attractions include whitewater and other outdoor activities along the Green and Yampa Rivers, as well as various festivals and celebrations, rodeos, cross-country skiing, and more.

Photo courtesy of the city of Vernal.

Interview with Ken Bassett, City Manager of Vernal, Utah

As a small town city manager, Ken Bassett is certainly unusual, perhaps unique. He has been the city manager of Vernal, Utah, for thirty-six years. In fact, he echoes the voices of others in this research when he speaks of his family: he has six children, all of whom left for bigger cities and four of whom have returned to raise their families. "Quality of life is everything."

Vernal exists in a valley that holds thirty-five thousand residents, a little less than one-third of whom reside in its largest city, Vernal. The city was originally settled in 1898 by Mormon pioneers and others moving westward to seek land and adventure.

Over time, the city grew as the result of discoveries of abundant natural gas and oil reserves in the area. Also over time, the federal government elected, in the interests of environmental protection, to apply a range of regulations and restrictions to the extraction of those natural resources. These superimposed requirements, coupled with the peaks and valleys created by the international economy and its impacts on the prices of oil and natural gas, have in turn created constant fluctuations in the economy of Vernal and the budget resources from which it provides services to its constituents.

City Manager Bassett notes that many other cities have similar interests and similar concerns. But Vernal is impacted even more than those cities because the oil and gas reserves in its region are located on federal property and subject to regulation without any congressional authorization. Once again, the changes are completely out of the control of the locality or its leadership, and even the representatives in Congress cannot control the issues. The administrators of the relevant departments and agencies of the federal government create the regulatory oversight at their level.

Because these forces are so impactful, and because they are completely out of control of the city's leadership, City Manager Bassett stresses the vital importance of setting aside as much of the revenues generated from those sources during the good times as possible. "Even though there is a temptation in those times to spend on large-scale projects, the city must save during the rich times. I will not leave the city with such incredible debt that they wonder how they will ever pay it off!"

Another reason for the great concern in Vernal over how these regulatory measures are applied is due to the fact that there are substantial remaining reserves in the area that can be the source of economic growth for well into the future. But, planning on that basis is difficult due to the external and inconsistent forces at play.

In order to ensure smoother economic growth, Vernal pursues additional economic drivers for its economy. The tourism trade is one such area. Vernal is home to the Dinosaur Park that is described above. State Highway 40 runs right through the city and brings with it trade for the local merchants. The city's objective is to keep some of that traffic in the city to patronize the local hotels and restaurants, and to see some of the local sites.

Of course, much of the city's economic development outreach is aimed at the retailers the city's population wants and needs. They provide jobs and needed clothing and other items, and they contribute to the city's tax base through the sales taxes, which constitute roughly 80 percent of Vernal's general fund expenditures. The larger contributions to the sales tax base come from the oil and gas extraction and sales (in the good times). The advantage of the retail trade is that much of it comes from travelers to Vernal from other places. Even so, City Manager Bassett advises developers and merchants to be very careful in doing their due diligence before establishing a presence in Vernal because the area's economy has historically been subject to such peaks and valleys.

One of the impacts of those fluctuations has been the attraction of workers to the community when times are booming and their departure when times get bad. In one example, Bassett noted that people "just left their homes and went on their way." This has, on occasion, left the city with unoccupied properties that require a range of public services without generating any of the revenue that helps to support those services.

Generally speaking, Bassett feels the residents of the area are a resilient group. He refers to the longer-term residents of Vernal as troopers. Many of the newcomers "expect greater consistency in these things and you just have to educate them. They will see: as we look forward, keep an eye on Vernal. Watch Vernal!"

Issues for economic growth	• Inconsistency of oil and gas prices
Strategies for economic growth	• Economic diversification
	• Market for tourism
Lessons learned	• Work hard to maintain the city's quality of life as you grow
	• Diversify the local economy

Chapter 3

Conclusions about Growth in America's Small and Isolated Cities

The Relevance of Lessons Learned in Micropolitan Cities to Those That Are Small and Isolated

The research conducted for *The Economic Viability of Micropolitan America* revealed lessons that were consistent across many of the seventy community case studies. Of course, variations were evident from one location to the next, but overall, it was possible to make several assertions about what enables or retards the growth of the local economies in cities of that size, given their distance from larger urban areas.

Clearly, not all of the conclusions derived from that research were exactly applicable to all of the case studies examined. Let's call it variations on the themes; the lessons are simply generalities that can serve other leaders in other cities of similar size and geography as indicators and guideposts. The extension of the variable applications of those lessons is whether they can be considered to be consistent when applied to even smaller cities: those that are small and alone.

Clearly, the thesis at this point is that there are sufficient distinctions between micropolitan cities and towns, and towns of fewer than ten thousand inhabitants that some or all of the lessons from the former do not translate well to the latter. In fact, Schaeffer and Loveridge (2000) wrote: "The lack of role models may contribute to a sense of helplessness that sometimes affects these communities." And, if such were not the case, this research would have been unnecessary. So, beginning from the premise that the distinctions are indeed real and substantial, it may be best to consider how that is applicable to the current research in two ways: community size and the degree of isolation.

A city or town that has between ten thousand and fifty thousand residents, despite its proximity or lack of proximity to an even larger urban area, may have sufficient size to be more self-sufficient than a small town. At some break point in size, the city is too small to provide all of that which is necessary for its survival. People in cities of any size will require a given set of personal services, retail, medical, educational, and other services. If only ten people live in a town, it is very unlikely that it can possess all of the necessary services and it must go outside to procure them. If they are close enough to another city, the critical mass grows and may, at some point, become sufficient.

Where is this break point? How many people is enough to ensure that all the needs of the city's inhabitants are provided? Of course, there is no specific number, but the implications are clear: some number will be too few and another will be adequate.

Now, let's introduce the notion of a very small city also being isolated (i.e., fifty miles from another city that is larger). The ability to add the demand created by several small cities in order to be sufficient to sustain those needed services disappears. Now, the inherent issue in both size and isolation becomes what critical services can be accessed by the residents of small cities and towns, what they can live without, and what alternatives can be acquired?

Will Technology Enable Small Towns to Survive?

An argument can be made—and is made—that small and isolated businesses can survive more readily today than in the past because of the advent of enabling technologies. The argument posits that one need not necessarily be physically co-located with all of one's colleagues in order to be maximally productive because the work can flow across high-speed communications lines and thereby permit work to flow in the same manner and speed as if one were at the next desk. Indeed, one writer noted, "Counties that had access to broadband services had lower unemployment levels, due largely to businesses being attracted to areas where they could operate through high-speed internet access" (Bilotta, 2009).

While there is certainly a case to be made for technology having such an enabling impact that people can work from extreme distances, one might also reasonably wonder whether this is possible in actual practice. And if it is, why has this trend not become more apparent than it has been? Certainly, the enabling technologies have been available for some time. In fact, if this is such an impactful trend, why are there so many technology and other workers still employed in our most dense downtown markets?

To some, the assertion may bring to mind the concerns of movie theaters upon the emergence of movies on tape that can be viewed more cheaply and easily at home. Some depicted the demise of movie theaters, which of course never happened. In fact, the opposite trend occurred: there were increases registered in movie going. It turned out that the social component of theater going was a vital component of the experience: people went out, got sitters for the kids, had dates, and enjoyed the big screen. You don't get all of that on the living room sofa.

In the world of work, there is a very strong collaborative element. The sharing of ideas, the common experience of working together on one project enhances the ability to team on the next project. Working with a team in Nebraska while you're at home in Delaware is not "just like being there."

This is not to say that technology cannot enable some people to work on some things from different places, but it may portend large-scale trends. In the long term, it is not the saving grace for small towns in search of better jobs for their residents. They will need to bring the employers to the community. To a large extent, if you want to draw your workforce from a small, isolated town in Wyoming, that's where you need to have your physical location.

Are There Advantages for Employers in Small, Isolated Cities?

Employers are comprised of people, and people have as many different sets of tastes as there are people to ask. Thus, if a company locates in an area, it must be mindful of the types of men and women who live in or nearby the relevant city. The people you will get to work for you must be those who wish to live in the environment selected, whether that's an urban area or a rural one. Those who live in small, isolated cities are generally thought to possess strong work ethics, positive family values, and a sense of reliability.

These are all good things from an employer's perspective, but there is an overlay for these rural residents: they are so intent upon those values that they are willing to forego the benefits of living in a more urbanized environment, such as cultural, educational, and other social opportunities and interactions. In the summation, employers must consider the environments available to them as well as the types of people they attract, and then select that which best fits their business plans. Small towns are great for some, but they are not for everyone. As such, that type of community can be both the blessing and the curse for small town economies.

Why Should We Care about America's Cities That Are Small and Isolated?

The potential for many of America's small, isolated towns to become ghost towns is considered to be rather strong. One writer, in reference to the 478 small towns in

North Carolina in 2000, said, "With little tax base and few other resources to help reverse the decline, towns are left wondering: Can they survive?" (Pulver, 2005).

Is there a reason that we should be concerned about the cities across this nation that are small and alone? After all, they are small so, by definition, the impacts of their losses will be relatively insignificant. And, if we are going to be able to compete head-to-head with nations like China and India and others where the costs are naturally less and the public sector supports private enterprise with investments not available in the United States, can we afford to prop up these cities and towns artificially? Could we not be more competitive if we did likewise, thereby implying that contributions to small areas might be foregone?

In brief, why not just let them survive if they can, and go away if not? From a purely economic point of view, the answer might be related to the need to have such communities as supports for those engaged in agricultural or other largely rural business pursuits. But, Carr and Kefalas (2009) wrote that their loss would be "ultimately detrimental not only to the region but to the nation as a whole. Put simply, without them, the country couldn't function."

From a broader, perhaps even philosophical perspective, small cities and towns that are not immediately proximate to larger urban areas are the roots of America. This nation has always been about freedom of choice. Thus, even though it may not be maximally efficient in economic terms, people need to be able to choose the settings in which to live or work if that is their personal preference. To allow them to decline when they can be supported—and sustained—would be a travesty.

One very important reason for assessing the economic vitality of these small cities and towns is that there is a great sense expressed in the literature that these towns are actually essential to the national character. People regard the presumed slower pace of life, the healthier and more wholesome environment, the lower costs and safer neighborhoods, and the longing for a sense of community that is not readily found in more urbanized areas, and express a tug to try that type of lifestyle and raise their families there. Having said this, the conclusion is that there should thus be sufficient demand for residences in these cities that the problems of size should be resolved.

Special Considerations for Small, Isolated Cities and Towns

The Brain Drain and Postsecondary Education

In urban areas with larger population bases than those represented in this research, the loss of a single large employer—or even an entire single industry—will be damaging but not necessarily devastating to the local economy. This may be simply because the communities are large enough to have other employment options for residents. Or, it may be because the workforce of the departing companies can sustain themselves long enough to become, collectively, an attractive asset for another employer to come to town.

For many of the communities included in this research, however, the loss of a large employer or a single industry may leave those employees without local options. The result is their departure to other, often distant, locations to find work. This is the so-called brain drain and is often next to impossible to forestall. The dual dramatic impacts of job loss and tax base decline can mean extremely difficult times for the community in question. In the case of isolated communities, the challenge is greater still because residents may not even have the option of driving great distances to work in other towns. In many cases, they have no choice but to move.

This brain drain means that the city is left without the very asset it needs to attract a new business. In cases like that, the community may have an option to upgrade the skills of those who remain in order to have a relevant workforce to entice new employers. In larger cities and regions, the training option often defaults to the local branch of a larger institution, often a public college or university, which can provide skills training for a variety of fields. In the case of small, isolated towns, the potential for training or retraining a workforce generally more appropriately falls to community colleges or technical schools that can provide the kinds of skilled employees that are required by the employers that are more typically found in these settings.

This raises the question of how community colleges can become engaged in the economic development efforts of small, isolated cities. As many of the interviews with mayors and city managers alluded to the importance of these partnerships for local growth, I selected a strong example to illustrate the types of things these institutions can do to help their communities grow.

Craig Fowler is the executive in charge of the Rice Lake, Wisconsin, branch of the Wisconsin Indianhead Technical College (WITC). His perspective is vital because he also served in similar institutions in larger urban areas and was helpful in identifying what programs work well in smaller cities and towns as opposed to more populous, connected regions.

WITC has four campuses throughout a catchment area that includes about three hundred thousand residents. Each of the campuses is different because they reflect the specific and very diverse needs and interests of the localities in which they are located.

The Rice Lake campus offers four areas of strength to the local business community. Continuing education includes the totality of programs that are made available to residents who wish to upgrade their skills in order to begin a career or to expand their options at a midpoint in their careers. Professional development programs are offered for men and women who need periodic training and review to achieve or maintain professional certifications. In the past, this has included EMT and other public safety employees. The college has also provided safety training for those who will be employed in mine fracking in the region.

Another area of support for local businesses is the WITC Conference Center, which is available for use by companies in the area. This has proven to work well for the companies but has also supported the local hotels and restaurants while the trainees are in town.

Finally, the customized training effort of WITC is designed to provide skills instruction to the workforce of a specific company, thus allowing the training to be highly tailored to the needs of that business and the exact equipment on which the individuals are working.

Training of the local residents is an important function for WITC because, in a recent five-year longitudinal study, it was revealed that after six months, 91 percent of graduates were still employed, and more than 72 percent were employed in a field directly related to their training. Nearly 80 percent of the graduates were still employed after six months in the state of Wisconsin, meaning that the investment in WITC by the taxpayers of Wisconsin is being returned many times over. Just under 70 percent of these graduates still resided and worked in the eleven-county region around Rice Lake, which means that there is a strong correlation between the training being offered and the employers' demands.

Fowler provided an excellent example of the customized training that may be instructive for other such institutions in small isolated cities and towns. A large paper manufacturer with seventy-five to one hundred employees moved into the county adjacent to that in which Rice Lake is located. The county into which it moved was the poorest in the state of Wisconsin. Before the training began for the residents who had secured jobs with the new employer, WITC paid to have the actual machine the workforce would operate shipped to the classroom. After the training was completed, it was returned to the employer's location.

Other communities can cite programs that have worked in their respective areas as well. Community and technical colleges can foster growth in these communities, help to sustain business operations, and contribute to the long-term growth of the area's economy.

If You Build It, Will They Really Come?

Many of the small town leaders interviewed for this text expressed what remains an economic development conundrum—sometimes cited in a conscious manner and other times in a subconscious way. The issue is whether to prepare now for possible growth or wait until there is a prospect with a given need that can be addressed on the spot.

Numerous interviewees mentioned that they felt strongly that a small city cannot wait until there is an active prospect to be in play to prepare the sites and infrastructure the employers require in order to select their area. Simply put, the competition is great for a relatively few economic development prospects, and if one town doesn't have everything to offer the employer immediately—or at least fairly quickly—it will opt to go elsewhere. There is a certain amount of logic in this point of view. It is the companion piece to the "build it and they will come" mentality: if you don't build it, they will not come.

In recognition of this need to be prepared for an employer that *might* give the city consideration as a place to locate a facility, many small towns have paid in advance to prepare an industrial park, complete with infrastructure. The costs are often quite high, and this can be an extraordinarily big gamble for a small town. The gamble lies in the possibility that no one will come, or that the time until they come is greater than planners had hoped. In the meantime, the city must carry the costs of the required debt service, maintenance, utilities, and more.

Those who are willing to take such a great risk will counter with the argument that this is an investment rather than a cost, and that the ultimate payoff will come in the form of jobs, income, expenditures in the community, and financial stability for the local government.

As the reader might suspect, both stories can be found in cities of varying sizes. It is likely that, for a smaller city or town, the costs represent a much greater proportion of local financial capability, and therefore a much greater risk. Of course, some cities proceed with such plans anyway either because they believe it will work or they believe they can hold out until it does. In some cases, they seem simply to find no other satisfactory option or they feel the need to do something, and this strategy is the best option they can identify. As an option, it is a sound approach if one understands and addresses fully the potential negative consequences in advance of starting the process.

But, just a comprehension of the potential downside of such a strategy—the wait-and-see period—is not enough. City leaders need also to fully appreciate the opportunity costs involved. That is, what will need to be sacrificed if this doesn't—or until it does—work? Debt service and the other costs associated with the interim period (until an employer makes a positive decision to locate in the park and begins to return the investment in the form of tax payments) can be high. Communities need to plan forward to decide what services they will *not* be able to support as a result. There are very difficult decisions to be made if one builds it and no one comes. Is this worth the equivalent expenditures for five more teachers, or a new police station, or a new fire truck?

Big gambles for large-scale projects entail risk. In a smaller city or town, the risk can be comparatively greater than for larger urban areas. And, risk requires careful planning, political and community-wide support, and a willingness to make potential sacrifices in other areas of public services. Perhaps the greatest element of the conundrum lies in the oft-cited need by interviewees to remain fiscally conservatives in small towns. In fact, many proudly stated that their cities had eliminated all debt in order to retain needed levels of public services in times when the critical budgetary revenue streams were down.

This fiscal conservatism is also a valid strategy, and there is no real clear answer to the level of acceptable risk to be taken in this way by a small town. The only legitimate answer is that if it works, it was a good strategy to pursue; if not, it was a bad idea.

This brings the discussion to the final element of risk: political. Those who set the city on the path of a risky strategy that paid a handsome return on an investment will be recognized for their vision and success. Those who pursue the approach of site preparation in hopes that an employer will locate to the park, but find that none do, may be forever associated with the failure and even with the loss of other public services in the interim. Economic development requires risk by the city and political risk by its leadership.

Chapter 4

A Special Case Study: Raton, New Mexico

What Happens to a City without Jobs?

One of the consequences of a city where the economy is on the decline is that it ultimately begins to lose the very institutions and pillars of the community that would be needed to re-create a vital and growing economic base. That may include the workforce, doctors, or other personal services. In one interview, it was noted that the city had lost its optometrist and residents now had to travel long distances for eyeglasses. In another interview, it was noted that the hospitals had downsized and patients who needed MRIs had to travel for that service. More serious medical treatment options were certainly located in larger urban areas.

A primary company in a small town is generally the most actively supportive entity in terms of supporting numerous types of community activities. These may include churches, Little Leagues, soup kitchens, scout troops, arts organizations, and more. What is left is a city with fewer jobs, a brain drain that has taken away the best and the brightest, a generally older population that may have greater public service demands, and a diminished local budget and diminished public services.

Not only can the amenities that make small towns attractive to many individuals decline, but also critical services can be diminished. This might include railroad or airline levels, hospital service, police and fire, retail offerings, and more.

But, these losses can be just the start of even greater losses for small, isolated cities or towns. When retail opportunities move away, people either have to travel to shop for clothes, food, or other essential items, or have to become significantly more self-sufficient. In the long run, residents begin to consider relocating to communities where these basic needs are available.

One loss that is less common but equally devastating is the loss of the local press. It is an institution that helps connect people in a small town and helps to promote the best of what it has to offer potential new residents or businesses. In July 2013, an article appeared in the Raton, New Mexico, newspaper, *Raton Range*. Its publisher wrote the heartrending piece that is included in part below. After decades of publication and numerous last-minute attempts to rescue the paper, it was closing—at least temporarily. An interview with the publisher of the *Raton Range* seemed in order because she had so eloquently made my case and because she had done so from the inside, looking out. In short, she had summarized the core thesis of this research: small, isolated cities and towns are constantly at risk of not being able to survive. One of the positive attributes of small towns is that people know each other and tend to pull together in crises. The means by which communications about others' lives is enabled is the local newspaper. To lose that connection means to lose a vital conduit for human interaction and the transmission of news about how best to work together to rebuild and revitalize the community. Without such an institution as the *Raton Range*, recovery becomes an increasingly daunting challenge.

Excerpts from an article that appeared in the July 19, 2013, issue of the *Raton Range* follow:

Range Sees Temporary Closure

By Paula Murphy, Publisher

> As some of you have noticed, *The Raton Range* did not appear in your mailbox, or store shelves Friday. I apologize for that. As many of you know, the population of Raton continues to decline. Many of the businesses that drove a tremendous retail town are no longer in business or are barely hanging on. The businesses that are able to remain open do so mainly because they have no debt. But that still doesn't mean that they are making it. They are spending their reserves in hopes that things will turn around.
>
> My hope was that things *would* turn around. I think we were all hopeful to get the racetrack back. We all remember the days of having five thousand people in Raton for the weekend. The days when all the shops were full, the restaurants had a waiting list; all the hotels and motels had to turn people away.
>
> We remember the days when five hundred plus miners went to work every day and spent their money in Raton.
>
> Those days are gone. My company is saddled with so much debt that it would take the glory days of advertising revenue to pay it back. I don't see that happening in the near future....

I tried until late Friday afternoon to finalize a deal with a group of investors to help me to continue to bring this community the local news of our area. But, that deal would not work for me….

My heart is breaking for our communities. I have worked at the *Raton Range* for twenty-eight years. And, I know its importance. I know how people rely on the information we have so thoroughly produced for them. We have struggled with issues that a lot of people didn't like but we did it because it was the news….

In my twenty-eight years, of working with this award-winning newspaper, I have never seen the economy so bad. I see the constant worry in the faces of my advertisers and my own reflection in the mirror. I have tried. Believe me, I have tried….

In closing, please know that I have to accept what is, to let go of what was, and to have faith in what will be.

Thank you all and may God bless you.

Interview with Paula Murphy, Publisher of the *Raton Range*

I spoke to Murphy by phone in May 2014. She no longer lives in Raton; she has moved across the border into Trinidad, Colorado. I told her that I had spent some time in Raton back in 1970. I remembered it as a pleasant town with warm and friendly people and a thriving downtown with busy shops and diners. I told her I could not fully comprehend her letter in the paper at first. Although I had theorized that this is precisely what happens in many small towns, I had thought of primarily how it affected cities and towns in decline. It was a bit of a shock to me that a town could fall so far.

What I learned was that virtually any small town can be potentially subject to some of the impacts.

The interview was not an easy one for Murphy. Her heart seemed still to be in Raton. She had been there for a long time. When she bought the paper, the advertising revenues had been stable over time. She worked hard and they grew to about $1.2 million per year. "That was when the advertisers could pay their bills and when Second Street, which is our main street, had had plenty of motels and restaurants that were packed."

The problems began in 1996 when the racetrack closed down and the summertime revenues to local vendors disappeared. Then, in 2004, with the closing of the local mine and the loss of five hundred jobs "overnight," people left; five hundred jobs meant the loss of up to five hundred families—potentially thousands of people.

Each loss of a company in town resulted in the loss of advertising revenues for the *Raton Range*. When the city lost its K-Mart store in 2005, the newspaper's revenues declined immediately by $96,000 annually. That was followed by the closure of the city's largest grocery store: $36,000 more in advertising had been lost. The "mom and pop" shops held on, but they didn't do much advertising.

Finally, the small shops also began to close their doors. The paper and its publisher were able to hang on for years, but the need for newer printing technology was the last straw and the paper had to close its doors. It should be noted, however, that hanging on meant that while the employees of the newspaper did get paid, its publisher did not. For six years!

In today's Raton, the largest remaining employers are the city, the county, the hospital, and the school district. Of course, as people leave Raton for jobs elsewhere, those institutions are also reducing their workforces and closing doors.

But the city, and the region in which it resides, was not finished with the various shocks to the economic system. The state of Colorado passed legislation that placed heavier regulations on the mining industry, and the local operations of El Paso Energy moved on to less restrictive Texas as a result. At that point, as Murphy put it, "All the employers that paid decent wages were gone."

And, they were still not done. The state of New Mexico agreed to issue five gambling licenses to Indian tribes and two to other municipalities. Raton won one of the licenses and saw a possible light at the end of the tunnel. Plans were drawn up in 2007 for a "Racino," a combination racetrack and casino, but the developer and his funding sources were questionable and the plans fell through. The city awaits word about the possibilities of retaining the license.

In Raton, Murphy asserts, the local elected officials were empaneled because they were popular and not because they could necessarily be effective. When the situation became seemingly irretrievable, the populace gave up. In the absence of leadership with a plan to move forward, "the impact on morale was horrible, absolutely horrible. Even the rich—those with old money—left Raton. One person had an enormous home on forty acres right in the heart of the city and they left. People would just leave … hand over the keys to houses they couldn't sell, and leave."

Her assessment of Raton's officialdom is given credence by yet another incident. At the height of the problems in Raton, the New Mexico highway department decided that Raton's main street (Second Avenue) needed a median strip. This rather surprising project took a stunningly long period of time to complete, during which the street in front of the shops that were still opened was entirely shut down. This meant that patrons would have to enter the shops through their rear doors. It turned out to be much easier for residents of Raton to do their shopping elsewhere. That, in itself, is a remarkable turn of events, given the distances residents had to drive to get to other shopping opportunities.

Then I asked the pregnant question: Can Raton survive? Long pause, deep breaths, a whispered answer: "I don't know. It's going to take a miracle. Every third house or building has a For Sale sign on it, and they've been there for years. People are so beaten down now. People are leaving in droves. The best of the citizens have left, the volunteers, the participants in almost everything good about the city."

Author's note: This was a very difficult and emotional interview for Murphy. I can only assume that the same level of emotion was felt by others who had to leave Raton. And, by others who have had to leave the other small, isolated communities in which they had spent all or much of their lives.

It could happen *anywhere.*

The resolution of these kinds of issues and situations lies in federal policies and programs. States cannot be expected to provide for these small, isolated cities. This decision needs to be made: Are these small, isolated cities and towns—that dot the American landscape—worthy of preserving? If not, we must prepare for potentially hundreds of new ghost towns.

If so, there needs to be a forward-thinking plan that makes these cities and towns both productive and sustainable well into the future.

Chapter 5

Issues for Future Economic Growth, by City and Region

Northwest

Emmett, Idaho

- Loss of retail
- Inadequate connections to major highways
- Seasonality of commerce and tax base
- Tax base dependence on real estate

Rupert, Idaho

- Brain drain
- Costs of infrastructure

Lewistown, Montana

- Tax base dependence on real estate
- Tax base to county; costs to city
- Retirees contribute little to tax base but require services
- Loss of retail
- Beautification of downtown

Lincoln, Oregon

- Tax base dependence on hotel tax
- Seasonality of commerce and tax base
- Need more high-end hotels and restaurants

- Ephrata, Washington
  - Remaining development areas not well located
- Cody, Wyoming
  - Seasonality of commerce and tax base
  - Brain drain
- Douglas, Wyoming
  - Availability of housing
  - Loss of retail

North Central

- Algona, Iowa
  - Planning for new stores in the downtown
  - Budget impacts of state tax policies
- Detroit Lakes, Minnesota
  - Greater development along highway frontage
  - Impact of state environmental policies
- International Falls, Minnesota
  - Workforce issues
  - No health care facility
- Montevideo, Minnesota
  - Workforce issues
  - Availability of housing
  - Inadequate connections to major highways
- Holdrege, Nebraska
  - Availability of housing
  - Loss of retail
- Sidney, Nebraska
  - Availability of housing
- Valley City, North Dakota
  - Availability of housing
  - Rising costs of infrastructure development

Great Lakes

- Carmi, Illinois
  - State legislation regarding fracking on hold
  - Brain drain
  - Retail needs
  - Impact of state tax policies
- Kingsford, Michigan
  - Concerns about growth altering the quality of life
- Ashland, Wisconsin
  - Community still recovering from major job losses
- Rice Lake, Wisconsin
  - Workforce issues
  - Impact of state tax policies

Northeast

Caribou, Maine

- Community still recovering from major job losses
- Impact of state policies
- Rail access poor
- Cost of utilities
- Remoteness

Titusville, Pennsylvania

- Community still recovering from major job losses

Southeast

Arab, Alabama

- Need for upscale restaurants
- Inadequate rail access

Hamilton, Alabama

- Community still recovering from major job losses
- Cannot compete for employers with larger cities
- Remoteness

Thomaston, Georgia

- Community still recovering from major job losses
- Vacant buildings
- Brain drain
- Tax base to county; costs to city

Kosciusko, Mississippi

- Inadequate access to highways
- Rail access poor
- Community still recovering from major job losses

Brevard, North Carolina

- Insufficient broadband access

Roxboro, North Carolina

- Inadequate access to highways

Covington, Tennessee

- Loss of small, family farms
- Loss of manufacturing

Lexington, Tennessee

- Community still recovering from major job losses
- Declining property values and the impacts on the city's budget
- Unfunded state and federal mandates
- Inadequate access to highways

McKenzie, Tennessee

- Poverty levels
- Walmart competition followed by its closing; loss of retail

Galax, Virginia

- Community still recovering from major job losses

    - Insufficient broadband access
  - South Boston, Virginia
    - Workforce issues
    - No "culture of education"
    - Brain drain
  - Elkins, West Virginia
    - Community still recovering from major job losses
    - Population decline
    - Decline in city's tax base
    - Inadequate access to highways
    - Insufficient broadband access
- South Central
  - Pocahontas, Arkansas
    - Community still recovering from major job losses
    - Brain drain
    - Retirees contribute little to tax base but require services
  - Colby, Kansas
    - Population losses
    - Brain drain
    - Walmart competition
    - Housing availability
  - Fort Scott, Kansas
    - Community still recovering from major job losses
    - Loss of population
    - Community malaise
    - Brain drain
  - Charleston, Missouri
    - Loss of small, family farms
    - Poverty
    - Brain drain
    - Inadequate rail access
    - Loss of federal aid
    - State tax policies
  - Chillicothe, Missouri
    - No institutions of higher education
  - Perryville, Missouri
    - Community still recovering from major job losses
  - Breckenridge, Texas
    - Need retailers and restaurants
    - Impact of state tax policies
    - Drought/water issues
    - Inadequate housing

- Beautification of city
- Aging infrastructure

Elsa, Texas
- Need for regionalism to reduce duplicative costs
- Inadequate housing
- Beautification of the city
- Improvement in city services

Pecos, Texas
- Need more retail
- Inadequate housing
- Abandoned building/beautification of the city

West/Southwest

Winslow, Arizona
- Community still recovering from major job losses

Fort Bragg, California
- Community still recovering from major job losses

Yreka, California
- Impact of state policies
- Workforce issues

Delta, Colorado
- Loss of small, family farms
- Community still recovering from major job losses
- Inadequate access to highways
- Impact of state policies

Gunnison, Colorado
- Remoteness
- No rail service
- Inadequate access to highways

Lamar, Colorado
- Effects of drought on ranchers

Salida, Colorado
- Not seeking growth

Winnemucca, Nevada
- Tax base dependence on sales taxes
- Remoteness
- Seasonality of commerce and tax base

Taos, New Mexico
- Seasonality of commerce and tax base
- Need for regional cooperation
- Impact of state tax policies

Vernal, Utah
- Inconsistency of oil and gas prices

Table 5.1 Issues for Future Economic Growth, by Region

	Regions							
Issues	*NW*	*NC*	*GL*	*NE*	*SE*	*SC*	*W/SW*	*Total*
Need greater retail, hotels	5	2	2	1	1	3		14
Inadequate transportation access	1	3		1	6	1	3	15
Seasonality of commerce/tax revenues	3						2	5
Tax base dependencies	3						1	4
Brain drain	2		1		2	4		9
Beautification of the city					1	3	1	5
Insufficient housing	1	4				4		9
State policies, taxation		1	2	1		2		6
State policies, other		1	1		1	3		6
Workforce issues		2	1		1		1	5
Community still recovering from major job losses			1	2	6	4	3	16
Remoteness of location				1	1		2	4
Poverty in the city					2	1		3
Inadequate access to broadband					3			3
Loss of family farms					1	1	1	3
Other issues	2	2	1	1	7	8	2	23

Table 5.1 further summarizes the issues confronting the fifty-one cities in the study by proving regional and national totals. The first thing one will notice from this summation is that there are twenty-three responses categorized as "other" at the end of the table. That would be a significant number, of course, and would bear further delineation if those responses were common themes or were of a nature that would contribute to this research.

However, the twenty-three "other" responses represent nearly twenty-three unique issues and therefore did not represent significant numeric replies. Further, many of the issues included in that designation are beyond the control of any city's leadership, and thus do not lead to lessons that can be learned by others. These areas include such matters as fluctuations in the world prices of oil and the effects of droughts on some local economies. They are included in the table primarily to indicate the magnitude of the issues confronting these cities and their leadership.

The second important realization from this summarization of issues is the line headed "remoteness." As the hypothesis of this research was, in part, that the remoteness of a city's location from larger urban areas would contribute to, or create, difficulties for economic growth, it is important to note that such was the case for only four of the fifty-one cities in this research. While it is very clearly an issue for those four communities, it does not stand as a primary issue for small, isolated cities generally.

One category of issues relates to those items that represent barriers to attracting employers to, or retaining them in, these fifty-one cities. The need for greater or higher-end retail, hotels, and restaurants is an important attraction asset recognized by numerous cities. However, there exists a chicken-and-egg situation because employers expect these things in a community, but without sufficient employment and earnings bases, there is no reason for these kinds of businesses to locate in a city either.

Inadequate housing is a clear problem for business attraction as the employer—and his or her employees—needs somewhere to live and house his or her family. Again, without the employment base, employers must build on speculation in order to have the asset in place for business attraction. Home builders are far more sensitive to the existing—not some potential future—demand than that.

The same conundrum applies to infrastructure projects, whether related to highways or rail. It also covers the community responses about having inadequate access to broadband, also an absolute requirement for today's employers. Unless state or federal funds are made available in order to create interest in a location, there is no reason to put the infrastructure in place until businesses arrive. More typically, states apply whatever infrastructure dollars do exist to more populated areas where there may be the implications of greater returns on those investments.

This brings the review to the issue of state policies and how they can affect the growth and decline of local economies. Local governments in several of the states indicated that state tax policies limit the ability of municipalities to generate revenues for public services. They also leave cities with a tax base that is not sufficiently diversified to withstand the peaks and valleys in commerce generally. It also means that cities in which the commerce is seasonal in nature also have to deal with the issue of seasonality in tax base generation and the planning for year-round public services. There were several communities that asserted that state policies can be particularly damaging to border communities. In those cases, employers can simply move across the border into more business-friendly states.

Additional state policy areas were also cited as being problematic in some states. Much of this related to environmental policies.

A major finding of this research came in the form of city leaders' descriptions of how they have recovered from major job losses or losses of entire industries, in many cases, seemingly all at once. This includes the category of responses related to the replacement of family farming and its replacement with technology-driven large-scale agribusinesses that employ relatively few people. While a few of those interviewed noted that people bore down and set their sights on new opportunities, sixteen communities out of fifty-one, nearly one in every three, indicated that—many years later—residents had either become risk averse or showed that they had not overcome the memories of those very hard times for themselves, their families, and their communities.

In addition to the direct responses to how cities had gotten past such devastating losses, other responses may be seen as directly related to dramatic job losses over a short period of time. This includes concerns about the brain drain and the costs of losing the cities' best and brightest. As well as losing the young people from these cities, those communities also lost one of their primary assets needed to attract new employers. Further, they were left with lower income levels, lower tax base revenues, greater poverty, and higher demands for transfer payments and other public services.

Layered on top of that issue is the issue cited regarding retirees. Their incomes come from other locations and are not always subject to local taxation. As such, they contribute little financially to their communities but increase the demands for public services, notably, transportation, health care, and recreation.

The final effect of these latter issues is often that, with a reduced tax base, city services suffer. This notion is reflected in responses about poverty, population loss generally, the need for beautification projects in the city, and the loss of businesses from the downtowns.

For America's small, isolated cities, this represents an extremely daunting list of challenges that must be overcome before economic growth can occur.

In response to the very issues that confront each of the cities in this study, the leaders who were interviewed cited a range of strategies that had been or were being put into place. These are summarized in Table 5.2 by region and city.

The table illustrates some commonality of responses but does not yield an overwhelming issue cited to a dramatically greater extent than others. Of the fourteen strategies cited, each was referenced between five and fifteen times. And, with one exception, no single response was cited significantly more than others in any given region. That exception was the construction of housing in seven of the North Central cities included. Thus, each example of strategies being employed can be seen as relevant to the specific city applications and not a generally accepted strategic solution.

Revenue sources for the city budgets are categorized in Table 5.3. This illustrates the sources allowed for each city to collect from as well as the potential for cities to confront challenges in providing public services when revenues decline.

Table 5.2 Economic Growth Strategies Cited by Case Study Cities, by Region and City

	Regions							
Strategies	*NW*	*NC*	*GL*	*NE*	*SE*	*SC*	*W/SW*	*Totals*
Attract tourism	1				1	1	3	6
Increase quality of life/beautify city	2	1	1		2	4	3	13
Diversify the economy	2	2	1			1	2	8
Offset nonpeak seasons with festivals, events	3				3	1	2	9
Use financial incentives	1				2	0	2	5
Train the workforce	1	3			3	1	2	10
Emphasize business retention	1	1			2	2		6
Attract retail, hotels, restaurants	3	2	1	1	1	1	2	11
Build housing	1	2				2		5
Build roads and infrastructure		4			6	3	2	15
Pursue regional solutions		1	1		2	2		5
Take advantage of natural assets		1			1	2	1	5
Grow businesses from within			1	1	4	3	1	9
Increase economic development professionalism/ outreach	3			1	3	2	2	11

Table 5.4 summarizes which cities have lost or gained population as a result of economic growth and decline, as well as those in which the population bases have held constant. That data is then summarized as well by region in the accompanying Table 5.5.

Finally, at the end of each of the fifty-one interviews, the leaders were asked the same question: If you were in a room with the leadership of other cities of a similar

Table 5.3 Primary Revenue Sources for Local Budgets, by Region

Region	*Property*	*Sales*	*Hotel*	*Fees*
Northwest	3	2	1	1
North Central	5	1		1
Great Lakes	4			
Northeast	2			
Southeast	6	8	1	1
South Central	4	6		2
West/ Southwest		9	3	1
Totals	24	26	5	6

Table 5.4 Population Change, 2000–2012

Region, City, State	*Directional Arrow*
Northwest	
Emmett, Idaho	↑ 10%
Rupert, Idaho	–
Lewistown, Montana	–
Lincoln, Oregon	–
Ephrata, Washington	↑ 10%
Cody, Wyoming	↑ 10%
Douglas, Wyoming	↑ 10%
North Central	
Algona, Iowa	–
Detroit Lakes, Minnesota	–
International Falls, Minnesota	↓ 5%
Montevideo, Minnesota	–
Holdrege, Nebraska	–

Table 5.4 (*Continued*) Population Change, 2000–2012

Region, City, State	*Directional Arrow*
Sidney, Nebraska	↑ 5%
Valley City, North Dakota	—
Great Lakes	
Carmi, Illinois	—
Kingsford, Michigan	↓ 5%
Ashland, Wisconsin	—
Rice Lake, Wisconsin	—
Northeast	
Caribou, Maine	—
Titusville, Pennsylvania	↓ 10%
Southeast	
Arab, Alabama	—
Hamilton, Alabama	—
Thomaston, Georgia	—
Kosciusko, Mississippi	—
Brevard, North Carolina	↑ 10%
Roxboro, North Carolina	—
Covington, Tennessee	—
Lexington, Tennessee	↑ 5%
McKenzie, Tennessee	—
Galax, Virginia	—
South Boston, Virginia	↓ 5%
Elkins, West Virginia	—
South Central	
Pocahontas, Arkansas	—
Colby, Kansas	—
Fort Scott, Kansas	—

Continued

Table 5.4 (*Continued*) Population Change, 2000–2012

Region, City, State	*Directional Arrow*
Charleston, Missouri	↑ 10%
Chillicothe, Missouri	↑ 5%
Perryville, Missouri	↑ 5%
Breckenridge, Texas	—
Elsa, Texas	—
Pecos, Texas	↓ 5%
West/Southwest	
Winslow, Arizona	—
Fort Bragg, California	—
Yreka, California	↑ 5%
Delta, California	↑ 10%
Gunnison, Colorado	↑ 10%
Lamar, Colorado	↓ 10%
Salida, Colorado	—
Taos, New Mexico	—
Winnemucca, Nevada	↑ 5%
Vernal, Utah	↑ 10%

Table 5.5 Summary of Population Increase/Decrease by Region

	Decline		*Relatively Constant*	*Growth*	
Region	*≥10%*	*5–10%*		*5–10%*	*≥10%*
Northwest			3		4
North Central		1	5	1	
Great Lakes		1	3		
Northeast	1		1		
Southeast		1	9	1	1
South Central		1	5	2	1
West/Southwest	1		4	2	3
Totals	2	4	30	6	9

size and a similar degree of isolation, what lessons would you offer them as they encounter the same issues? The responses are listed below:

Northwest

Emmett, Idaho

- Prepare for growth; don't wait for companies to consider your city
- Residential growth generally costs money; businesses help to pay for residential public services
- Make your city attractive to employers

Rupert, Idaho

- Prepare for growth; don't wait for companies to consider your city
- Make your city attractive to employers
- Pay attention to existing employers
- Diversity within a sector is also a stabilizing factor for a local economy; economic diversification does not have to be among several business sectors

Lewistown, Montana

- Montana needs to implement a local sales tax

Lincoln, Oregon

- Save surpluses for a "rainy day"
- Make your city attractive to employers

Ephrata, Washington

- Ensure community-wide involvement through constant communications
- Privatize city services when feasible

Cody, Wyoming

- Don't pursue "just any jobs"; be sure they are a good fit for your city
- Ensure community-wide involvement through constant communications
- Save surpluses for a rainy day

Douglas, Wyoming

- Save surpluses for a rainy day

North Central

Algona, Iowa

- Make your city attractive to employers
- Work constantly to ensure strong city–business community relationships

Detroit Lakes, Minnesota

- Prepare for growth; don't wait for companies to consider your city
- Work constantly to ensure strong city–business community relationships

International Falls, Minnesota

- Make the best use of the natural resources in your area
- Regional cooperation is critical
- Workforce training is vital; it is a primary asset you can offer businesses

Montevideo, Minnesota
- Ensure that there is sufficient housing for workers before talking to businesses about locations

Holdrege, Nebraska
- Make sure that new growth fits well with the existing community

Sidney, Nebraska
- Prepare the infrastructure before companies begin to consider locations
- Work constantly to ensure strong city–business community relationships
- Diversify the local economy as much as possible
- Cities either grow or die; there are no other options

Valley City, North Dakota
- Commercial growth helps cities pay for the growing costs of infrastructure
- Get the infrastructure in place before businesses consider locations

Great Lakes

Carmi, Illinois
- Grow small businesses from within your own community; do not rely solely on growth from outside

Kingsford, Michigan
- Act regionally for economic growth
- Diversify the local economy

Ashland, Wisconsin
- Improve services for tourism attraction
- Make your city attractive to employers and tourists

Rice Lake, Wisconsin
- Grow your own businesses from within; you cannot rely solely on growth from outside
- State policies need to regard smaller cities distinctly from one another; there is no "one-size-fits-all" solution

Northeast

Caribou, Maine
- Business growth helps to pay for residential public services

Titusville, Pennsylvania
- Small towns need to produce consumable products; they bring revenue into the city

Southeast

Arab, Alabama
- Grow your own small businesses from within
- Communicate your plans to citizens and businesses constantly
- Work constantly to ensure strong city–business community relationships

Hamilton, Alabama
- Economic development incentives are a must for small towns
- Prepare the infrastructure before companies begin to consider your city for location

Thomaston, Georgia
- Diversify the local economy as much as possible

Kosciusko, Mississippi
- Communicate with the business community on a regular basis

Brevard, North Carolina
- Take advantage of the natural resources in your area
- Work on retaining existing businesses as you seek to attract new businesses

Roxboro, North Carolina
- Work to attract smaller companies; larger companies cause more disruption when they relocate away
- Work to retain existing businesses
- Communicate with the business community on a regular basis
- Regionalize economic development outreach
- Professionalize the economic development program and make it full-time

Covington, Tennessee
- Diversify the local economy
- Regionalize economic development outreach
- Beautify the downtown; it is what potential employers will see

Lexington, Tennessee
- Prepare the infrastructure before businesses consider locations

McKenzie, Tennessee
- Work regularly with local businesses and institutions, such as colleges

Galax, Virginia
- Encourage residents to support local retailers
- Work regularly with local businesses

South Boston, Virginia
- Economic growth requires all of the community working together as a team, including the young and the old
- Cities must put things in place for growth before companies will come; exercise patience

Elkins, West Virginia
- Work regularly with local businesses

South Central

Pocahontas, Arkansas
- Work regularly with local businesses and institutions, such as colleges
- Old and young people in the community must work on economic development plans together
- Diversify the local economy

Colby, Kansas
- Prepare the infrastructure before companies consider a location
- Communicate and interact with businesses and residents regularly about plans for economic growth

Fort Scott, Kansas
- Beautify the city; employers are looking for attractive locations
- Work regularly with local businesses

Charleston, Missouri
- Grow your own small businesses from within
- Beautify the city; employers are looking for attractive locations

Chillicothe, Missouri
- Retail follows industry; attract employers and the retail will follow

Perryville, Missouri
- Work regionally to attract businesses

Breckenridge, Texas
- Beautify the city; employers are looking for attractive locations
- Work to retain the existing businesses in the city

Elsa, Texas
- City services must be responsive to citizens and employers
- Beautify the city; employers are looking for attractive locations

Pecos, Texas
- Attract retail to support business growth
- Have the infrastructure in place before companies look for locations

South Central

Winslow, Arizona
- Pursue economic development on a regional basis

Fort Bragg, California
- Take advantage of natural resources in the area
- Have infrastructure in place before businesses consider location
- Communicate and interact with businesses and residents regularly about plans for economic growth

Yreka, California
- Communicate and interact with businesses and residents regularly about plans for economic growth
- Diversify the local economy

Delta, Colorado
- Diversify the local economy
- Take advantage of the natural resources in the area
- Put the infrastructure in place before companies consider location
- Beautify the city

Gunnison, Colorado
- Put the infrastructure in place before companies consider location

Lamar, Colorado
- Communicate and interact with businesses and residents regularly about plans for economic growth

Salida, Colorado

- Not interested in further growth but, where they are, be careful not to allow growth to alter the quality of life

Winnemucca, Nevada

- Use economic development incentives to attract employers
- Beautify the city

Taos, New Mexico

- Economic development must be regional
- Economic development needs to be a full-time, professional operation
- Cities cannot rely on government help; you must do it on your own

Vernal, Utah

- Quality of life is everything
- Diversify the local economy

There are nine significant responses from the fifty-one interviews to the question about lessons learned. The most consistently noted comment is that growth must be considered a team effort in small towns and that every part of the community must be on the team. Further, the sentiment was expressed that the team cannot be assembled at the last moment, that is, when a prospective business arrives. Rather, the team must be an ongoing group, and that requires regular communication about planning from the city to the business community, residents, and institutions. Seventeen individuals made this comment, representing more than one-third of the interviewees.

The second highest number of lessons offered concerned preparing the infrastructure for future development. It is always a conundrum for communities, especially small towns, whether to prepare now in the hopes that a user will someday arrive. In the meantime, the city must carry the costs without the benefit of revenues from the properties. However, to wait until there is an active prospect will likely mean that another location will be more appealing because it is already prepared. In this research, fifteen respondents addressed this matter. For thirteen of them, the lesson was that you must act before a prospect arrives and the city must simply carry the costs until a user is identified. Two others took the more conservative approach and recommended saving surpluses for the inevitable rainy days.

One of the appeals of small cities to prospective employers is the charm that many such locations have as well as the small town atmosphere many people enjoy. As such, it is not surprising that twelve of those interviewed noted that employers want attractive locations for their businesses and their employees, and that makes city beautification projects critical. There is no implication herein that the other thirty-nine cities did not consider this as a paramount lesson. It may simply imply that they feel their cities already meet the necessary attractiveness standard.

Eight responses related to the need to diversify the local economy in order to avoid a single business loss from becoming a sudden collapse for the entire economy.

Again, there is no implication that others did not also feel this way; many simply felt that their cities' economies were already fairly diversified.

A number of responses can be seen in multiple cities. These include the use of the natural resources in proximity to the city for commercial purposes, the use of incentives to attract employers, more regionalized approaches to economic development programs, the focus on retaining existing employers as well as attracting new ones, and the emphasis on growing new businesses from within as a good way to restore a local economy rather than only focusing on business attraction. Many of these can make sense for some, though not all, similar communities, depending upon their degree of isolation and the individual circumstances of the communities.

Bibliography

Books

Avey, Loren, and Person, Gary. 2006. *Lynchings, Legends, and Lawlessness: Nebraska's Original Boot Hill Cemetery*. Sidney, NE: City of Sidney.

Carr, Patrick J., and Kefalas, Maria J. 2009. *Hollowing Out the Middle: The Rural Brain Drain and What It Means for America*. Boston: Beacon Press.

Duncan, Cynthia M. 1999. *Worlds Apart: Why Poverty Persists in Rural America*. New Haven, CT: Yale Press.

Huston, Kim. 2009. *Small Town Sexy: The Allure of Living in Small Town America*. Lexington, KY: The Clark Group.

Kageyama, Peter. 2011. *For the Love of Cities*. St. Petersburg, FL: Creative Cities Productions.

Lessinger, Jack. 1990. Penturbia: *Where Real Estate Will Boom after the Crash of Suburbia*. Seattle: SocioEconomics.

Lyson, Thomas A., and Falk, William W. 1993. *Forgotten Places: Uneven Development in Rural America*. Lawrence: University Press of Kansas.

Moltz, Barry J., and McCray, Becky. 2012. *Small Town Rules: How Big Brands and Small Businesses Can Prosper in a Connected Economy*. Indianapolis: QUE Press.

Norquist, John O. 1998. *The Wealth of Cities: Revitalizing the Centers of American Life*. Cambridge, MA: Perseus Publishing.

Schaeffer, Peter V., and Loveridge, Scott. 2000. *Small Town and Rural Economic Development: A Case Studies Approach*. Westport, CT: Praeger Publishers.

Speck, Jeff. 2012. *Walkable City: How Downtown Can Save America One Step at a Time*. New York: Farrar, Straus, and Giroux.

Storper, Michael. 2013. *Keys to the City: How Economics, Institutions, Social Interaction, and Politics Shape Development*. Princeton, NJ: Princeton University Press.

Tumber, Catherine. 2012. *Small, Gritty, and Green: The Promise of America's Smaller Industrial Cities in a Low-Carbon World*. Boston: MIT Press.

Urbanska, Wanda, and Levering, Frank. 1996. *Moving to a Small Town*. New York: Fireside Publishers.

Vidich, Arthur J., and Bensman, Joseph. 2000. *Small Town in Mass Society: Class, Power, and Religion in a Rural Community*. Urbana: University of Illinois Press.

Whyte, William A. 1988. *City: Rediscovering the Center*. New York: Doubleday.

Wood, Richard E. 2008. *Survival of Rural America: Small Victories and Bitter Harvests.* Lawrence: University of Kansas Press.

Wuthnow, Robert. 2013. *Small-Town America: Finding Community, Shaping the Future.* Princeton, NJ: Princeton University Press.

Zukin, Sharon. 2010. *Naked City: The Death and Life of Authentic Urban Places.* New York: Oxford University Press.

Internet Citations

Arts, David. September 24, 2013. What Is Next for International Falls? http://minnesota.publicradio.org.

Bass, Frank. November 16, 2009. Census: Small Cities Have Better Quality of Life but Economic Picture Is Steadily Worsening. http://greattimes.com.

Benfield, K. September 7, 2012. The Death—and Life—of Small Downtown America. http://www.theatlanticcities.com.

Bilotta, Frank. October 21, 2009. Rural Broadband: Internet's Effect on Small Town Economies. http://business.ezine9.com.

Blackwell, John Reid. October 9, 2013. Small Cities Like Richmond Could Capture Population Shift. http://www.timesdispatch.com.

Brown, Aaron J. October 4, 2013. Building Small Town Economy with New Attitude. http://minnesotabrown.com.

Can Statues of Killer Bees and Storytelling Festivals Stop the Country's Smallest Towns from Withering Away? December 19, 2006. http://www.economist.com.

Census. November 16, 2009. Small Cities Lose Luster in Downtown. http://msnbc.com.

Chura, Hillary. January 9, 2009. Lacking Airlines, Small Cities' Economies Suffer. http://nytimes.com.

CNBC. 2014. Top States for Business. http://cnbc.com/id/101758236.

Corey, Russ, and Delinsky, Bernice. December 6, 2010. Small Town. http://www.timesdaily.com.

Dayley-Smith, Lisa. January 19, 2014. Rupert to Expand Urban Renewal District into County. www.minicassia.com.

Decatur Daily. May 22, 2005. Small Town Not Afraid to Finance Its Growth. http://archive.decaturdaily.com.

El Nasser, Haya. June 27, 2004. Small Town USA Goes Micropolitan. http://usatoday.com.

Forbes. 2013. Best States for Business List. http://www.forbes.com/best-states-for-business/.

Freeman, Michael W. November 1, 2010. Small Town Businesses Struggle. http://www.theledger.com.

Green, Mark. July 14, 2013. Big Economic Development in Small Towns. http://www.lanereport.com.

Halseth, Greg. July 7, 2010. Rural Renaissance: BC's Small Town Economy. http://www.bcbusinessonline.ca.

Jonsson, Patel. July 6, 2004. Small Cities Cope with Crime Surge. http://www.csmonitor.com.

Kotkin, Joel. May 8, 2012. Small Cities Are Becoming New Engine of Economic Growth. http://www.forbes.com.

Luijn, Van. Infrastructure Deficit in Rural Canada: Is It Time for a Marshall Plan? http://economicdevelopment.org.

McCray, Becky. 2013. Small Town Economic Development Idea: The Tour of Empty Buildings. http://smallbizsurvival.com.

Messick, Molly. February 18, 2013. Emmett, Idaho Sawmill Closes Its Doors—Again. http://stateimpact.npr.org/Idaho.

Neistadt, Shawn. May 23, 2012. Small Town Economies Strong in the Midwest. http://www.keloland.com.

Olley, John. November 30, 2008. Wal-Mart and Its Impact on Business of Small Town Economies. http://yahoo.com.

Portuguese Fruit Company Picks Rupert for First US Plant. October 16, 2013. http://www.idahostatesman.com.

Prevost, Ruffin. March 4, 2013. U.S. Budget Cuts Force Yellowstone to Delay Opening. http://newsstoryus.com.

Probert, Cameron. November 9, 2013. Ephrata Council Prepares to Vote on Asking for Tax Increase. http://www.ifiberone.com.

Schorpp, Doug. February 27, 2014. Summit Lays Groundwork for Small Town Growth. http://qctimes.com.

Spence, Rick. April 15, 2013. How to Keep Small Towns from Disappearing. http://business.financialpost.com.

Traynham, Linda Brady. April 10, 2009. The Inherent Sustainability of the Small Town. http://dailyreckoning.com.

US Department of Commerce. June 18, 2013. Economic Development Administration Invests $1 Million to Help Build Critical Infrastructure and Create Jobs in Carmi, Illinois. http://www.eda.gov.

Yen, Hope. March 14, 2013. Census: Record One in Three Counties Now Dying Off, Hit by Aging Population, Weakened Local Economies. http://www.huffingtonpost.com.

Presentations

Kures, Matt, and Wise, Greg. November 5, 2008. The Role of Small Cities in the New Regional Economy. Presented at 17th Conference on the Small City and Regional Community, Steven's Point, WI.

Person, Gary. May 1, 2014. Verbal Statement for the Record. Presented at US Senate, Agricultural Subcommittee on Jobs, Rural Economic Growth and Energy Innovation, Washington, DC.

Unpublished Papers

City of Taos. 2013. Updated Community Economic Development Strategic Plan. Taos, NM.

Gem County. March 2010. Gem County Joint Comprehensive Plan: City of Emmett, Idaho.

Homsy, George, and Warner, Mildred. 2012. Defying the Odds: Sustainability in Small and Rural Places. International City Managers Association, Center for Sustainable Communities.

Lambe, Will. December 2008. Big Ideas: Case Studies in Small Town Economic Development. University of North Carolina School of Government, North Carolina Rural Economic Development Center.

Miller, Kathleen. March 2010. Why Definitions Matter: Rural Definitions and State Poverty Rankings. Columbia: Rural Poverty Research Institute, University of Missouri.

Pulver, Robin et al. November 2005. Small Town Fact Book. Raleigh, North Carolina: North Carolina Rural Economic Development Center.

Putting Smart Growth to Work in Rural Communities. 2010. International City Managers Association, Smart Growth Network.

Ricketts, Thomas C. et al. June 1, 1998. Definitions of Rural: A Handbook for Health Policy Makers and Researchers. Washington, DC: US Department of Health and Human Services.

Woods, Mike D., and Sloggett, Gorden. Strategic Planning for Economic Development in Rural Areas and Small Towns of Oklahoma. Stillwater: Oklahoma State University, Division of Agricultural Sciences and Natural Resources.

Index

T

U

V

W

Y

For Product Safety Concerns and Information please contact our EU representative GPSR@taylorandfrancis.com Taylor & Francis Verlag GmbH, Kaufingerstraße 24, 80331 München, Germany